Also by Jill Johnston: MARMALADE ME

LESBIAN NATION

THE FEMINIST SOLUTION

by

Jill Johnston

NEW YORK   SIMON AND SCHUSTER

ACKNOWLEDGMENTS

I wish I could say I had a number of wives who cheerfully read my manuscript and made the most helpful suggestions throughout and contributed invaluable encouragement and criticism at each stage of work as well as untiring help typing and retyping and reading proofs and assisting in bibliographical work in various amerikan and european libraries and without whose loving inspiration this book would not have come into being and so on but I can't. However I can say that I'm thankful to Danny Moses for encouraging me initially to write the book and to Diane Harris and Vicky Wilson for key suggestions in progress, and that without the continuous infusion of confidence and political insight of Jane O'Wyatt and her communication of the urgency that such tracts be written it's true as they say that this one might not have come into being. I thank also many women and friends in struggle. And my paper The Village Voice *whose pages continue to provide a vehicle for my stylistic outrages and journeys in consciousness.*

Certain portions of this book appeared originally in The Village Voice, *in many cases in a slightly different form. These include: "Bash in the Sculls," "'The Kingdom of Holy Insecurity," "Lois Lane Is a Lesbian," "The Second Sucks & The Feminine Mystake," "Sigmund: An Analysis of a Case of His-teria," "Who Is the Father of Her Child?" "Teach Your Angels Karate," "Anybody Dying of Love," "Movement Schmoovement," "An Amazon in the White House," "Her Command of Impermanence," "On a Clear Day You Can See Your Mother."*

This book is for my mother
who should've been a lesbian
And for my daughter
in hopes she will be

REMARKS

This book should read like an interlocking web of personal experience and history and events of the world forming a picture of an evolving political revolutionary consciousness of one who was female who emerged from straight middle unconscious postwar amerika.

All speculations of biological destiny and social reality and the complexities of cause and effect between the two are true explanations of personal history and understanding reading back from the individual life into the dim archetypal past of our collective memories. All explanations work, and explain each other.

All repetitions of thoughts ideas material projections plans reflections reveries fantasies in the same or varied phrases in different contexts constitute my way of working circles within circles, like the quadriga, the four horsed chariot, constantly returning to its point of origin. Every departure from a point of origin carries with it a renewed approach to it. Each return to the point of origin completes the cycle of one existence and begins another. The style and the subject are the same: the return to the harmony of statehood and biology through the remembered majesties of women.

CONTENTS

TARZANA FROM THE TREES
AT COCKTAILS

The Town Hall affair of May 1971 billed chiefly as a dialogue between Norman Mailer and Germaine Greer was a disaster for women and a minor triumph for me since my notoriety as a swimmer was briefly eclipsed by the greater infamy of public sapphism. I had adjusted myself in the preceding year to being regarded as a swimmer instead of a writer so this new claim to honor required merely a slight shift in adapting to the demands of a career as an amusing personality. I was sorry to leave my swimming reputation behind but we have to move on in life. We have to become whatever we do next. We have to be whatever they like to say we are when we do something. We can be whatever we like. My career as an impromptu clown is studded with glorious exploits. It's necessary in order to attract attention, to dazzle at all costs, to be disapproved of by serious people and quoted by the foolish. If anyone should think my exhibitionism is a symptom of my neglect as a writer they're wrong because this behavior is an art form derived from my early years with my mother and my grandmother who encouraged my efforts to please them by laughing at me and applauding all my inventions even the phony grimaces. And from my slightly later years in boarding school where I refined my performances somewhat to suit a new environment of spinster teachers and episcopal nuns and beautiful competitive female schoolmates. Naturally I became both

15

more daring and more selective and on many occasions secretive in order to impress a chosen few peers and not offend the authorities in defiance of whom such underground exploits were intended to especially enhance my status with potential admirers. Possibly my most impressive happening was a double disruption of the religious life in a carefully planned saturation of the priests' vestments with perfume and the inundation of the organ pipes with ping pong balls designed of course to make havoc during the chapel service as soon as the nun who played the organ sat down to perform. I don't know what the newspapers would've called me after that. My best number really was a random investigation of the bureaus of the nuns while they were on retreat in order to find out what sort of underwear if any they were into inside all the black stuff. But most of my exhibitions truly were spontaneous and public inspirations like singing too loudly at grace or whispering in line or passing notes in study hall or walking too fast in the refectory or making faces at inappropriate times or teasing the french teachers and generally enjoying my habits of delinquency and irresponsibility. Anyone could judge from these descriptions that such a person later on in life would have evolved a sophisticated form of these reckless projects and expect naturally to see their perfection in such a masterful event as an impulsive dive into a swimming pool in East Hampton on a hot August afternoon in 1970. A lot of people said and wrote that I went into the pool to protest the discrimination against lesbians by feminists, but I wasn't nearly so organized. I was hot and drunk and I like empty swimming pools and I'm a very good swimmer so I like to show off my skills. I wouldn't entirely deny my contempt for the event and the maxi decolletage or radical chic uptown depravity of its sponsorship and the pressing need to subvert such charities (the party cost $25 a head) and the temptation to upset a few silly prudish old culture people who have a new reason for their lives in feminism. But basically I was delighted to have the opportunity to impress a bunch of

strangers with my 10 point Australian crawl, and to douse off a
few strong drinks in a pretty pool. The reason I took off my shirt
after the second lap was that it interfered with my stroke. I was
rather embarrassed when I emerged since I was brought up
modestly. As we all found out there were more press and photo
people there than people and so I became a swimming star
overnight. Of course nobody praised my technique. It was simply
hailed as a disruption. Nevertheless, a swim it was. So town hall
at least gave people something else to think about. After all, before I was a swimmer I was a pipe hanger. I mean I had an
underground reputation for hanging upside down off pipes at loft
parties. Before that I was a dancer. Before that an athlete. Anyway never a writer. My original intention for town hall was to
launch my career as a boxer. I had plans for renting a pair of
Cassius Clay shorts and one glove and appearing somehow after
my speech in said shorts and with the glove on my left hand and
wearing my reddish combat boots from fort brag california and a
female symbol upheld in my bare right hand. Just standing there
that way. I dug the image for myself. And for the photo hounds. I
wasn't sure I wanted to expose my breasts live for that many
people or males. I like my breasts but I was brought up modestly
as I said. Mostly I wasn't sure I wanted to further acknowledge
Mailer by making the obvious reference to his sport. If Hemingway was the moderator I might've been projecting my new career
as a matador and I would've felt the same way. Why even
parody these characters. I liked the idea and I didn't. I was conflicted over the whole thing. Just appearing at town hall was to
acknowledge mailer. And to concur in the tacit premise of the occasion—that women's liberation is a debatable issue. In this sense,
that the event occurred at all, it was a disaster for women. As a
social event it was the victory of the season. The lobby before
curtain time couldn't have been more electrified if the performance people were coming to see was the Martians' first press conference at the Hilton. I never saw anything like it. It looked as if

there was no other place for anybody to be on earth at that moment. It looked as if the whole world thought this was the only place to be. The whole world extremely smug and satisfied and excited to be at the right place in the right time. Obviously someone had spread the word that you just didn't count if you didn't make it to this one. I was standing in the lobby leaning against the stairs gaping at the commotion holding my coffee-to-go in one hand and a baby bottle of martini in the other exchanging confused astonished inanities with a small raggedy contingent of my friends supporters who had escorted me to the Algonquin beforehand to celebrate the unknown. Even in the lobby we still had no idea of the heroic dimension of the thing. In the din and clatter I was concentrating on the immediate problem of how to appear on stage late. Who appears late has other important things to do. I assumed the curtain would be open the way it is for any ordinary panel. But this wasn't a panel. It was a command performance. Still, I thought it might be open, and we kept checking at the doorways to see if it was, and it wasn't, and the clock was running out and the lobby thinning down too. I had planned to make a flying leap Fairbanks style over the orchestra pit and gallantly demonstrate my affection for Germaine by kissing her or something as innocuous or exciting before taking my place at the table. As it turned out I kissed her behind closed curtains after Shirley Broughton the organizer of this thing had found me loitering in the lobby and towed me backstage upbraiding me for holding them all up. They were waiting at the table. Jacqueline Ceballos of NOW and Diana Trilling of Trilling on either end and my empty chair to the left of mailer flanked on his right by Germaine who was sort of leering smiling friendly at me sideways over her shoulder dripping the dead fox that she had worn for fun and satire and cost a pound she said afterwards. Mailer was standing and turned as I approached and reluctantly shook my extended hand and said in greeting that I had to speak second. I said no. Shirley Broughton had me scheduled for third as I requested, when Diana Trilling beat us all to being last. Mailer repeated the command. I said no. And he very gracefully assured me that everybody there had come to hear and see Germaine. I didn't care. And I didn't believe it anyway. I thought they came to see me. I think I'd think that if I was on the platform with the Queen. I put my coffee-to-go and baby bottle of martini and record book down on the table next to Diana's briefcase prepared to speak third and I did. I had never seen Diana before and I supposed she despised me like the rest. I had met Ceballos the week before at a talk gig in longisland at hofstra college and she seemed to have the same attitude as Betty Friedan who'd declared the year before over the mikes at the swimming bash that I was the biggest enemy of the movement. I didn't know much what the movement was at that time so I guess her accusation was a rare compliment. Possibly it was remarks like these that gave people the idea I was protesting the discrimination against lesbians by feminists. Possibly I was. Betty wasn't nice to me at all. And she had said that the two movements (gay and feminist) had nothing to do with each other. From the people point of view that was okay by me, if these were the people who were called feminists. Anyway I imagined every woman who lived above 14th street thought lesbians were sick dirty and dangerous. I thought almost every woman who lived above 14th street was frigid furious and unimaginative. So here was a sick dirty dangerous lesbian appearing on sacred puritan anglo jewish territory and by their own invitation. For Shirley Broughton was a Mailer fan. And her Theatre For Ideas always sponsored culture stars with fancy credentials. So the question was what was I doing there. I was a culture star from the bowery and the bellevue. I was not a feminist in any proper sense of the term whatever that was, either by activity or by consciousness, although I was moving along in my consciousness. I did think that the only true feminist was the lesbian and I still do although at that time I was adamant and obnoxious in my assertions and intolerant of

all the moderate approaches. Anyway no lesbian was audible
above 14th street and I think the Theatre For Ideas wanted their
token lesbian and I was just recently notorious for exposing lois
lane as a lesbian in *the village voice* and there's no question the
Theatre for Ideas was having difficulty persuading people to
participate. Already several well known feminists had declined
the invitation. The popular view around town was that women
should boycott the panel. I wondered how that was supposed to
takes place since the event itself was obviously going to happen.
For any bunch of women who wouldn't participate there were a
number who would. For any number of women who wouldn't
go to it there were just as many who would. It seemed to me the
only effective boycott is the kind that stops a thing altogether.
Clearly this couldn't be done by dropping out. As Valerie Solanis
said dropping out is not the answer; fucking up is. She said most
women are already dropped out; they were never in. Dropping
out gives control to those few who don't drop out; dropping out
is exactly what the establishment leaders want; it plays into the
hands of the enemy; it strengthens the system instead of under-
mining it, since it is based entirely on the non-participation, passivity, apathy and non-involvement of the mass of women. Endquote. I wish I could say I was thinking along these lines myself
but I wasn't. I was to be honest hardly thinking at all. I had no
rationale for either participating or not participating. I did rather
lamely agree that it was outrageous for a panel on women's liberation to be moderated by norman mailer or any man for that
matter and that the whole show was a bad deal for women and I
thought it up myself that women's liberation is not a debatable
issue, but as an exhibitionist in my own write it was a hard invitation to turn down and it was not at all clear to me that it was
possible both to participate and to arrange a destruction of the
event from within, thus my position was merely that of a person
in conflict over wanting temperamentally to do something that
a lot of other people disapproved of. Nobody convinced me that

it was correct to drop out. They did make me feel guilty over going ahead with it. Or at least extremely uncertain of my motives or something. Not that I didn't question theirs. Why would anybody want to dissuade their friends from doing something they knew somebody else would do if their friends didn't and very possibly not do as well. I think my low feminist consciousness and non-involvement stood me well. I thought I had the true message and the style in which to deliver it, so better me than some other joker. So I never seriously considered not doing it. For appearances sake I threw the ching to see what some neutral source of wisdom would decree. The ching excels in pointed generalities, it rarely indicates any single course of action, if it does in one passage it suggests another in the next and so on in a series of alternatives that leave things basically up to you which is where you started before you threw it, so it's hard to say why it can be so reassuring when you already know what you're going to do especially when it merely confirms the confusion you think you feel regardless of what you're going to do; but it is (reassuring), and in this case it didn't let me down. The reading was 60. Chieh/Limitation. It said that a woman who would like to undertake something finds herself confronted by insurmountable limitations. That sounded right. It went on If she rightly understands this and does not go beyond the limits set for her, she accumulates an energy that enables her, when the proper time comes, to act with great force. Discretion is of prime importance in preparing the way for momentous things . . . If germinating things are not handled with discretion, the perfecting of them is impeded. *Therefore the superior woman is careful to maintain silence and does not go forth* (my italics). That didn't sound good. But the next passage went *Not going out of the gate and courtyard/Brings misfortune.* When the time for action has come, the moment must be quickly seized . . . It is a good thing to hesitate so long as the time for action has not come, but no longer. Once the obstacles to action have been removed, anxious hesitation is a mistake that is bound to bring disaster, because one misses one's opportunity. —That was it. Seize the time! And I was on the phone telling excitedly what the ching said to one friend who said yes by all means I should do it and the ching was always right and I was on the phone relating the same thing to another friend who said it didn't matter what the ching said it was wrong to do it and anyway the ching said it was wrong too and so forth but it didn't matter I was a performer and an opportunist and I couldn't think of anything more drastic and wonderful than appearing at town hall before thousands of people who lived above 14th street to tell them that all women were lesbians. I thought the invitation was a real coup. It isn't every decade that the enemy invites its opposition right into its own camp to tell it off. Not that I fully grasped as I've indicated the nature of my opportunity. If I thought the invitation was a coup I was far from clear on the political significance of my lucky break. I mean it seemed I'm sure more like a personal break than a politically significant opportunity and there was nobody except Valerie Solanis whom I didn't take seriously at that time other than as a dangerous woman to help me into a broader view of the situation. I had the correct instinct to fuck things up but no political philosophy to clarify a course of action. And had I had such a philosophy it's doubtful I would've been able to educate enough people in a short time to make a real difference. As it was the most radical people I knew were the radicalesbians and the message I got from them was that they had already done their lavender menace actions and they were tired of them and they didn't work anyway since the media always distorted everything and the best thing to do was to retreat and get your own shit together and build lesbian nation from the grass roots out of your own community of women. I couldn't disagree with that, but what about the actions, why couldn't we do everything, anyway now that I was ready to do something why was *I* supposed to feel that it was no longer the thing to do. The reason was that I wasn't a member of the group or of any group and only the group can make up its mind about how things should not be done. I was still a flourishing free enterprising capitalistic individual and as such I could do what I wanted to do but I could hardly expect support from a group that for me didn't exist. The group that did exist for me was a loose collection of friends who were no more political than me and I think less so. The irony here was that they would have done what only the radicalesbians could envision as an expedient political action and wouldn't do themselves. I mean neither me nor my friends could see what had to be done if anything was to be done since we were not politically sophisticated. One group was informed and unwilling, the other was willing and ignorant, is one way of putting it. Of course the willing and ignorant group, to which I belonged, was not really a group, we were as I mentioned a bunch of friends engaged in private pursuits who could usually count on each other to appear at critical personal moments like just before a performance to offer moral support over a couple of drinks which is more or less what happened for town hall. One might ask at this point what all the fuss was about and why I'm even telling the story. In oakland california the winter of '72 I read the town hall speech to mills college women who asked me what was the town hall thing all about. I think some of us were under the impression that it was an intergalactic event. Certainly in new york the event was accorded the kind of front page attention you might expect to see for a new episode in an alice crimmins murder trial or the sinking of the queen mary. Which are not exactly apt examples perhaps of what I mean considering that many people although nobody actually said it were looking forward to the town hall affair as the great matchmaking epithalamium of the century. Considered in this way it had nothing to do with me and indeed the moderator himself suggested as much when I arrived at the table. Apparently I was there like Ceballos and Trilling to complete the pretense of a panel under the guise of which the moderator and our new exotic feminist from abroad could bloom into the first public episode of their intercontinental courtship and betrothal, or something. Hadn't the moderator said plainly in his armies of the night that he had had a love affair with england for his third wife, so one could easily suppose that as an anglophile in women at least that he was looking for another. In which case I don't know why I wasn't suitable myself since I was actually born over there whereas the prospect in question was an unlikely provincial from australia. Not that I had the slightest interest in the moderator except as a familiar mug that occasionally appeared on the newsstands. Nonetheless it was the preference of the moderator for a glamorous impudent foreigner from australia which made this event very much what it was supposed to be. The prospect herself satisfied everybody's expectations by her advance interest in the moderator. Germaine's obsession with norman seemed to me in fact foreign and embarrassing. She had already told me she wouldn't mind fucking him. Coming from wherever she did I think she saw him a lot larger than we did. Not that he hasn't been a literary hero to many amerikan women too. Anyone with such a reputation is impressive at some brute level in any case. I could appreciate him as clown and celebrity. I thought he would make an interesting mayor. But local and alive heroes are much less exciting than foreign or dead ones. Local or dead or dismissed or whatever the important thing that had emerged about this little bean of amerikan litters was his indisputable claim to championship as a sort of king of the chauvinists. So this basically was what the fuss was all about. The event itself could be viewed retrospectively anyway as the first shot like fort sumter of the male retaliation to the new wave of feminism. I don't think this was Shirley Broughton's intention in any conscious way, to help out the men. Like many women who still considered themselves people she just saw this particular man as a writer and he happened to be one of her favorites for whatever reasons I don't know although I suspect she was no different than other admirers who learn to like what's best advertised and what represents in this way the normative literary structure of a culture or a nation which remains substantially male. Certainly she had given me no illusions that the event she was arranging was in the interests of women's liberation—rather it was to be a farce in the tradition of the amerikan debating team society, a vehicle for mailer to star and to make box office. She wasn't interested in other words in helping *either* men or women, but inadvertently she provided the instrument for the first official male backlash if by official you mean the setting of a date time place price and subject and a suitable cast of characters which attracts an inordinate amount of attention. The timeliness of it all being its chief claim to official status. So much for officialdom. I was very impressed afterward when I heard that people like stephen spender and sergeant shriver were there. I thought it was impressive enough that susan sontag was there. Actually everybody was there, except for the leaders of the movement. What was happening in a way was that women's liberation was being co-opted for a sort of literary cultural commercial venture. What mattered was not anything to do with women and liberation but the social extravaganza for which the subject was a pretense like the window dressing of ecology programs sponsored by our greatest polluters the industrial firms. Something like what radical chic meant to black liberation. This was in effect radical chic for women. Backlash defined as instant conversion of a movement for revolutionary social change into an expensive gladiatorial performance. Into a nuptial ceremony celebrating the amorous public encounter of the chief representatives of the warring factions: the educated goddess from abroad and the general of books and machismo at home. The warring parties found each other attractive. Here possibly was the essence of the reaction: the pacification of lysistrata through the presentation of a trophy. The liberation of women is accomplished immediately by their proper

seduction. The shining example of this couple would put an instant
stop to the feminist complaint. The angry feminists after all all
they needed was a good fuck might be a line you'd expect to
find in the very article that brought us all together. I don't think
this particular brawling cliche can be found in the prisoner of
sex but it doesn't matter it's the message of the article anyway. It
was the article of course that had provided the foreplay for the
orgasm of our appearance at town hall. For myself I had no intention of copulating with the hero and to that (non)end I
plotted a demonstration of my own position followed by an
evacuation after I said my piece and before the hero was scheduled to erect himself by asking questions and making dialogues.
I had in other words no intention of indulging the hero of the
occasion any more than I was by my first crime of agreeing to
make an appearance. The organizer had indicated over supper
one evening in chinatown that the panelists would shape their
delivery around an appreciation of norman's hot controversial
attack on women and Millett in particular in his just published
prisoner of sex in harper's. In that spirit she sent me her last copy
and like most mailer stuff I was unable to read it and I knew
what it said anyhow although I must say now that considering
how all feminists around town were foaming and fulminating at
the thing had I read it myself I might've approached my entry
into the lists with more righteous indignation and intent to murder if not simply destroy but I didn't. My instinct to fuck up was
fine as far as it went but it went into schemes for theatrical stunts
and sideshow in the tradition of dada the absurd and the happenings not strictly to epater le bourgeoisie but in that spirit
somewhat anyway falling discouragingly short of any masterful
plan to tear the place apart. One meeting of a committee dedicated to destruction would've been sufficient for determining the
proper invasion tactics and takeover. As it was I had abandoned
my plan to become a boxer and all I could think of was to speak
and disappear leaving behind an advertisement for myself in

form of a huge poster of the jacket of Marmalade Me or to try
and wire the hall and convert norman's voice into instant static
every time he spoke or to try and rise on a swing or a platform
by pulley or helium balloon and demolish the stage with water
bags and paper airplanes and jelly beans and confetti and rice
patties from astride the beams in the flies and unfortunately
none of these things happened and what I ended up with was the
most vaguely formulated plan for demonstrating my message by
making love with a couple of pals which wasn't so bad after all
considering the apparent total capitulation of the goddess from
abroad it behooved *some*body to show in some way that the subject of the panel was women and that the liberation of women
is about women not men by the obvious display of women relating physically illustrating this fundamental truth hopefully coun-
tering the embarrassing attraction between the warring parties
although I knew we'd probably just come across as degenerates
like the sick dirty dangerous lesbians we were it didn't matter it
was still the most satisfactory plan short of bombing the place
and that isn't true either now that I think back on it. Now I
realize I could've stopped the show singlehanded. A filibuster
could've included an auction of my manuscript (I wasn't paid
for this performance) and a repeated plea for all women to vacate on the repeated premise that women's liberation is not a
debatable issue over and over vacate vacate and women's liberation is not a debatable issue until pandemonium developed. The
problem all the way around was that norman himself has had a
lot of theatrical experience so he seemed equipped both by experience and by the power invested in him as moderator not to
mention the anticipated sympathy of hordes of his brother comrades eager to support the seduction of lysistrata he seemed
equipped to upstage any of my own designs. Primarily I think I
was afraid of the man. If so many women were visibly affected
by this thing in harper's magazine what was anyone to think.
Mostly however the image I had was of a drunken bloody brawl

between the moderator and a young antagonist in the dense crowd of an annual village voice xmas party in '62 or '63. The moderator bloody and flailing. The crowd pitching to and fro in its attempt both to escape the disorder and to disentangle the assailants. Wasn't he thought to be a frustrated pro boxer? Or a knife artist? After I'd heard he'd stabbed his wife I knew he was the sort of man my mother always told me to watch out for walking down the street. I should cross to the other side when I saw a man like that she said. So I knew. And even at a place where some of your worst behaved artists would be conducting themselves like apologetic criminals for a couple of awesome wealthy hours I found the man at an elegant french dinner party in honor of truffaut in 1968 feinting and jabbing in contemptuous amusement and swaggering pomposity for such an amerikanized untitled lipoleum and reserving what modicum of graciousness he permitted himself exclusively for the beautiful elderly hostess or so it seemed since his attitude toward me was just obnoxious. I suppose he wanted to like me but I didn't fit any of his categories. And I turned down an invitation to be a "lady reporter" in the movie he said he was getting ready to make. Now although it was quite clear to me that here was just your ordinary disgusting person, the sort you avoid in your daily life, it never occurred to me that the man was a chauvinist—in other words a person of a particularly disagreeable character shared to a greater or lesser degree by the male sex, and in this one's case of the less subtle variety. I didn't know this because the word chauvinist had not yet been invented here. Like most women I had seen both women and men in strictly individual terms or as part of a race or class without respect to sex. The difference between class and caste had not yet been defined. My innocence was something of an asset since it permitted me the illusion that one disagreeable character was just that, one disagreeable character, or *person,* and not a member of a whole threatening class of people like the class of men, and this particular one didn't threaten me as a literary entity since he was not only never a model but I never read a thing he wrote except for the white negro about which more soon. For artists I admired jackson pollock and franz kline and philip guston and even de kooning and a few male poets like o'hara and duncan and olson and others I guess but hardly a single male amerikan novelist I preferred the french and british and the women all the female sensibilities whether by men or women but mostly the women and instinctively found amerikan cock so transparently after mother dragon in their managainsttheelementsadventures distasteful and unreadable. Certainly in any case by the nineteen hundred and sixties having come of age by a narrow margin at least I found people and their work separable entities and no longer seriously expected to be impressed by a person no matter how much I admired their work so I'd say that in the case of norman although his reputation was imposing even if his work was negligible he was personally as offensive as all those crazy artists who drank and made too much noise at the cedar and fucked (up) too many women no matter how much I like a pollock or a de kooning I didn't want to get in their way and in fact one time in the country at a summer's pig roast I learned my lesson well when de kooning lunged and swore at me in a particularly loathsome manner I suppose he wanted to fuck me and insult me if he couldn't and he did both at once in a sense by lunging and swearing and I don't know what all but it's one memory I don't treasure and now I'm beginning to wonder about these guys' work too but I don't want to get into it. As for norman I just wrote him off as an undergrown bully, the kind of boy wonder from yer P.S. 94 days whose one exploit was dipping the pigtails of the girl at the desk in front of him into his inkwell. You forget about those boys. The ones who grow up to become a pest of major dimensions. The irony of the town hall affair was that it forced me to think about one of them. The times had changed. The author of these books I'd never read had become a Chauvinist. By the date of this infamous event

May 1971 I confess I was not all that certain what a chauvinist was. I guess I should've read his article. The article after all was just a substantiation by quotes of his own work and of miller and lawrence of what Kate Millett had already discovered in his (their) novels by quoting them and commenting on them and mailer fully cooperated in Millett's judgment by defending to the hilt as it were the very masculine mystique that she was exposing as sexually politically degrading to women. So really what he was doing was saying yeah that's the way I am and that's the way we were made and that's the way it's going to continue to be and hail joseph and jehovah all glory to the male mystique and right up on the backs and into the cunts of women. It's a curious kind of rebuttal where you affirm what you appear to be contradicting just by hollering. It's like having a tantrum objecting to what they're saying about you and going right on to say what they're saying about you. What it amounts to is that the mailers can't find anything wrong with what they're saying and doing and the women were beginning to say it was all wrong which is the latest chapter in the old war between the sexes with the critical difference that the women now are making this broadside attack on the entire heterosexual institution which they analyze as the root cause of all oppression or at least I do and many do I think see the sexism of the institution as its modus operandi which through its domination of one sex by another is the prototype for all other dyadic structures of oppression. This sort of analysis I believe completely eludes men like mailer who would not be expected in any case if they did see it to see anything wrong with it or rather with the object of the analysis since their own position is the superior half of the manmade bargain. Defending old henry miller mailer virtually yells and drools and pisses over his rights to the barbaric modern custom of mortifying women: . . . in all the indignities of position, the humiliation of situation, and the endless revelations of women as pure artifacts of farce, asses all up in the air, still he screams his barbaric yawp of utter adoration for the power and the glory and the grandeur of the female in the universe, and it is his genius to show us that this power can survive any context or any abuse. Endquote. His genius. His defense of the exclusive right of men to go on saying what women are, defending poor lawrence, a son despised by his father and beloved of his mother he says, a boy and young man and prematurely aging writer with the soul of a beautiful woman he goes on, claiming for lawrence that "It is not only that no other man writes so well about women, but indeed is there a woman who can?" It's almost hard to believe norman would've been writing this sort of presumptuous garbage in 1971, I mean where had the man been, saying things like "Yet whoever believes that such a leap is not possible across the gap, that a man cannot write of a woman's soul, or a white man of a black man, does not believe in literature itself." Indeed, I think for many it had come to exactly that that it was difficult to believe in literature any more. For myself as I began to say a ways back I had an instinct for any literature that *was*n't the literature of the tradition of mailer and miller meaning the amerikan cult of virility and violence. farrell dos passos steinbeck wolfe hemingway fitzgerald these were not my heroes. I read them or a little of them along the way but it just wasn't my swig of whisky or whoopee or anything and if there was any amerikan male I liked I don't mind saying it was henry james who was a eunuch or an (in)active homosexual and at least a gentleman whose novels of manners I still prefer to such dribble as miller ". . . once she got the taste of it in her mouth, you could do anything with her . . . he'd stand her on her hands and push her around the room that way, like a wheelbarrow . . . he'd do it dog fashion, and while she groaned and squirmed he'd nonchalantly light a cigarette and blow the smoke between her legs" or mailer explaining miller ". . . that there were mysteries in trying to explain the extraordinary fascination of an act we can abuse, debase, inundate, and drool upon, yet the act repeats an interest

—it draws us toward obsession, as if it is the mirror of how we approach God through our imperfections, *Hot*, full of the shittiest lust." I think I really think james went and lived in england because he couldn't stand what was going on here in amerika. If it was miller and mailer (and manson as gore vidal suggested) that we were coming to it must've been pretty bad when old henry was growing up around here too. Anyway at least now we know what it's all about. Kate prepared the indictment and the accused pleaded innocent using the evidence of the prosecution. The accused rounded up quite a lot of other evidence to use against himself. To his credit for example he even delved into our feminist folk hero Valerie Solanis courageously quoting one of her best passages about how the male is an incomplete female and spends his life attempting to complete himself to become female by constantly seeking out fraternizing with and trying to live through and fuse with the female and by claiming as his own all female characteristics etc. in short how the male has pussy envy. The accused somehow incorporates this notion beautifully into his elocunt plea for understanding how his pal miller has captured something in the sexuality of men as it had never been seen before when he says sweepingly for all his sex I suppose things like it is "precisely . . . man's sense of awe before woman, his dread of her position one step closer to eternity (for in that step were her powers) which made men detest women, revile them, do everything to reduce them so one might dare to enter them and take pleasure of them" or "So do men look to destroy every quality in a woman which will give her the powers of a male, for she is in their eyes already armed with the power that she brought them forth, and that is a power beyond measure— the earliest etchings of memory go back to that woman between whose legs they were conceived, nurtured, and near strangled in the hours of birth . . . So it is not unnatural that men, perhaps a majority of men, go through the years of their sex with women in some compound detachment of lust which will enable them to be as fierce as any female awash in the great ocean of the fuck, for as it can appear to the man, great forces beyond his measure seem to be calling to the woman then." I don't care if he ever said it before, in the context of his article it perfectly illustrated Valerie's point. The accused was perfectly right. I don't know why the feminists were so upset. The accused had corroborated the testimony of the prosecution and the jury in the form of apparently thousands of literate people had swept down on the newsstands like a school of piranha to devour the evidence in every last issue of the march harper's magazine to regurgitate the verdict of guilty. I suppose then that it appeared unseemly for a convicted criminal to be offered the opportunity of presiding over a function the subject of which was a debate over the treatment of the victims of his crimes. Possibly women's liberation to somebody like him was whether or not the victims of the war crimes will be taken care of in some way. Reparations. Child Care and Equal Pay and Abortion Rights. The victims are people being held (women are still down) and the debate is about shortening their sentence somehow. I dunno. People will do anything for excitement. Rent a big hall and invite your friends. I felt rented and excited. I didn't relate to the subject very well. I'm certain this is because as a realesbian my position as woman or victim was relatively remote like that of a ghetto minority to the center of action, I mean there are varying degrees of intimacy in relation to the oppressor and child care and equal pay and abortion rights are the issues based on the greatest intimacy and such issues no longer concerned me personally and my position in fact was to disengage from the oppressor such that these issues would no longer be issues but practical problems in a woman's society. My message in other words was all about women and not women in relation to men. Yet there I was on the platform with the man in front of a huge audience that was half male. I didn't have much of a chance. I wasn't really anybody's representative. The representative for women of course was germaine. The convicted criminal was still at large and stalking his prey like all the guilty and accused feeling cornered but with powerful resources back in the strongholds of life magazine aroused to unplumbed heights of revenge and ambition. The criminal required a sacrifice. The best specimen for the sacrifice out of the hordes of victims was a giant godiva rising out of the celtic mists with a better education who had written a book admiring the types of victims the criminal himself had written about. The choice was perfect. The amerikan male had had enough of its ordinary looking indigenous feminist stars. The amerikan male was not anybody to appreciate the looks of any old mature and accomplished straightforward woman as beautiful. Nor was or is the amerikan female we could be sorry to say. The image is glamour and Kate according to the criminal had a pug nose and the pest from P.S. 94 would especially pick on a pug nose to dip her braids in his inkwell we all know that. Kate had qualified as the literary quarry of the criminal's hysteria, as the object of murder I should say, but the object of seduction was essential to complete the picture of a happy retaliation, the object sent by the masses of dubious women to capitulate to the charms and genocidal genius of the criminal. Kate had been disposed of. She had written a book "as unwittingly obsessed with the nature of men as a child born blind from birth might be absorbed in imagining what a landscape was like." The criminal had learned "little which was new about women in the pages of Sexual Politics." The choice of the day was made by mcgraw hill and life magazine ("a saucy feminist that even men like") and by advance word of the prisoner of sex who had singled out the english lecturer from warwick and upper james st golden square as representative of a new style by women he thought were writing like very tough faggots with a wind in the prose that whistled up the kilts of male conceit is the way he put it. He thought some amerikan women were writing raunchy funky prose too, in fact he thought it started here and that "the style

had crossed the atlantic." Possibly he saw the women's movement exclusively in terms of its prose style which was good if it
sounded like tough faggots with a wind whistling up the kilts
of male conceit. Whatever he saw he joined the media men at
that point in assisting a certain setback to feminism by exalting
a book that was distinctly low brow compared to the monumental
criticism and quality of Millett's Sexual Politics, not to mention by
the way another amerikan book Shulamith Firestone's Dialectic
of Sex which if widely read and seriously considered would I
believe along with Millett's book and other movement documents
have projected feminism into a position less debatable than it
appeared to be at the time of the town hall affair. In any case the
natives really wouldn't do and the glorification of Steinem had
not yet taken place. The imported brand besides was a lot bigger
than the criminal and a lot sexier and wittier and more stylish
and with a command of extemporaneous rhetoric that every
amerikan is seriously deprived of. The land of pioneering immigrants is still struggling with its english and the real mayflower
anglos are by now too far descended from the oratorical expertise
and artificial elegance of their origins and just realistically the
mixed tribes of amerika don't too much give a damn how they
spit it out because they don't need a finely turned phrase to bank
all their money and consume all their goods. But england is still
the land of ancestral status and prestige. The end of the british
empire and the rise of the amerikan has in no way gravely affected the respect and awe with which the old mother country
is still regarded here. The death of the duke is top news in amerika. I know whenever somebody asks me where were you born
and I reply there in england they say oh really and remain impressed for at least five minutes. I know the first thing I did at
town hall when I arrived at the podium to deliver my portion
of the women's allotment was to try and give myself some instant credentials to better advance the cause of lesbian nation I
suppose by making some offhand remark across to Germaine at

the table to the effect that wasn't it amusing or something hoho
that we were both from over there me from england and her
from australia forgetting to add that beatles line we've come a
long way baby but anyway intending not altogether unconsciously to discredit the central attraction by placing her as a
provincial. But the genuine article was still a sick dirty dangerous
lesbian so what could I do. I gave a fine speech. I made everybody laugh. I got a lot of women excited. I made a lot of men
furious. I gave them a floor show. I provided some good copy. I
enjoyed myself. I felt victorious. I thought it was right to walk
off and all. But there was that one thing that happened if I had
better repressive faculties I wouldn't remember any more and
that was the vote the moderator called for when he suddenly
decided I had talked enough on the ostensible grounds I was
exceeding the time limit he stopped me and said I should read
my last sentence and later after a lot of confusion involving the
eruption of my two friends from the wings when they misunderstood the break in my speech as their cue to enter he called this
vote from the audience to determine if I should finish my speech
or not and the reaction and results of this maneuver clearly indicated how favorable my position was in the line-up I just wasn't
a potential bridesmaid to the godiva and the groom. It was as if
not one but three dykes in boots and overalls had come happily
stomping into the wedding reception to eat all the cake and
drink all the champagne and muss up all the bridal sheets. I wish
actually we *had* been as disturbing. Robyn and me were pretty
sedate, probably we looked like grable and gable in an old movie
in the goodnight kiss outside the lady's apartment, SK did more
justice to the intention, coming barrelling out yelling hey Jill
what about me and throwing the three of us to the floor which
was described variously by the papers as an affectionate tumble
or a hunter locker room happening or etc., but I think now we
were compromising all over the place and the three and more of
us should've stayed and crapped up the stage going raving naked

and orgasming our way through the rest of the verbal garbage is what I think and that's to add to my list of grievances over my own dearth of creative vision and experience in the medium of destruction. Anyway that vote had a ring of social truth about it. The men still command the lower register. There may've been just as many yeas in favor of my continuing speaking but the male voices made a resounding no noise. It was fitting that the criminal element in support of its head mobster should negate the right of the victims in their most alarming and obnoxious mutation to speak at their own forum. The idea of course being to drive us back into our ghetto minority. All women are lesbians? Get that woman outa here! And by my own volition I left. My prior decision to walk off and the message I wished to communicate by doing so became neutralized by the coincidence of another intent implicit in the imprecation (vote) of the vocal majority at the performance itself. I think if my computer hadn't been tangled up at that moment I would've perceived the new turn of events and reversed my decision to walk off since by walking off I seemed to be complying with the male intent and not saying what my own intention was which was to demonstrate by the gesture my compromised contempt for the event. But maybe I did anyway, or for some at least. (It's been pointed out that women at *this* date would not permit such an outrage as the interference of a speech by a woman by male members of an audience; nor, I might add, would such a panel ever be permitted to occur again, at least in a sophisticated city like new york.) Certainly at the time I thought it was fine. Naturally I did because I was still politically unsophisticated. And my friends thought it was wonderful. The radicalesbians wouldn't speak to me and the feminists never spoke to me anyway and my mother hasn't spoken to me for three years but there were always a few friends . . . and a couple of lovers. And then there were the repercussions: all those women above 14th street bewildered and furious and uptight and happy and amazed and hot and wet and wacky thinking about what to make over such a lowdown disreputable unsavory character appearing under such fancy expensive auspices and this was a satisfying if disorienting development. The point after all was to enlarge our constituency. The question the moderator addressed to me in my absence was what was I he was asking *me* what was *I* going to do about all 90 per cent of him or them to which I replied in my column I was just exploring my own ten per cent but already right at his own performance our constituency had been enlarged if only by a fraction of a per cent that was a good beginning because he's through and he don't know it yet but the women are on their way and the next town hall is gonna be an international convention of the amazon generals and lieutenants to discuss what should be done if anything to alleviate the suffering of the males who survived the holocaust of stag nation and are no longer fit to assume any leading responsibilities. The survivors of the female gender will be instantly rehabilitated and educated into their inheritance "one step closer to eternity" to control the destiny of that which passes between her legs. The missed opportunity this time became a mere line in my speech: A lord was not considered defeated in a local war until his flag had fallen from the main tower of his castle . . . svastickles falling outen da sky . . . the current dispute would be settled if the central figure was no longer present. Right on cue the moderator interrupted as soon as he heard this line to tell me I'd better read the end of it in other words shut up and sit down or as the new york post reported he said Come on, Jill, be a lady. I guess he was right. The company was park avenue and cocktails. But I wasn't invited to the dinnerparty beforehand, and I wasn't greeted by the moderator as though I was anything more than a filler to complete the pretense of the panel, in fact the moderator inferred that I was dispensable as soon as possible, and the great godiva from the east (or west) displayed more interest in the convicted criminal than she did in her jury of peers her sisters, and the organizer didn't pay me or thank me for the awful time I gave

them, so town hall was just another swimming pool at easthampton, just another random investigation of the bureaus of the
nuns at boarding school, just another swanky artists loft party
at which to ruin yer dress and lose yer shoes hanging upside
down from the pipes, just another readymade set to practice
the improbable art of being a public nuisance and a maverick or
a martyr at the service of the principle of chaos and corruption
or whatever we can call the urgent necessity of swinging from
the trees at cocktails and clacking hideous noises to stop all the
polite chatter and see the faces register amazement or disgust or
*some*thing behind the tin foil masks at the disturbance in the
trees, I dunno, I could say other things about this mode of inspir-
ing social change, I could say I just had sour grapes is an old
expression or that I was getting off a frustrated career as a dancer
and the bitterness of being a critic or that my mother adored and
abandoned me which is true of me and everybody or that I hate
the rich but that's sour grapes I think or I could say I really enjoy
being scene and herd and that is true although it scares me to
deaf and I might rather be dumb but here we are and I remain
my own most avid interpreter. The evolution of an art form like
the impromptu performance derived from one's early years of an
appreciative audience of the two important people in your life
is a whole lifelong study. For me the sixties was the great opportunity. The fifties was hopeless everybody knows that. The fifties
you had to do something *reg*ular and *dis*ciplined. The sixties you
could do your own thing was the phrase. You could look silly and
irresponsible and stop working for other people. You could do a
whole lot of things you couldn't do in the fifties but you couldn't
do that much and that made it exciting too. I practically never
misbehaved in the fifties. The fifties was a closed scene. The
poets ginsberg and corso and their pals were taking their clothes
off to read their poems in the coffee shops but they were the
only ones, nobody else did anything like that, certainly no women
did. The beats opened things up but hardly anybody knew about

it, not until the sixties, and then a bunch of other things happened too. The fifties just sucked. All I ever did was get fired
from jobs. That was the trouble, you had to have these jobs, you
you had to be a responsible adult, you had to have credentials
and titles and degrees and affidavits and be a worthwhile citizen
it was really awful. The sixties was the ocean after the desert. So
along we came into the sixties. And one small irony about the
town hall affair was that one notorious survivor of that decade
was sitting next to another who had styled himself "the first
philosopher of hip" and had written an essay (the white negro)
which the first survivor had actually admired for it helped define
a world she was becoming if a definition is necessary anyway she
liked the essay and who had emerged in the meantime apparently
as the arch enemy of her besieged sex. This I think is not insig-
nificant. It took me for one until 1970 at least to suspect never
mind be convinced that those wonderful hipsters and hustlers of
the left come to bring us all freedom and lollipops by doing
something about "the system" were just some old wolves in new
sheep's clothing with due apologies to wolves. Again our folk
hero Solanis was very advanced saying in 1967 ". . . in the case
of the 'hippie'—he's way out, Man!—all the way out to the cow
pasture where he can fuck and breed undisturbed and mess
around with his beads and flute . . . the 'hippie,' whose desire to
be a 'Man,' a 'rugged individualist,' isn't quite as strong as the
average man's, and who, in addition, is excited by the thought of
having lots of women accessible to him, rebels against the harsh-
ness of a Breadwinner's life and the monotony of one woman. In
the name of sharing and co-operation he forms the commune or
tribe, which, for all its togetherness and partly because of it (the
commune, being an extended family, is an extended violation of
the females' rights, privacy and sanity) is no more a community
than normal 'society' . . . The most important activity of the
commune, the one on which it is based, is gang-banging. The
'hippie' is enticed to the commune mainly by the prospect of all

the free pussy . . ." All the free pussy! Isn't that what miller and
mailer were talking about ("somewhere in the insane passions of
all men is a huge desire to drive forward into the seat of creation, grab some part of that creation in the hands, sink the cock
to the hilt, sink it into as many hilts as will hold it") (Mailer,
Prisoner of Sex, 82) and why vidal was updating them with
manson? I mean mailer was no commune man but he had the
right idea, and his essay the white negro explained what the boys
were after in old fashioned terms like in terms of reich and the
ultimate orgasm which was popular in the fifties. The new breed
of urban adventurers "drifting out at night looking for action
with a black man's code to fit their facts." The competition for
pleasure in a world where "the truth is not what one has felt
yesterday or what one expects to feel tomorrow but rather truth
. . . being what one feels at each instant in the perpetual climax
of the present." Urban adventurers. No longhair country freaks
turning into the sixties. The style was evolving. The war novelist
turned jazz and black enthusiast was neatly compiling the evidence of a new culture around him. I don't know what he was
doing about it himself except looking for the next most terrific
orgasm and occasionally stabbing a wife or running for mayor. I
know better what ginsberg and larry rivers were doing like rivers
was in the *middle* of a lot of that stuff shooting up and playing
sax with his black friends besides painting and fucking women
and possibly men too. I know also at that time it was not clear
to me that the hip jazz beat black white world of the new psychic
outlaws was a world of cock roost strut sturm and drang or else
why would mailer have been so interested in it and in becoming
the "first philosopher of hip." In 1966 susan sontag ironically was
putting down leslie fiedler for putting down "the new mutants"—
the new breed of youthful androgens, turned-on kids "from
Berkeley to the East Village . . . both lumped together as representatives of the 'post humanist' era now upon us, in which we
witness a 'radical metamorphosis of the Western male,' a 'revolt

against masculinity,' even 'a rejection of conventional male po-
tency.'" Susan rightly I suppose viewed the phenomenon as a
healthy "natural, and desirable, next stage of the sexual revolution" moving "beyond the discovery that 'society' represses the
free expression of sexuality (by fomenting guilt), to the discovery that the way we live and the ordinarily available options of
character repress almost entirely the deep experience of pleasure,
and the possibility of self knowledge" she said. But the whole rap
was about boys and susan's disagreement with fiedler was based
on *fiedler's* assumptions regarding a new disturbing style so I
guess she knows now like the rest of us that the sexual revolution was a sort of downwardly mobile and in mailer's case upwardly new mystique of masculine aggression. Nor was there a
shift as some say. The love ethic that went to chicago and came
out a fuck ethic was a fuck ethic to begin with. I was fooled along
with the rest but none of it seriously affected me personally. I
mean I wasn't jumping into bed with any bearded freaks. The
women were following their men and I was following the women.
The style was grand and dangerous but for me as for many of the
women who were following their men and waiting up for them
there was no "paradise of limitless energy and perception just beyond the next wave of the next orgasm." The women may've been
potent orgastically they were exponents of reich certainly and
they weren't like the frigid new england types who had been my
sole reference previously but how much did these women have
left over after they'd kept the house kids money and sanity together for the best part of any piece of waking time I mean how
could a woman just "hang around" staying loose and cool thinking
about the next perfect or apocalyptic orgasm. They couldn't and
didn't. And the philosopher of hip's white negro was a man like
the philosopher. I don't know why we didn't know that but we
didn't. I do know why we didn't know that. We were all people
not men or women so as people naturally we women thought that
anything we said about ourselves was about people meaning both

men and women but we were wrong because it was men mostly
who did the talking and what they were talking about was themselves although they used such generic terms as people or mankind these terms were really a euphemism for men but we didn't
know that since the men didn't think it was necessary to say so
and the women permitted the men to do most all the talking it was
easy to conclude that we were all humans and when one human
spoke that human spoke for all of us all of which means that until
recently very few of us realized we were women. So the white
negro, like the amerikan indian or the black puerto rican or the
dutch puritan, was a man. And by some neat turn that we didn't
know about the very black man we had emulated by example of
our white brothers was a soul on ice whose prime fantasy was
rape of the white woman. We were twisting and smoking and
thieving and using the lingo and having a very good time but
still we were experiencing the fringe benefits of a man's revolution which meant basically more and better women to fuck and
more shit on the women's heads for doing everything they always
did as well as taking care of the new pleasure oriented freaks. I
wasn't personally taking care of any freaks and I was having a ball
hanging upside down from the pipes, but nobody was paying me
to be such an interesting character and nobody was dying to be
my wife to make my life as a writer any easier either. I couldn't
say like the philosopher "He could love a woman and she might
even sprain her back before a hundred sinks of dishes in a month,
but he would not be happy to help her if his work should suffer,
no, not unless her work was as valuable as his own. But he was
complacent with the importance of respecting his work—what an
agony for a man if work were meaningless: then all such rights
were lost before a woman" and ". . . so did the housework of
women take on magnitude, for their work was directed at least to
a basic end." I couldn't say that and it showed. The parties I was
going to were everybody else's. The people I was writing about
were people like the writers of the white negro or the painters

of those paintings of dots and stripes whose wives were so helpful and so dispensable apparently in the gush of success that they
might do you the wonderful favor of coming after your girlfriend
whose love for the writer writing about the others doesn't easily
withstand the pressure of the successful artist who needs all the
wives he can get including his writers and his writers' girlfriends
to continue to be so successful. I wasn't very successful in other
words. I was writing about the work of other people. I did decide by 1967 to make the subject of my writing myself so by
1971 I was feeling a whole lot better about things, but as to
leverage in the world, or who thinks you're worthwhile listening
to, I was at a distinct disadvantage next to the first philosopher
of hip who in any case had written about the war and the moon.
Anyway the swimmer and pipe hanger and dancer and athlete
who was never a writer was a survivor. And she was a little
amused to be sitting next to a dirty old man of a generation that
had wiped her out and whom she had invoked just six years
before walking out of new york's infamous depot for revelatory
casualties blinded by the sun after three weeks in the dark proclaiming that *some*thing (she didn't know what) should be done
about a man who had received better treatment than her in the
same dungeon after going around and stabbing somebody. She
came pleased enough to think that as david dalton said of janis
joplin her presence seemed to corrode everything other people
took for granted and that to approach too closely meant the possibility of some kind of personal detonation. She came both as a
celebrant and as a victim of the second wave of the beat generation. She came as one who had seen the best women of her generation destroyed by madmen, starving hysterical naked, dragging
themselves through the negro streets at dawn looking for an angry
fix. She came as a warrior in the ginnunga gab wearing armor of
faded denims and rose patches and tin can jewelry held up by a
lanyard made by her son and missing a medallion of Joan pur-
chased in Orleans cathedral on a drive through france. She came

bringing libations of coffee-to-go and baby bottle of martini in honor of the resurrection of Amazon Nation. She came as a survivor from the dark ages of her own submission. She came thinking she was beautiful and all that and she came. Like Janis said of herself— . . . the lights, cameras, and I was standing up there singing into this microphone and getting it on, and whew! I dug it. So so much for how I felt at the time about who I was and what was going on. I was happy and thought the solution was fine. The three of us walked out and left the marriage ceremony intact. A crazy manic man grabbed me in the stone corridor running parallel to the orchestra and leading to an exit and wildly invited me to a party he said he was arranging at edward albee's. He was wild and crazy. SK and Robyn hustled us out to the lobby and the street and a taxi down to max's and I was flushed and flying. A social disaster was a personal triumph in the worst old tradition of bourgeois individualism. I don't know what happened to the couple of the century. I saw Germaine at the party afterwards surrounded by willing bridesmaids and she kissed my hand and I suppose she went home alone. I know she eventually recanted in esquire, disillusioned by the opportunism of the general of books and machismo her prospective something or other or not really who was eager in the amerikan fashion to pursue the commercial aspects of their relationship. The engagement was broken and the appetite of the criminal remained unappeased and feminism lives. The prisoner of sex himself thought women had breached an enormous hole in the line is the way he put it, and wondered how far back the men must go before they are ready to establish a front. That was before town hall which wasn't such a bad front. It wasn't such a good one either and we all went down into oblivion in such wonderful reportage as Rosalyn Drexler in the Village Voice saying " . . . would Norman, Germaine, and Jill pose for modern sex tableaus, each taking the sexual position which suited them (or their cause) best? Would Jill go down on Germaine, while Norman, poised above Germaine's head, attempted to give her 'head' . . . Or would Germaine straddle both Jill and Norman at the same time as if riding two magnificent white horses around a circus ring?" The image or collection of images was as good as the event to describe its decadence.

A SERIES
OF GREAT ESCAPES

I. THERE WASN'T A DYKE IN THE LAND

Now a survivor from old dykedom Phyllis Birkby says we should go into the deep south with a lesbian nation bus and collect all our old friends and bring them up to date. We don't remember who to rescue so much but Helen Marie Parks. We assume Helen Marie Parks is lushed flat out on a catholic work farm someplace the far side of the mason dixon. Phyllis said she heard she went catholic anyway. Phyllis says we should research the reasons why so many old dykes went catholic. I said I think it's because of the virgin but my thinking stops there. I went catholic once myself when I was out of my mind because I didn't know what else to say I could be and be acceptable. I knew Christ was crazy and possibly I could seek refuge in his name since it's still a going thing institutionally and I could explain it to myself personally as an identification with the real Christ, who was crazy. I don't know. I abandoned the idea shortly after I thought of it. Helen Marie Parks was never mad so far as we know. She was an original from missouri. A nice godfearing lovable impetuous nailchewing unmistakable dyke from hillbilly land. She told me some fascinating tales about missouri and shotguns and her big older brothers that I don't remember. I guess I thought she was a dyke because of her big older brothers but I don't remember if I thought that either. Whatever we thought in those times we didn't say anything. Growing up in amerika was to grow up not talking about anything that meant anything. We talked a lot but not about the real things. I never said I was a dyke even to a dyke because there wasn't a dyke in the land who thought she should be a dyke or even that she was a dyke so how could we talk about it. Helen Marie Parks was my best friend in north carolina that one whole year and we never talked about it as I said there was nothing to talk about. Growing up in amerika was growing up completely unconscious. We knew certain things were wrong and certain things were right and we were probably wrong since we never questioned the right and wrong code if we had we might have been talking about something as it was we couldn't exhibit our wrongness by saying it out loud or we would be admitting the inadmissible so we kept being wrong to ourselves and in that way were able to largely deny being wrong when you know only by some cultural osmosis that certain things are wrong and certain things are right that is all you know and that is enough and there's a tacit agreement about pretending that everybody is right. Whoever wasn't really right was off in a mental place someplace and we didn't know anybody like that. But we were certainly a bunch of wonderful bandits in north carolina. The place we all ended up at that year was the women's college in greensboro where apparently many young women flocked from all over the carolinas to study mostly home economics. The bunch I fell in with were the sensitive fucked up poet and painter types, a readymade contingent of tightlipped lesies, a whole nest of queers. I wish I could say I was happy to meet them. I wasn't happy to see anybody. I was making my first trip south of new jersey except for florida when I was eight and that doesn't count. I was lonely and desolate in a new place of strangers. I was on my own but I wasn't old enough to be. I wasn't grown up yet but I was past nineteen. I didn't know what I was doing or why I was going anyplace. I was gawky and erratic and unmanageable to myself. I had no reason to go south except by advice of an obscure dancer woman in minnesota who said I could undoubtedly obtain a graduate assistantship meaning another degree by exchanging my services doing a little teaching for room board and nine hundred dollars at this particular college is the reason I happened to be going. I was unhappily adrift ever since I left boarding school which was my last true home. The only thing worthwhile about college after boarding school was my first lover who was an extremely impressive older woman of the world. I was still in love with her. She was the home of my college years. After those years I went to minnesota for a year and hated being so far away from the atlantic ocean. I was a river and ocean person so the middle west didn't agree with me at all. If there were any rivers in minnesota I never saw them. I think really I missed my first lover and later on made up the story that the middle west was disagreeable for being so far from rivers and oceans. I've never lived in the middle west since. The only worthwhile thing about it was my second lover with whom I was not in love but with whom I experienced my first orgasm. She was another older woman although not so old. It was very worthwhile and she was very handsome and sexually exciting but all of it didn't finally make up for being so far from the rivers and oceans. I mean I was still in love with my first woman and somehow I began to develop the idea that something was wrong with me and I'd better take charge of myself and do something about it. Obviously something was wrong. I had never been to bed with a man and here I was on my second woman. Possibly I would not have begun to develop this anxiety had I been in love. Being in love the first time made it absolutely all right apparently. It wasn't all right but it was. It wasn't all right because it was completely hushed up, I never could mention it to my collegemates, even my close friend or two, even my roommate; and my lover herself, being one of my teachers, was in mortal fear of disclosure. So naturally it was not all right. It couldn't possibly have been all right when all the others were boasting about their boyfriends and even flaunting their relationships in public or making big fusses about a date or a blind date or a letter or a phone call. I made my affair all right to myself in private by the sheer undeniable extent of my passion. This woman was a greatly respected teacher too. So of course it was all right. I was actually very proud to be involved with such a woman. Thus I was able to overlook being wrong but in minnesota somehow probably because I was not in love I lost my confidence and thought I should do something quickly or I might truly go wrong. This should be clear. The dilemma of it. And since growing up in amerika as I was saying it was understood we never talked about real things I had nothing to say to anybody so I did something. We were quite oriented toward doing things. We put no value to speak of in talking. Talking was idling away a lunch hour or a bridge game. Talking could be some important damaging information about somebody. Talking in any case was primarily information. Like requests commands and denials or affirmatives. Talking was just not done as an interesting form in itself as in england and it was not done to convey the real things that were going on behind the information and directives or the idle chatter over lunch hours and bridge games. We were completely unconscious active ablebodied privileged white middle class women of amerika. The real thing was doing things. Since we had no tradition of talking about things as they were we didn't know what things were. We instinctively knew things were right or wrong and that was all and that was enough. What was impressive was the doing of things. We never sat around talking if we could be doing something. Altogether then naturally that year in minnesota since I was not in love with my handsome and sexually exciting woman although we got along very well and amused ourselves I began to develop the idea that I was going wrong and I immediately did something. I called my male poet correspondent long distance, a rather drastic measure at that time you didn't just call anybody long distance for the hell of it, and ordered him to meet me at such and such a hotel in new york city at a certain time when I planned to be in new york for a vacation. I had no interest whatever in my male poet correspondent except as a male poet correspondent. I was flattered by his love poems and fancied myself a Maud Gonne to his Yeats whom I might marry platonically in my old age and that was all. But I went directly to new york to the hotel at the appointed hour and got into the bed with him naked and nothing happened because I found him physically repulsive. He had a beautiful soul and a kind face and he wasn't even so bad looking but I couldn't do it. I wanted the romantic fantasy in distance and letters. Having failed to lose my virginity to a beautiful poet I returned to my second woman in minnesota to enjoy the rest of my wrong year. I'm enjoying remembering this. I couldn't complain that much having that much good sex. It was my first totally good sex. So it was a good year after all, even without the rivers and the ocean. A good lover is a certain kind of home. The endless dry white winter of minnesota was an occasion to learn about real sex. I became a sexual somebody. I could do it with somebody else or with myself too. Since I experienced an orgasm accidentally I could reconstruct the site of the excitement to make it happen myself and this was a great discovery as everybody knows. I had never heard of an orgasm. When I had one I was as surprised as if I'd heard the Martians had landed. I had it and made the most of it. I worked it out very well. It was the sort of toy you don't lose interest in. If I didn't know what I was doing or why I was going anyplace at least I had a dependable longlasting pleasure. Why I so impulsively ran off to new york to climb into bed with a repulsive man is a question nobody could answer at the time. I had a handsome sexually exciting somewhat older woman who didn't oppress me so it didn't make real sense to go dashing off in wild pursuit of the obviously unpleasant. All this was the background to my troubled arrival in north carolina. I was saying I arrived there lonely and desolate surrounded by strangers. I was still in love with my first woman and I had no regrets over my second and for all social purposes I was a virgin and long past the beginning of my time of reproductive usefulness and I think the notion was strongly developing in me that although the further pursuit of my education and accomplishments was a good thing I had a very dimly conceived destiny as a woman as well. My mother never said I should do anything in particular, but she had me, and everybody else I knew was had by somebody, so clearly there was something in it. I didn't think about it, I just know the notion was developing inside me and as it developed a certain vague awareness along with it that my passions of the last two years were not the way people were had if having and being had were the truly basic things that made the rest of what we were doing possible and even meaningful. So I think then I must have been troubled by a clear contradiction. Not to mention that I didn't really think I was a dyke anyway. We never said it so it didn't exist. And it was impossible to be wrong. Since we never questioned the right and wrong code we had to be right. If we had been questioning anything we might have been talking but we kept ourselves in check by not being able to talk or rather knowing anything about talking or realizing that talking was a possible way of finding out what we were about. We didn't even know it was wrong to be a woman. So in a way we were superbly right. We were white and moderately privileged. Talking in north carolina was as much chitchat as it was up north. It was always a joke in the north that you never discussed politics religion or the civil war. One might say that down south you didn't discuss race either. I never heard any race talk. That isn't true, I did. I think there were rumblings that year in greensboro of a race problem, something about property or real estate and white folks discussing legal actions or moving out of some neighborhood or other. That was all. Nobody I knew personally was interested. I was interested and appalled by the segregated rest rooms I noticed in bus stations on my way to north carolina but if I wanted to talk about it and if I did nobody encouraged me so all in all we were still growing up unconscious in amerika. My first trip south except for

florida when I was eight was depressing and vacant. And de-
praved. I never saw so many dykes collected in one place before.
I thought the carolinas must be rank with sick family life. I
thought family life was basically healthy so any product out of
the ordinary was sick. I satisfied myself that Ann Polling's father
was a drunkard which made Ann Polling a poor unfortunate and
that Helen Marie Parks had some big older brothers and that
made her drink and smoke too much and chew up her nails and
like her own sex and other such explanations about other people
including I suppose about myself that I never had a real family to
begin with. But if Helen Marie Parks was sick she was sensational. She was a real original. Phyllis Birkby says Helen Marie
Parks was the first person she knew who went to Ocracoke every
year with a frying pan, a typewriter, and a shotgun. I remember
Helen Marie myself racing out into the carolina ocean in all her
clothes at midnight yelling about the almighty sea or something.
I remember her mostly in her everyday sense very dark brown
nearly black hair almost in a duck tail cut anyway the unmistakable dyke look and deep brown eyes and a deep urgent voice that
she brought up from the kidneys that broke into a frequent nervous staccato machine gun laugh and the straight well defined
features and the chain smoking nicotine fingers and the one leg
pumping up and down constantly like a vibrating cement drill
that was Helen Marie Parks everyday. Sometimes she shut herself
up drinking with a typewriter and a monkey that shat all over
everything. She bit her nails so I used to tease her she'd bite herself off to the elbow. She was an extremely nervous and a very
good person. She was your friend to the death. Phyllis was thrown
out of school one day and Helen Marie drove her up home immediately to new jersey. Phyllis says she made it with her once
and I think I did too but I'm not sure. If I did it was in new york
city after I left down there and Helen Marie came to visit if so that
was the last I ever saw of her. We all knew she was in love with
Barbara the poet and much later on we heard that Barbara mar-

ried a man and now Phyllis tells me Helen went catholic. Possibly that's the reason why so many old dykes went catholic. Certainly many old dykes gave up and married a man. Certainly I turned out to be an old dyke who gave up and married a man. So maybe the ones who couldn't do that had no other recourse in all their terrible disappointments except to go catholic. The catholic worker in new york was considered a fine courageous place to go and do your first social service. There were no knights of columbus for women and there was no daughters of bilitis no nothing really to join and drown in a higher purpose or comfort and reassurance of better things in another world. Old dykedom wasn't the best place to be. You were better off trying to get it on with a repulsive man. Unless you were unusually lucky. There might've been a few like that in north carolina. But even this tall gorgeous Rita somebody I knew who lived with a Charlotte somebody in a cozy little house on a nice green street was trucking out surreptitiously having an affair with an old male professor and probably disrupting her home life and making Charlotte desperate. I mean just superficially to look at them you might think they were getting along alright. I don't know really if they were or they weren't. As I keep saying nobody was talking. So we didn't know if they were actually lovers even. Anyway the place was rampant with faculty women living together and looking suspiciously dykey. The faculty women you couldn't be dead sure about even if you knew (and people really know), but the students!—the sensitive fucked up poets and painters from all the hillbilly towns of the south were definitely queer! The biggest building on campus was the home economics building. But the south was producing some interesting females besides its future homemakers. No scientists or engineers or politicians maybe. Just crazy exciting creative women. I met my first crazy exciting creative women and except for Helen Marie Parks who remained my friend I withdrew into a twilight of plato and ivy and tweed and tea and toast on a quiet street sitting at the feet of wisdom who was an imported professor of philosophy formerly of wellesley harvard heidelberg manchester and liverpool in that order reading backwards. I know I thought he was great because he was decrepit and english. It didn't have all that much to do with plato. I mean plato was an experience but I needed a real old man and apparently he had to be decrepit and english. No ordinary bloke my own age interested me in the least. And he had to be short. Short and decrepit and english. And wise and gentle and with impressive credentials. Anybody english had fine credentials. But this one also had been a friend of alfred north whitehead and bertrand russell so how could I go wrong. I was permanently impressed. I sat around being impressed that whole year and lost my virginity over it. If you had to give up dykedom you might as well give it up for somebody short and decrepit and impressively english. I didn't reluctantly give up dykedom. I seemed to be fleeing from it. A common phenomenon. No sooner had I arrived on campus than a sensitive sad beautiful painter appeared to be stalking me in the library. I think it happened in the library. Ann Polling was in that plato class so we knew each other and I liked her a lot and I probably went over to look at her delicate drawings in some abandoned building she used for a studio and stuff but I was definitely not looking for sex with another woman. But I remember now she was staring at me infinitely sadly from her large deep blue longing for something eyes under the exaggeratedly arched eyebrows fixed that way from the longing and pleading eyes and I didn't know what to do. I think suddenly I found her terrifically attractive and swelled up and ran away to the lavatory to masturbate. Then I don't know how but somehow sometime a little later we fell into bed and did something and I was very unhappy about it but I couldn't have told anybody why since I thought she was beautiful and all that. I remember crying over it out at the ocean in beaufort. I think I just was unable to tolerate a third woman without having slept with a man even if I didn't want a man, so somehow I contrived to want one and that turned out to be the short decrepit englishman who seduced me under the guise of being a counsellor to my problem. So I did talk after all. A philosopher apparently is convertible to a psychiatrist and they're all after pussy. Possibly I thought this one was enamored of my gawkiness. More likely he thought he was saving me from a life of certain tragedy and frigidity. Even though he assured me in his best philosophical equanimity and sagaciousness that I was free to choose my fate in this world after all I was a free spirit and suchlike liberal enjoinments, it was puzzling but encouraging, although as I've said I succumbed to his charms so I didn't have much time to test out this liberating view of my predicament. To be fair however I should say that I was already unconsciously so far along in my flight from my true vocation of women that the slightest encouragement from an impressive decrepit male was probably enough to send me into his bed. And that is the true story of how I became disengaged from my short past and turned in the proper direction of social neurotic womanhood and eventually became one of those old dykes who gave up and married a man. I didn't give up so easily. Regarding myself now retrospectively in some heroic light I can see myself struggling singlehanded for a half dozen years after leaving north carolina against all of society with not a word spoken by me or anyone in my defense, a silent unconscious warfare, until I lost, in the battle of new york city, without even having known that there was anything to win or lose. Possibly some of those who stayed in hillbilly land fared a little better, even if they did go catholic. Going catholic was never so bad for a woman if the church offered her some protection from the other alternative if the church itself didn't turn into the devils of loudun. I know I think for myself I went catholic for a couple of days or so long after north carolina and getting married and returning again to my true vocation of women when I seemed to be wedged in a vacuum between the pressure of the society I was giving up meaning men and marriage and the reconstructed society of women not yet validated by the lesbian/feminist revolution. Going catholic is a way of transcending both impossibilities until some clarity is established. The reason I didn't stay catholic is that I was certain I wanted women, so I went genealogical instead. My unconscious dredged up a genealogical solution to a vast social problem. It was really a holding tactic. If I lost before I would win this time with a giant fantasy designed to impress everybody with my incredible credentials. It's the best personal historically recorded solution. It has worked very well for men. There isn't a man who doesn't know what it means to go and slay the dragon. The definition of the objective for a woman is naturally more difficult. The conception and the execution both are extraordinary problems. My unconscious correctly aided me by dredging up the material guide for examination and action. As a holding tactic it served me until the revolution began and concrete external social support for a hitherto untenable position was at last at hand. Alas in the days of old dykedom we were all on our own. And alas we left many of our sisters behind. That's why Phyllis Birkby one of the survivors and one of the creators of lesbian nation says we should charter a lesbian nation bus and go and collect all our old friends and bring them up to date. It may sound presumptuous but we don't care. Mostly we agreed we both loved Helen Marie Parks and we'd like to see her again. I saw the one I forsook for the decrepit englishman not long ago on a return trip to new york driving up through the southlands. I think she made her peace with herself still encased in the excruciating privacy of our old world, she is one of the ones who didn't go catholic and didn't give up women to marry a man either, she went shrinking you might say, she went I suppose to some liberal minded representative of the profession which will help a person "adjust" to their situation in the private individual sense of adjustment, on the freudian premise that a common unhappiness is better than a suicidal misery or something. A compromise therapy stopping well short of the affirmation of sexual identity. I wouldn't try to collect her in our bus because she must have so carefully and at such great pain and sacrifice arranged a little plot of peace and a functional framework for herself. I mean we'd like her in the bus, but how do you start saying you're a dyke even to another dyke when there wasn't a dyke in the land who thought she should be a dyke or even that she was a dyke and out there in lots of outposts of amerika that's the way it still is, still growing up unconscious in amerika.

II.   A NICE WELL-BEHAVED FUCKED-UP PERSON

I was way ahead of myself with my genealogical solution. Such solutions come at the end of the line when the real world seems totally improbable. I had however intended to pass blithely over a dozen years hoping nobody would notice. The fifties was the bleakest decade of all and not particularly worth telling except what there was in it to illustrate the total failure of sexual identity for thousands of nice young dykes like myself trying to become responsible adults. I say thousands because I know now what I didn't then that I was one of many and in fact all if it's true as I very often think it is that all women are lesbians. Whether you think so or not you have to agree there was no lesbian identity except a criminal one so it is almost impossible to estimate the numbers who might have been had there been any social recognition of the state and who were but who were guilty and unacknowledged. The conspiracy of silence prevailed. Identity was presumed to be heterosexual unless proven otherwise and you couldn't afford to be so proven and so for all social purposes we were all heterosexual. There was no lesbian identity. There was lesbian activity. For most of us the chasm between social validation and private needs was so wide and deep that the society overwhelmed us for any number of significant individual reasons: not running off at 20 or so with yr one true love forever like the ladies of llongollen; not being able constitutionally or by naivete or distaste or poor location to become a bar dyke; not falling by chance into a fugitive salon a la paris in the twenties and colette and rene vivien and romaine brooks and radclyffe hall and the like. Those were three good reasons. For all three I was one of those who didn't make it. Phyllis Birkby came up from north carolina and somehow encountered a little society of new york city dykes but I didn't and I never went looking for one either. I went straight to columbia and the dance studios and the book stores and museums in further pursuit of my education and accomplishments. My life as a sexual somebody almost literally hung in the balance for at least five years. I was going to say my sexual identity but I don't think that's accurate. As I said we were all heterosexually identified and that's the way we thought of ourselves, even of course when doing otherwise. By hanging in the balance I mean I wasn't moving toward women or men and neither sex was doing very much about me either. The identity that concerned me clearly was that which came from the command of techniques and information—work identity. The important thing was doing things. The question of identity really was not a question. I was born a female, that was clear. Other distinguishing charactcristics were assets or embarrassmcnts I didu't seriously contemplate in between doing things if there was any in between. By that time I was dimly aware that as a female I was not receiving preferential treatment but the awareness was too dim to affect my undertakings by halting my progress in any way or by making me smarter and thus less likely to fall down hard when the momentum of my activities met the institutional prejudices of my male society. Basically I accepted my lot as a person. I made no political classification of myself whatsoever. A person was white and middle class but I didn't think of it that way either. A person was what we all were and we would do the best we could and if we didn't do so well it was just a failing as a person and that was all.

Equipped with that dazzling generalization I was prepared to take on the world, which reminded me often enough that as a person apparently I left something to be desired. The word my mother had for it was unstable. I was unstable. Whatever it was it was all my mother's fault. Whatever went wrong it was her fault. The way we all had was to blame our parents for everything. I never talked about myself except when I was in trouble and then it was to say it was all because my mother had made these terrible mistakes. The project of course was never to be in trouble. Most people I knew contrived never to be in trouble. If they were they never told me about it and you didn't read about it in the papers. The people in the papers didn't exist. The people who existed were the people you knew or the people walking down the street, these people lived day to day living normal natural lives and nothing ever went wrong. It was quite a fiction. Somehow I was the only person I knew who was ever in trouble. Even when my friend Sally Brinsmade who married Billy Bramlette was obviously in trouble when Billy left her for somebody else I refused to see her as being in trouble. For that reason I suppose such a person like Sally would go to a psychiatrist which is what she did. Nobody liked hearing about anybody else's troubles because you weren't supposed to have any. That's how I see it now looking back at it. I imagine nobody thought I was in trouble either. The fact is we were all in a whole lot of trouble but we didn't know it. The fifties was no time for a woman and new york city was the worst place. But for all we knew the fifties was no special decade. The war was over so what. We had no national or global or even city local consciousness. We just didn't care. We were good women in that respect. And we were instinctively correct not to care too. I mean we were so remote from the sources of power that to care would have been foolhardy in the extreme. Caring is an emotion impelling action and action was out of the question so all we could conceivably care about was immediate personal survival. We were abysmally unconscious of political affairs. I didn't

even know that men ran the world. Men were people so people
ran the world. All we were intent on was personal gratification
and survival. It seems important now to realize that it was for this
reason we were terrified of being in trouble, for to be in trouble
was to fail *personally*, there was at that time absolutely no political significance to being in trouble. To admit failure was to ostra-
cize oneself as a transgressor just short of the criminal element
proper by virtue of not actually being in jail. The conspiracy of
silence made us all guilty of personal troubles by which we suffered isolation in all but the communion of work. What you did
share was a common interest in some medium. As artists or
apprentice artists we had common cause for complaint in our
economic struggles, but even the political significance of our
economic plight was obscured to us, and so this was a personal
struggle too, there was no way to make things any better because
we had no collective complaint. Really there was nothing to do
but to consider men and marriage and the liberal arts and avoid
as many evil people as possible. We were all people and people
were good and evil. This assessment of people was how you got
along, how you figured things out, how you summed up your day
—did they treat you alright. My mother always used to say was
so and so nice to you. The relative niceness of everybody was the
essence of reality. Besides the sheer expenditure of energy in
doing things. You went along doing things and expecting people
to be nice. As soon as somebody was not nice you were in trouble.
new york city was not a nice place so I was in trouble as soon
as I got there. I had nightmares and claustrophobia and chest
pains and constipation and paranoia and daily harassments and
weekly disasters and yearly major catastrophes. I still think the
others survived better than I did but I know that isn't necessarily
true and they might well have thought the same of me. That any
of us survived at all is the fact worth pondering. I'm convinced
that if the others *were* surviving better than me it was because
they were better prepared to cope than I was. I think they were

more realistic about themselves as women. I know they thought of themselves as people the way I did, but women people did have a destiny as women, that was understood, and these other women I knew appeared to be pleased about or resigned to their expected orientation toward men and marriage. Sally Brinsmade was already married. Betty Jones was married. June somebody was married. Melissa stopped dancing and went to vermont and got married. Pauline Koner was married. Ruth Currier was always involved with a man somehow. So was Pat Christopher. Lucy Venable I think wanted to be if she wasn't. It went like that. And since I had come up to new york from north carolina prepared by my decrepit impressive englishman to be turned in the proper direction of social neurotic expectant womanhood I should have been doing the same but I wasn't. My natural vocation of women was still not utterly squashed. No sooner had I left the old englishman than I fell in love with Ruth Currier. That was all very well, but it was a classic of unrequited love of the tragic lesbian variety, Ruth was no north carolina dyke and in fact there just weren't any dykes in new york that I could see so there weren't any. Much less myself. It was the perfect nothing affair to finish me off as a dyke. It was so nothing that I never expressed my feeling or ever once seriously tried to do anything about it. So for me there was not only no lesbian identity but no lesbian activity either. I was very active in the best western tradition of sublimation. Studying dancing reading, and working at any dopey job to keep myself going, rushing from university to dance studio to job to book stores to museums and to coffeeshops to read and back to my rented rooms like an activity machine. I had become a sexual nobody. Moreover I really didn't know where I was going, what I was doing all the things I was doing for. Dancing was exciting and challenging but if somebody had asked me what I really planned to do with my life I wouldn't have said dancing and I didn't have any other idea either. Possibly the culture had already closed in on me and my strongest if inarticulated feeling was that I was doomed for men and marriage. I don't know. Certainly I was finished off as a dyke. I was so finished in that respect I was climbing into bed sometimes with any repulsive man, no man sexually seemed better than repulsive, the boyfriend of a roommate or some stranger in a coffeeshop, it didn't matter, there was no reason not to, there was actually now that I think of it every reason why I should have considering that every woman I knew in new york seemed inclined that way and there wasn't the slightest indication of anything out of the ordinary except for the queer males and for the first time in my life I was surrounded by every cultural persuasion of heterosexual identity, not least of which was the unnerving and taken for granted daily lowdown assaults by the public freaks. There was no end to this sort of harassment. Men everywhere were extremely insulting making remarks at you out of their car windows, whispering obscenities passing you along any street, sidling up to you on busses, feeling you up in the movies, goosing you on subways, pulling their pricks out at you in restaurants, I wonder that none of us complained, but none of us did, we might even have assumed such attention to be flattering, if not outright dangerous. If anybody else questioned this behavior I never heard of it. You might say to a friend there was this *horrible* man who did such & such and that was the end of it. The horrible man just being of course an evil person. We knew some evil women after all. Evil women didn't assault you in this manner but we didn't differentiate the types of evils to arrive at any sort of classification and discrimination in other words any rudimentary feminist analysis or consciousness. Nor did we associate all this public freak behavior with our private voluntary encounters although I for one had every reason to. I was beginning to get myself in a whole lot of trouble. I think now and I've said regarding myself retrospectively in some heroic light that I was engaged in a great battle singlehanded against all of society with not a word spoken by me or anyone in my defense, a silent unconscious warfare, until I lost, without even having known that there was a battle or anything to win or lose. So what are we coming to. To the story of the end of my real world as a busy person. To the story of the traumatic confrontation between me and the male corporation. To the story of the end of these stories in a melodramatic genealogical solution. I have to make it clear that I was not at all prepared to deal with society at large. I still think most of the others were prepared. None of them seemed to come from such an exclusively woman centered background as I did. I had undoubtedly a culturally imposed internalized low opinion of myself as a female, if from no other source but from the original one of my mother and my grandmother who were self sufficient but abandoned women, women abandoned in the sense of living through whatever complex combination of circumstances without the support and recognized status of the male provider and protector, yet by virtue of these same demoralizing origins I was a female of a certain uninhibited chauvinism about my identity as female or person uncorrupted by male influence. I think thus I was even more aggressive than the others about being a person, a person being that idealized transcendent member of human animalkind long before or after the corruptions of political sexual discrimination. Anyway I'm fond of thinking I was a delinquent and outrageous adolescent in boarding school because I didn't have the super-ego daddy in me and that later on the same license served me well in being in turn a rebellious critic, an innovative writer, a revolutionary lesbian. That's getting way ahead of myself. I see me now in the effort of memory back in the fifties moving into the sixties a hopeless case in new york city. I had met the male corporation and I was knuckling under. My complete naivete was the measure of my inability to cope. I had after all been nothing much more nor less than the beloved daughter of my mother and my grandmother and the various woman centered institutions I attended although hardly sympathetic to my every whim did have a tendency to reinforce my sense of myself as a noticeable entity.

Everybody was my mother and my grandmother in the expanding theatre of activities and reactions. The main thing was doing things and attracting enough supportive attention to make the doing appear to be as worthwhile to others as it was to me. I appealed to various audiences who would hold up a mirror to my image by reflecting me themselves in their own reactions. The symbiosis of me and my maternal parents was the internalized model. The mother and her child must be the original theatrical pair. Performer and audience in reality the same person. I didn't think any of that out. Like anybody I was on automatic computer and the plug in or the combination in my particular set like I suppose many another nice young dyke was just totally out of synch with the general social computer which was perhaps located in new york city. My last feeble claim to be a dyke was rapidly evaporating in the unexpressed and unrequited romance of the Ruth Currier affair. My first claim had already been seriously deflected by the old man in north carolina. If there was at one time some shade of doubt as to my heterosexual identity it was now gone in the overwhelming phallic city of the world. Naturally the conflict of my inside potential identity and the pressures of normal regular society out there resulted in some serious trouble. It was one thing going along rushing from one activity to another pursuing my education and accomplishments, in the process it was impossible apparently to ignore the demands of sex and intimacy and the invisible inaudible but omnipresent commands of the corporation to shape up and make the conventional marriage. I know that's what was happening. My destiny was out of my hands. I didn't seem to be doing anything by any choice or influence of my own. Even the activities themselves seemed to be carrying me along of their own accord and there was no sensible reason why any activity would stop and go veering off in a different direction until it just as unaccountably stopped again and resumed in some new mystifying guise or other. But worst of all of course was the alarming lackadaisical aspect of my private encounters with men. Out of these encounters occurred my downfall. I took no precautions and I turned out to be a real fertile myrtle, one screw and I was done for. The first time wasn't so bad. This Tony somebody who was actually a boyfriend of my then roommate took moral and financial responsibility for his part in the accident and saw me through this my initiation into the abortion racket. It wasn't so bad. Still, it was sordid and upsetting and depressing. And the second time was the end. It should've been the end of me too. In a sense it was. It was the beginning of my being one who was an old defeated dyke who gave up and married a man. It was the beginning of my saying silly things such as well I'll have to do it the right way, I'd have to find the right sort of a man and do it all properly, things like that. I said it and that was the beginning of it happening. Saying it is imagining wanting it and it was the first time in my life it seriously occurred to me that I had a destiny as a reproductive woman. At last my social destiny as woman had made a conspicuous impression on me. I was a woman like other women, these accidental pregnancies proved that, and since my education and accomplishments were not proving anything in particular beyond being educated and accomplished, and since I was virtually finished off as a dyke, and the culture with its insistent persuasions of heterosexual identity by which a woman is defined as wife and/or whore had by that time easily closed in on me, I was going the way of all women—the grave of marriage and the hell of motherhood. And toward that end I got myself into the worst sort of trouble. The second abortion was an interminable bloody and dangerous and humiliating affair. For my friendly rapist I had chosen the most bizarre character, an Oswald somebody who materialized suddenly up around columbia as a friend of a few of my friends there, claiming an obscure noble french lineage and a fascinating life as poet and adventurer. In reality as it turned out he was a pathological liar and imposter who hailed from a little immigrant ghetto in brooklyn. Now here was an evil person.

Here was your genuine evil person. Right inside your door in your private spaces in living awful color, no better than those public freaks whose daily harassments at least didn't send you to the hospital in an ambulance. That's how I ended up. Carried out on a stretcher into an ambulance. Not that this particular last act form of my second error was the fault of this particular villain. But a villain he was. Whose moral flabbiness compounded my desperate situation of accumulating confusion and terror and ruination to whatever remained of my self respect as a person getting along in the big city without any trouble. I was about to become a bona fide failure. I was involved in so much trouble it was no longer the sort of trouble you could keep to yourself. I had not exactly kept my troubles to myself, but I had not spread them abroad either. But here I was almost in the kind of trouble that gets in the papers. I might have become one of those people in the papers who don't exist. The only people who existed were the people you knew and somewhat the people walking down the street. There were three kinds of paper people who didn't exist: the men who ran the world, the movie stars and sports heroes, and the murderers and rapists and suicides. Possibly I was the closing the gap. I think really I was an overlyprotected white middle class not unprivileged young female experiencing life at more drastic levels than losing a boarding school soccer game or arriving as a troubled student in a strange new state lonely for her first two women. I mean I had never even seen a dead person. The photos of nazi victims in wheelbarrows just didn't mean anything to me. The novels or movies of tragedies for me were all a fiction. I could cry over them, but what did they have to do with me really. In truth I was involved in a great extended personal tragedy, the perversion of my original identity as a woman's woman in the phallic subliminal persuasions of the biggest baddest city in the world, but I didn't know it so it was a fiction just like the fictions of death and disaster in the papers and the movies and the novels. I should correct that word identity. There was

lesbian activity, no lesbian identity. Everybody understood identity. When you filled out application blanks for schools or jobs
you found out who you were or who you could be. You were
male or female, single married or divorced, protestant or catholic,
old or young, white or black and anglo or jewish. And you had a
name. Identity is what you can say you are according to what
they say you can be. And not least of the categories of identity is
that of sexual status under the law which allowed of no other
orientation than that of heterosexuality. Lesbian identity was a
criminal or non-identity. The conspiracy of silence was to prevent
such an identity from emerging. Why certain dykes persisted in
the fugitive life against all the social tacit evidence of their
criminal definition and others like myself didn't is a question I
still can't answer to any satisfaction, what I'm more certain of is
that both types but I think especially the type that stopped doing
it or couldn't get into doing it in the first place anyway both types
were seriously dissociated from themselves. Both types being all
women if you agree that all women are lesbians. On the general
principle of the romance between the mothers and the daughters.
That forgotten romance. The continuity of it or the recovery of it.
I can't ultimately differentiate my oppression as a woman from
my oppression as a lesbian. Whatever you think, and it's impossible to estimate the numbers who might ever have been and who
might be now were it not for the fact that the law of man recognizes only a woman's prime commitment to him, we know it is
essential to be an integrated person to be unified in the belief of
the rightness of one's needs and interests and the doing of them.
So in order to continue to be right you had to pretend you were
and in this way any natural dyke like myself was in a state of
internal dissociation over what you thought you were and what
you were doing or wanted to be doing, and then even if you gave
up wanting what you were once doing and you were now merely
wanting you were still dangerously dissociated from yourself in
the sense that you were repressing your potential identity and

your real needs and interests. Looked at in this way every lesbian
was a sick person. The internalization of the taboo was so great
that you didn't think you were what you wanted or were doing. In
the sense that every woman is separate from herself is she ill. For
all daughters once primally attached to their mothers it is a general social illness to be turned in the direction of a prime commitment to the fathers. I'm way ahead of myself. As it is it isn't easy
just to think back into how I was as a very active unconsciously
conflicted person in new york city. I had plenty of warning in the
form of symptoms but that's as far as I got: troubles and chest
pains and claustrophobia and constipation and paranoia. And the
confirmation of myself as an unstable person turning into a
failure. Clearly something had to happen, and it did. I think I
nearly died significantly enough in the apartment of my friend
Ruth Currier with whom perhaps I was still secretly in love anyway I happened to be in her place hemorrhaging over the spontaneous delivery of this four and a half or five month old fetus
after a couple of weeks of visiting one of these abortionists who
attach a device to the cervix to somehow electrically induce labor
and I thought I was done for. This was the upshot of the Oswald
affair. Nobody was around so while I was bleeding to death I
managed to call the hospital bureau which arrived with all their
emergency and towaway equipment and that's how I became a
kind of public casualty in a city depot, it was very embarrassing.
I had made a grand personal demonstration of my inability to
cope. My mother was turning out to be right about me. And it
didn't help matters to blame her either. And I didn't go to a
shrink which was the obvious recourse in such melodramas as
mine. That's what new york was all about. An army of head doctors just waiting for everybody at the natural end of the line. But
I was far from finished with myself. The final touches involving
of course a man and marriage, the real thing. Never mind that I
went on to break my foot and later suddenly stop dancing for no
apparent reason and unaccountably take a musty job sorting out

clippings and photos in the dance collection of the public library from which I was predictably fired and to become more completely than ever an isolated and alienated struggling young lost white middle class female unprotected in a big city. Never was a person so clearly driven into the desperate expedient of marriage as the illusory solution to a problem I didn't know was much bigger than me. Some people say now but why did you do that and what can I say, I didn't know what else to do and that was always a thing to do in fact a basic thing to do, it was all around you, and I suppose since I had embarrassed myself, I had to legitimize myself, and nobody seemed so happy as when a person especially a woman was making the contract called marriage. Thus I entered the final phase of my complete capitulation to the male corporation. And I picked a perfect male dope to make sure I did it up fine. To tell the truth I just picked the first handsome intelligent sounding male that came along after I knew there was nothing else to do. Handsome and intelligent didn't mean a thing. Four years and two kids later I might as well've made a cross atlantic solo flight in a balloon for all my marriage meant as a solution to anything whatsoever. To be fair however I should say it performed an extremely important function: it brought me back to my lesbian senses. It was about time. As it turned out I'd made the perfect choice. The marriage was an exercise in violence interrupted by short periods of violence. I had made certain that nothing short of a desexualized rhubarb for a male specimen would ever please me again. That I survived to ever think the thought was one of the minor social miracles of the day. I should've won a lavender heart for survival. By the time I was through I had experienced all new york had to offer short of jail. If I had arrived in new york a sort of institutional domestic geranium unfit even for walking down the street at last I resembled somewhat those heartier indigenous weeds growing up through the cracks of the broken sidewalks. I suppose you think I had it all together by this time. Well certainly I didn't. I had the sense to fall in love with a woman again, and I had something called Experience, the novels and movies of tragedies were not such a fiction to me any more, and I was by then embarked at last on an activity I enjoyed that had some social personal direction to it and that was writing; but I was still a private person, still an individual with no political sense of myself whatsoever and thus responsible for all my actions in that awful ultimate sense of democracy and the freedom of choice or enterprise and upward mobility that made even that oldfashioned concept of fate an obsolete one, I mean there was not even fate to blame for yr troubles, and I was for a short but interminable time an impoverished tenement bound stranded mother of two with a typewriter and a few assorted salvation army dishes and a beatup escape vehicle for which you sacrificed food money if you needed the gas, and a palpable physical reminder of yr disaster in those periodic paralyzing attacks in the chest which drove you to the nearest emergency clinic and a bunch of x-rays that suggested you were a case for the shrink. Moreover, I wasn't through with men yet. Naturally I was under the impression that the character I married was just one of those bad people, so I had had a piece of bad luck, and I might do better the next time or if there was no next time I knew there were better deals around and I could agree with my friends in the popular psychology of the time that I was just a masochist and had *chosen* the agent of my defeat, something like that. Now I think it's true that on the scale of boys the one I chose was a particularly bad one, I mean at least there were those who were restrained in their violence by the gentleman's code of manners about never hitting a lady and all, and who were older than a sexually demanding explosive 21 & so forth; but I had not the slightest idea that marriage in itself was just a bad deal for a woman and that from that point of view it wasn't that the bloke I married was so terrible as that I was constitutionally unable to submit to my proper role as woman in the contract, I was ill prepared for such a role, I didn't know what it was, as I've said the

exclusively woman centered life of all my early years had given
me a certain uninhibited chauvinism about my identity as female,
and although this identity was drastically at odds with the social
discrimination against my sex, I remained oblivious to what that
discrimination meant in terms of innate inferiority and the behavior required to suit that preconceived notion of myself, and
as such a female ran straight up against the role-playing aggression of a young male whose chauvinism was, unlike mine, socially
cultivated and sacrosanct. I had grown up it seems in a kind of
fugitive hothouse of a matriarchy. The word chauvinism may be
inaccurate to describe the feeling I emerged with. I don't know.
I don't recall emerging with any specific attitude of being *superior*
to the man, nobody audibly put men down, it's just that we went
on as if men didn't exist more or less, I had no occasion to observe
and to feel their privilege, so I think my chauvinism was people
chauvinism, I met the male world with a naive sense of equality,
that pure sense of nature antecedent to the corruptions of culture
in its political sex race and class discriminations. The young male
I married was not the individual I thought he was so much as an
excellent representative of the system at whose hands I had already been diminished. But once again, not understanding any of
this, I had failed personally, still all out of whack with myself and
society. I'd like to've skipped over these dozen years without anybody noticing. It was a dismal time and there wasn't much help
for us. The feminist revolution was still a few years away, gay
liberation even more remote. There *was some*thing however, and
that was the cultural revolution of hip and beat and black jazz
and the twist and the drugs: all the incipient makings of drop-out
and the later radical left and a woman's movement. And I almost
forgot—I was becoming a writer! And I had fallen in love with a
woman again! There was devastation, but there was hope. Most
hopeful of all was leaving behind me that overall fifties mono-
chromatic peck&peck and lord&taylor life of skirts and *blouses*
and the entire wasp outfit of proper well educated sensible young

women who never had a good time but who functioned superbly, who were responsible and dedicated artists or whatever they were, always in control of themselves meaning if they were in trouble you never noticed it, the main thing was *appearances,* and I was incapable of keeping them up, so at last I met some other floundering disorganized people. Who were having a good time!

My port of entry into the wild sixties was the leftover beat generation on east broadway where new york's original jewish ghetto was still flourishing. Ferlinghetti's east broadway. I don't know where ginsberg and corso and burroughs were by then, and I never met ferlinghetti, but here was a far out scene of people mixed up with the poets and painters in making "Pull My Daisy" with script by kerouac and whirling around themselves in the slums with thrift store finery and the new underground culture, whatever that was for anybody. The new happenings. The new chorcography. The new paintings not yet called pop or op. The new music. The new mixed media. It was very exciting. And my wasp thing was at last contaminated first hand by the children of the children of new york's great population of disenchanted immigrants. These people I met were the sons and daughters of some real original amerikan outsiders and they were getting it on culturally with another group of outsiders—the amerikan blacks, and as a misplaced person with a forgotten history of rebellion of my own, the halcyon years of boarding school delinquency, I could relate to all this chaos and craziness. I became a beatnik in thrift store gear. I became an impromptu entertainer at loft parties. I had joined the historical company of eccentric bohemians now called beats or hipsters. Apparently I was so overwhelmed by my new life that I outdid everybody in the sheer extent of conceivable silly exploits. I was delighted with my new reputation and seized every opportunity to enhance and enlarge the scope of it. It was just like boarding school with the added

complexity of poverty and mudderhood and a serious involvement in writing. It didn't solve a thing sexually, even if I was in
love with another woman, but at least I was running around
again and acting as if the whole world was my mother and my
grandmother in the original expanding theatre of performance
and reactions. Sexually in fact this little society of crazy artists
and beautiful spunky women was as straight as any other in new
york city, straighter for that matter than the uptown world of
dancing I came from in which at least many males were queer
and kinky even if they didn't say so. So I remained as heterosexual as ever, not unlike the earlier days when I would climb into
bed for no good reason with any male dope who really wanted
to while being secretly mad for a woman in another hopeless
quest for an unattainable object. The difference being that I was
encouraged by the more expressive histrionic nature of this new
society to be a little assertive about my needs and to risk something in the folly of exposure as I went down finally in one more
battle against straight society and my own heterosexual identity.
The difference also being that these people didn't condemn me
outright, they were modern bohemians after all, and they con-
ceded the possibility of being queer if you could just get to it, I
think they were exasperated by my own unresolved conflict, they
allowed for an individual solution, that is if it was maintained as
strictly individual, and they could say well this friend of ours was
fucked up somehow and this is what they have to do and so be it.
In any event there wasn't much point in secrets among these people. Unlike the wasp they didn't come from families that made
big pretenses over things. They yelled and scrapped and loved
their way through life, everything surface and up front. If this
second wave of beat and ripoff was colorful and exciting the life
was also desperate and precarious and the troubles of everybody
were just as declared and manifest as the daily good times and
the celebrations of the parties. Here was a more integrated kind
of existence. My odyssey as a dissociated person was coming to a

close. It would not be through or within this milieu of hippiedom that I would sort out the discrepancies of my life, but it was through them that I moved on to the next, the concluding phase of an untenable conflict and a highly personal spiritual solution in the shattering experience of schizophrenia, that time of going catholic for a couple of days and of going better than that with some grand creation of a genealogical explanation, a kind of holding tactic until the revolution began and concrete external social support was at last at hand. Nobody should wonder why I turned into a revolutionary lesbian. I had done practically everything there was to do. My case was a paradigm for a revolutionary consciousness.

iii.   LOVE AT FIRST SEX

In january & february 1969 I was travelling in a vw squareback south and west and back east again 12000 miles in seven weeks with a lover and partways with a friend of hers from canada and finland who weighed over 200 and protected us through the badlands of the south. In el paso we sent him flying on. We were in love and he was a jealous party. We stayed in every holiday inn along the way. We arrived los angeles feb 20 and cut back east about a week later not having gone up to big sur as planned. Driving route 66 thru flagstaff and albuquerque into sante fe we steered north into taos and settled there for a week in a sagebrush inn below the mountains. We were tired and confused. It was a wonderful aimless trip. I was still quite mad from a third schizophrenic freakout that had taken place back the second week in january in new hampshire and although I was keeping the delusions at bay I never stopped talking and I was stimulated by every bush rock sign or human incident along the way to rhapsodies of association and excitement over each new piece of evidence related to the cosmic plan. I think the initial purpose of the trip was to keep me out of the clutches of the psychiatric profession. Presumably by the time we returned I would be less sensitized to my environment. Other than that we were involved in the personal drama of another one of these secret impossible relationships. For me the drama was a kamikaze trip to live happily ever after with yer one true beloved or perish in the effort. I was to perish. I just couldn't figure it out by myself. The Stonewall Riots in new york that launched gay liberation were five months away so we were still a fugitive pair so far as the world was concerned. Even so, I was furious and determined. Here I had a young rich beautiful storybook princess who would make my life worthwhile forever. This was my second heiresstocrat and they both loved me but they both thought it was wrong and so did I. We all thought it was right to be in love but that was all. By this time I was convinced I had to be a dyke but how. There was still no salon, there was for me still no underground bar dyke world, and I wasn't being very successful at running off with my one true beloved forever. I was running off and everything, and the vague plan was to get a big house out in the boonies someplace as soon as we returned, but I knew it wouldn't happen and I didn't have the sense to realize it shouldn't. Anyway if I thought that was what I needed I didn't really deserve it. I was doomed to a life of adventure as a writer and of tragedy as a lover. With that highly constructive opinion of my situation I persisted nevertheless in waging one last war toute seule against society. I didn't have a real strategy but I did have a goal or an objective and that was to somehow buy up a lot of space and establish a chain of lesbos on the mainland and invite the lesbian population and introduce the rest to the mysteries and just forget about the men, leaving them to their own devices destroying themselves with their machines and frozen foods. That was the cosmic plan. I had conceived the mission and my lover had the money. The lesbian population was completely invisible at that time, I knew nothing but straight people and gay men, but I thought we were such a dashing couple that the world would turn on at the very sight of us. Especially since my chemistry was so beautifully fouled up. An asset that was proving to be more of a drawback in our crosscountry escape tour I found it impossible not to read the mind of the barbaric amerikan psyche so that more than two days in any one place was a luxury we couldn't seem to afford. The texan stormtroopers. The vanquished indians. The spanish christian flaggellantes. The bible belt yahoos. The hot rod cowboys. The big mean mommas. The gas pump abners. Either there was really a menace out there or it was all in my paranoid lesbian mind. I think it was both. But basically I thought the world was after us and we had to keep moving. And basically I was right. We were an illegal couple. The law of man which recognizes only a woman's prime commitment to him could not make us right no matter how right it felt sexually and no matter how much we were in love. It was impossible therefore to think that what we were doing was what we were. So what were we then. We were not women and we were not lesbians. We were people. We were people with a difference. But all people from a liberal point of view were individuals or exceptions or special cases. Since we were all special cases we all had special justification for our actions as individuals. As white middle class people in fact we were expected to be upwardly mobile and individually accountable to ourselves and society. Individuality is released by privilege. If we thought of ourselves for a moment in any political sense it was as part of a privileged race and class. Never mind even that many of us were not directly the beneficiaries of the industrial wealth of our puritan anglo ancestry. The inherited sense of ourselves as the right sort of people was not significantly diminished by our original particular circumstances of genteel poverty. A circumstance that my mother for one rectified somewhat by sending me off to the right sort of boarding school. What we had overlooked completely was the erosion of our confidence as the wrong sex. That's why I say we were not women. And why I didn't really deserve what I wanted. Why in other words we viewed ourselves in strictly individual terms without respect to sex. For the key element in the design that was obscured to us was our sexual position as a politically inferior caste. It was not at all clear that although we were encouraged enough to pursue our personal ends we were at the same time under implicit regulations to go just so far. The young woman with whom I was travelling was an heiresstocrat as I said so she was certainly a superior person as people go and she was smart and beautiful besides but what was she supposed to do with her life if not breed more of her kind and especially the male kind even if nobody specifically said so and nobody did because it was understood and we never talked about it either. So what was she doing being in love with another woman. She was going through a phase is what the psychology people would have to say about it. So what was I going through. The second stage of my own arrested development I suppose. And the corruption of the young. And the depravity of the species. Altogether the solution of one who would never grow up and make the proper entente with society. So how did I come to all this after those years of being such a nice well behaved fucked up person minding my business trying to be a writer and a somebody in new york city. I came to it through precisely that description. I had come apparently to the very end of my possibilities of going on existing in contradiction to myself and in august of 1965 on my own behalf I went totally mad. In 1966 I went mad again and in january 1969 I did it again and in that condition having escaped the clutches of the psychiatric profession and its penal colonies I was travelling about the union in style convinced at last that it was the world who was fucked up and not me and that if I didn't do something about the world it would continue to mess with me and all the mes like me wherever they were who didn't know yet that it was the world making us all such normal neurotic people but I didn't have a real strat-

egy as I said and how could I when I was still a solo case attempting to make myself a political group of two. And that isn't
true of course in that I still didn't know that people and in particular the two sexes were politically defined, politics meant
republicans and democrats or tories and whigs which meant one
man trying to beat another man into being president of the class
so he could decide on the color of the bombs and the names of
the hiways, yet I had the right idea in a way to consolidate myself as a team of two in so much as the base political unit of society is the marriage of man and woman although I didn't think
of it this way my instinct for the power in such a union was correct as was my traditional attitude toward the greater claim of a
storybook princess with an inheritance. One thing I'm trying to
say is that most of us didn't know yet that it was wrong to be a
woman but we did know it was wrong to be lesbian and that it
was wrong for people to make us wrong and in this way some of
us were acquiring the rudimentary emotions of a gay consciousness. I was in fact generating a lot of unauthorized fury. The way
it felt at the strictly personal level was that society had an almighty nerve telling me that what I liked and wanted was sick
or sinful or illegal or criminal. Nobody had to use these words.
It was clear enough in the gestures and attitudes of everybody
everywhere. The women disapproved and the men were after us
and I wasn't making that up. They were after me and my woman
but primarily my woman because she was a desirable princess
and I had no right to her whatsoever except in the privacy of our
minds through the accident of a street meeting and love at first
sex. I can't say that by this time I was politically enlightened at
all, I was just personally furious and armed with an extremely
amorphous outlandish plan for saving the world. Meaning I suppose a plan to save myself. The world just continued not to give
me any reasonable demonstration of its interest in my welfare
apart from forty dollars a week for a column in a village newspaper. Thus the world needed saving. I think I had become se-

riously interested in saving myself and that was a healthy sign for me and the times. I wonder what adjustments people in the past in furious isolation like myself made to their situations if they didn't give up as I once did that first time as a young dyke not knowing any better or knowing only too well you might say anyway what did they do I wonder. I think they were rich like Gertrude Stein and set themselves up in big houses in liberal cities and made some approximation to the heterosexual model by supporting another woman in a stimulating protective menage. I don't know. I suppose there were many variations. But whatever they were they did not exist as dykes. So far as the world was concerned such women were companions or roommates and they were identified by their careers and salons. Dykedom was not a reality for the world nor was it real for any of us who were actually doing it. The person you were involved with was very much a person or a special love object about whom you rationalized that it just happened to be a woman and could as well be a man and although it was a woman it might be a man the next time if the right *person* came along. People will remember an interview in a feminist publication concerning two good friends "coming out" together that was very offensive to revolutionary lesbians. That's because although we could be happy enough that women were getting it on together the tone of the interview was an appeal to that personal private place so many of us came from where we were without any identity in that essential political sense of belonging to a tribe in its mutual understanding and protection and collective means of changing society. The old style lesbian marriage by the way being a part of that personal isolated place from which we'd come, the marriage I thought I had to make in 1969. Anyway one woman in that interview said sure I could have a relationship with a man if he were the right kind of person, qualifying that by adding if he rejected playing "the man" with her, which made her think that left out a lot of men, although if a man had the right combination of qualities she saw no reason why she shouldn't be able to love him as much as she loves her. Living as we still do in a sexist society defined absolutely by the norm of the heterosexual institution by which sexist practices are cultivated and sanctioned such statements are politically reactionary for women whose love for other women can now be viewed clearly as revolutionary and subversive and whose very articulation as a political group is the prime instrument of refusal to participate directly in the institution of our oppression and thus ultimately of overthrowing the institution. Such advanced thinking was remote to me in those desperate days 1969 travelling west and east across the country trying to legitimitize myself in the only way known to private people which was to approximate the heterosexual model by running off with yr one true beloved forever in a fugitive marriage or marriage without legal contract. The standard of respectability for persons was a durable marriage. Most persons seemed respectably married. I don't know if I wanted to be respectable so much as I wanted some assurance of the private urgency and reality of my involvement through the continuity promised in the social affirmation or blessing of marriage which amounts to respectability I guess. Whatever it was I was pursuing a classic contradiction. For one thing a fugitive lesbian marriage was not compatible with my temperament. Already I had been writing home dropping the news of my romance obliquely in my column such that a gay person certainly could detect the subject behind the references. Either I was constitutionally incapable of keeping a secret or I was angry enough to defy all the taboos regarding such confessions made even indirectly, actually I think I was so angry that I was conducting a one woman revolution through a very slow calculated but unrelenting exposure of myself in the guise of a literary code hopefully so challenging and fascinating and entertaining and difficult to read that any premature retaliation from a hostile society would be discouraged, and in this sense from the standpoint of anger I was certainly no longer çapa-

ble of keeping a secret. Such exposure also perhaps was my only
means of marriage in an unmarriageable situation. Had I known
we were just four months away from the Stonewall Riots I might
have been more daring even. As it was I was greatly emboldened
one sunny monday in taos new mexico by the appearance of a
lead article in the drama section of the new york times entitled
Why Can't We Live Happily Ever After written pseudony-
mously by a man and concerning a recent bunch of movies on
the lesbian and homosexual subjects treated in predictable stereo-
types as the sick unfortunates with a dismal outlook that indeed
society had made of us but which this man in the times was contesting in his film criticism it was very exciting reading off in
taos new mexico as I was floundering through a hot and hopeless
romance. It was in fact just the tonic we needed. Why Couldn't
We Live Happily Ever After. Exactly. And it was in that spirit
that my lover in the initial flush of romance back in new york
had enthusiastically introduced me to her sophisticated but conservative and unsuspecting mother who reacted like a solid
mother a bit unhinged running off consulting psychiatrists and
wiring her husband to fly in from spain until she was assured
that her delinquent daughter was merely going through a phase
and that she would do more harm than good by interfering and
overtly disapproving. And it was in that spirit that all naive lesbian lovers have expressed their feelings naturally and have
been informed instantly of the consequences of their criminal af-
fections. Anyway, inspired by that article in the times I sat down
right away and wrote the most explicit column I had yet written
and sent it off to new york in frightened jubilance under the title
Pubis Est Veritas. It was still convoluted and obscure. But any
half literate reader should've been able to see what I was saying.
It seemed explicit enough for me to feel somewhat safe in our
distance from the scene of publication. My terror over a silly column and my concern for safety in distance surely was the measure of our severe and internalized repression as women and les-

bians. Possibly for many like me there was no way left to save ourselves but to risk everything by breaking that conspiracy of silence by which we had been so consistently destroyed. Surely many of us were psychically mobilizing at the barricades. Certainly our revolution was already ensured by the spadework of radical feminism and all that was required was an event like Stonewall for gay liberation to materialize. Had I known I might not've been so tenacious in my efforts to be married happily forever to somebody much less somebody so vulnerable to the blandishments of male prerogative and so clearly cut out for being a vessel for the continuity of the mayflower line of anglo aristocracy in amerika. I think she was the last beautiful daughter of her particular line. I was as impressed as any upwardly mobile wasp of dubious origins was supposed to be. I thought it was wonderful. The estate in new hampshire. The town houses in new york. The mansions in boston. The stocks on wall street. For all I knew they owned the country. An asset that was central to the cosmic plan. Which would originate in some big establishment involving a continuous lesbian extravaganza. Which we discussed idly on the journey as nothing more than a little house for two in the country. I couldn't tell you as I'm writing this if I really had such a startling fantastic scheme in my brain. I can tell you I was quite crazy and nothing was beyond me and I was definitely waking up at six every morning full of new symbols and diagrams explaining the relativity of the universe. I don't think I dared actually to conceive too much for my personal cause. Being crazy I knew somewhere in my head my personal cause was far bigger than me but I was still after all a woman unconscious of my own oppression and so in most parts of my head I remained a private person struggling to survive and without any political affirmation of the vision of my crazy part. In any case the vision transcended political discrimination. I suppose I might've come out of orbit if somebody had given me an elementary political lesson or two. Going crazy has always been a personal solution in extremis to the unarticulated conflicts of political realities, a way of transcending these conflicts by going into orbit and settling the world to some terribly private yet collective and archetypal satisfaction through the imaginative construction of interrelated unified systems. I had indeed become a dreamer awake. I slept deeply and dreamlessly and woke each day to spin out my symbols and associations of names, numbers and concepts in vast constantly changing webs of multiplying interdependencies and frightening cancellations. The many and the one. I could talk myself outward in circular expanding ripples that included everything and then back again by cancellation to the void in the center. My terminology was a mix and a jumble of whatever I had stored in my head from all the disciplines I knew and when I met somebody with an unfamiliar discipline like say diamond cutting or watch mechanisms I would press the secrets of their crafts out of them plying them with questions until I felt satisfied that one more discipline was subject to the great immutable laws of related unified systems. The exercise was to crack the code and find the essences. One could surmise correctly that my head was very big from all these exercises, and I rarely stopped talking as I said I was so sensitized to my environment I was in a state of suspended or arrested stimulation. Every tree was the tree of life, every child the original child, every sign the ultimate portent. If this is schizophrenia schizophrenia is a remarkable event, a highly evolved personal down under substratum solution to the impossibilities of social reality. If nothing could be changed I could change myself and rise up out of my destruction like the well known phoenix. For there is certainly destruction in madness. Real madness is a rite of death and resurrection. In 1965 in true crazy style I had written I am the resurrection and the life. I had gone catholic. I had become christ herself or the angel gabriel or any combination of the messenger and the figure of sacrifice. Probably I was christ and mary and gabriel and magdalen and the apostles and the child I thought I had conceived miraculously to be de-

livered somehow 9 months hence by my lover whom I projected
as prototypical virgin. Probably I was certainly all the figures in
this popular story assisting at the imminent birth of myself. Certainly I used the only allegory I really knew that remained more
impressive than alice in wonderland or rumpelstiltskin or peter
pan or the snow queen and even the later christian variations of
sebastian and theresa and joan to explain and dramatize my own
rite of passage. Certainly I enacted the whole story. I was holy
and I was dying and my lover and my friends were consecrating
my death by making sure I was crucified in the snakepit of bellevue. The allegory completed itself as I struggled against darkness
and the derangement of my senses to survive the brutality of
captivity and realign myself with objective reality. This is a long
story. It's a story very much related to the total story of being
one politically unconscious and sexually confused however determined and accomplished person moving through the nineteen
sixties in new york city. Nevertheless it's a long story in all its de-
tails and complications quite a story in itself and what I'm doing
here is going along discarding certain aspects of the story such
as what people did to me or about me and extracting the essences appropriate to the quest for sexual identity. Actually my
insanity is the axis of the total story, the event that catapulted me
out of the sleep of repression into the second life of consciousness so well recorded by saints and philosophers, the spiritual
event that prepared me for politics, yet a spiritual event it remained, and since I had no social authority or credentials, I was
never congratulated for it, and in fact I had become of course
nothing more than an official mental case, and so the event in
itself although of great transitional importance was not in any
way socially viable. I mean unlike black elk of the oglala sioux
there was no role awaiting me upon my recovery. In our society
revelations are consigned to the bin and the psychiatric textbooks
or translated by the few fortunates into the symbols of an art medium. Either you went under in the social judgment of yourself

as a case or you put your experience to some private constructive use. I did both. I was a real case off and on for a couple of
years until I figured a small way out of my final failure and public disgrace by very slowly converting that column of mine into
a sort of literary facsimile of my experience and a confessional
defense of myself. Concurrently I employed myself as a private
detective to investigate my case and collect the evidence to present on my behalf at the imaginary but always continuous trial
of the accused called crazy and I began in fact to exploit my
crazy trip and to make a kind of career out of it by presenting
the evidence in my column as a celebration as well as a defense.
All of that was happening beginning the fall of 1967 and continuing through 69 in January of which as I said I went crazy
again and completed my trip for the first time unmolested by the
psychiatric profession with the aid of my lover who provided the
getaway car and the supportive company which included some
essential assistance in controlling my delusions. The delusions
are the dream material of grandeur and grace that conflict with
reality and lead to your capture. The delusions like the dreams
of nighttime of which they are the daytime counterpart provide
the crucial material for interpretation. Without the delusions I
still might not really know what the trips were all about. The
delusions constituted a dream code to be cracked and analyzed
and rendered as the mythological substance of an event that can
ultimately only be conveyed by this substance—the words and
symbols of myth. The one deluding is not the best investigator
of her delusions while deluding and so although the more outrageous joan and jesus and william the conqueror type delusions were being kept at bay during that crosscountry 1969 vw
squareback and holiday inn affair I was still way out there and
deluding in the abstract and thus not in any condition to comprehend what I was doing dying over this young princess attempting to validate myself by making myself a political group of two.
Certainly it wasn't any clearer when the delusions proper re-

turned in the form of that genealogical construction to which I've referred, when we came full circle back to new york and the princess fled to spain to her mother and I was left by myself three harrowing weeks settling my writing affairs and putting everything in storage before flying to europe myself. The meaning of the genealogy I created was never clear in fact until I became a revolutionary lesbian with a feminist consciousness. I should say until I became a lesbian, meaning a woman loving woman with a political definition. Lesbian identity in truth is political identity. All identity is in fact political identity. There was as I've stressed no lesbian identity, only lesbian activity. One could describe the activity but it had no name for traditionally homosexuality has been the crime without a name. Names are political. As a miss or a mrs. we were all heterosexually identified and as such further classified under the aegis of the man whose names we were all required to assume. I never met my father and my mother never married him but I had his name anyway and if I didn't have his I would've had my grandfather's or my mother's father's and in fact I was born in england with that very name although later on in amerika my mother assumed the name of my english father so in a sense I still have both names which are her father's and mine and so far as I'm concerned neither of them ever existed. Who was my father? It's a political question. And who is my mother, the other political question. For me the mother was the big important figure, but not so far as society was concerned. This I think perfectly sums up the problem. The ignominy of illegitimacy really meant something. It meant something more than a vestige of victorian prejudice. It meant the entire question of legitimacy through paternal identity. It's all very clear now. It's the essence of the problem of being a girl in the first place. A girl must move from father to husband for legal identity or be more or less damned, that is absolutely the position of women in a patriarchal society. Women are not legal, not alone they're not. So if for me the mother was the big important figure what was my mother's mother to her and my mother to herself and how could you characterize the three of us living in a culture virtually without legal status. We weren't living very well and my mother supported us working in a service career and my mother and my grandmother appeared most of the time to hate each other and I guess I was the central attraction that made it all worthwhile. And central though I was surely I suffered the same deprivation that my mother and my grandmother inherited from their own mothers and grandmothers. As Phyllis Chesler has said women in modern Judeo-Christian societies are motherless children . . . Neither mother nor daughter can redeem the other from certain harsh realities that define the female as "mother" and "loser" under bio-patriarchal rule. Yet we were in truth an anachronistic family, a fugitive matriarchy of three. I mean that in some ancient sense. Me and my mother and my grandmother were a beautiful study in fallen aristocracy. I knew they were aristocrats. Not just from one or two generations back, but from back to the beginning. We came from a race of stunning important women. And that was all very well and we sustained ourselves on a sort of vagabond affection of three generations of outcast females, . . . but outcast we were, for "the principle of legitimacy" was formulated to insure that "no child should be brought into the world without a man—and one man at that—assuming the role of sociological father. By this apparently consistent and universal prohibition (whose penalties vary by class and in accord with the expected operations of the double standard) patriarchy decrees that the status of the child and mother is primarily and ultimately dependent upon the male. And since it is not only his social status, but even his economic power upon which his dependents rely, the position of the masculine figure within the family—as without it—is materially, as well as ideologically, extremely strong." (Bronislaw Malinowski, *Sex, Culture and Myth*, 63) And so he was within our own fatherless family, by his very absence he loomed large and mythological and although my mother explained him away as dead she also evoked his image as dashing and debonair and romantic and a man of honor and position and wealth in his own country and of no small reputation in amerika and of heroic dimensions to my childish mind, for however we appeared not to need the father and it never occurred to me we might not have wanted him even though as a child my world of a mother and a grandmother being all I knew was quite sufficient and undoubtedly superior for that matter insomuch as we were uncorrupted by the disturbing male factor we did constitute after all three generations of the primal unity of mother and daughter intact and unimpaired it is also true that we were not socially respectable and we suffered that insecurity and low opinion of ourselves of the inferior caste or outcast woman doubly outcast by our situation of living without the socially credible father. A situation that my mother remedied somewhat by posing as a widow and assuming the responsibility as a provider in a respectable profession. I'm caught sometimes between thinking a woman was better off with a man or she was better off without one, it depends I suppose on many factors like class and race and age and capabilities and temperaments. There's no question in my mind a woman was better off without one if nature was the only consideration, the problem I'm outlining here is the conflict between woman-nature and father-culture and the difficulty for the woman of living under the imposition of the latter and especially without even knowing it. Since for both women and men men were the important figures the woman committed woman was not living her expected role and was thus like my mother a classic example of a precociously independent but unfulfilled person, for almost no woman fulfilled herself outside the projected identification with a man living through him as it were and somehow my own mother was constitutionally incapable of doing that and at the same time she was not sufficiently confident to conceive the kind of ambition it took for a woman to become a success or a token in a man's world, thus the woman committed woman was committed in a vacuum or with no sensible direction to her commitment. A commitment to ourselves as women could only be partially or furtively realized. A woman committed to herself and I mean by that the woman as combined image of mother daughter and sister was absolutely at odds with society which has been in the modern western world organized around the principle of heterosexuality which in effect means the prime commitment of woman to man who is committed to himself. By this organizing principle we know now that woman as a sex class has been stigmatized and outcast, for her needs at every level of society have been secondary to the male, and as such the lesbian is merely a rebelliously woman committed woman, a pre-revolutionary feminist as Ti-Grace Atkinson has said. If we were doubly outcast as lesbians we were also doubly extended as women doing basically the right woman committed thing. It's impossible to separate our oppression as women from our oppression as lesbians. All women are lesbians. And I see that I'm not asking your indulgence anymore by qualifying my assertion with a whether you think so or not yourself type of phrase and I think that's because an unqualified assertion is the natural outcome of the logic of this development thinking out of my own experience from a woman centered family eventually meeting the male corporation and the consequences of this conflict and what it all means to me now as I locate the experience within a context of feminist analysis I feel in a position to assert that the lesbian with a political definition is the woman committed woman par excellence and that this is the goal of feminist revolution. That's bringing myself way up to date. I'm still supposed to be travelling as a private desperate person. It's hard not to bring myself up to date when I see myself back there now wishing I knew better. Not only didn't I know any better but I thought I knew everything and I did. That is I knew everything it was possible to know outside of a political education. And even in that respect I wasn't doing too badly. It was becoming clearer for example that I had a natural enemy and that was the man. I was still inclined to see the man in two distinct classes as the good guy and the bad guy much the way the women in a violent revolutionary country like ireland line themselves up with the good guy to fight this mystical invisible entity called "the system" we too imagined ourselves a common victim with the good guy alongside whom we would somehow join forces to eventually overwhelm this system or bad guy by our very goodness or something which is not the irish technique but which in amerika at least was an idea embodied in bea(r)ds and flowers that predated the activist movements of campus radicals and weather people. Anyway in one form or another as artist or yogurt or flower boy or beat poet or beautiful jesus and of course for a while the new blacks and the weather types the men were acceptable as allies in the struggle to overthrow the metal men and free us all for dope and good sex and a life of continuous festival and infatuation. I had every reason to know better but I persisted in this dream right through the last alliance with males in the gay liberation front and I still think some of them are okay and in fact I could consider a few my friends but that doesn't mean much because although they may be the most harmless of males they still aren't for women and they never will be, they'll continue to thrive on their own male image as long as that image dominates the culture and why shouldn't they. No reason why not at all. The liberation of women is for women, not for men. We don't have to have anything to do with the men at all. They've taken excellent care of themselves. The trouble was we always thought since we were all just people that the man could be saved and we never thought of saving ourselves first. This really I think is the political revelation of feminism. The mothers after all had for centuries by this time given their best services to the sons and what in the end have the sons done for us. My artist friends in new york were sometimes my friends and even my supporters but they were never my friends over my woman not even the gay ones so it was in respect to my new life with a woman having come back to my lesbian senses in 1964 and 65 that I had begun to suspect the man as my natural enemy. If they liked my work and needed my services they were apparently without any sensitivity to my personal life whatsoever. I had another one of those beautiful heiresstocrats who loved me and who thought it was wrong although we never said so and it was understood that we were a special case for each other and if the proper man came along then of course a man would be more suitable although I knew somehow by 1964 that the man thing was basically all over for me for my young lover obviously it was not and it rarely was for any marriageable female in our culture in the dark ages of our political unconsciousness as I've said the person you were involved with was first and foremost a person or special love object with no certain significance as to gender so that if it happened to be a woman it could as well be a man the next time if the right *person* came along and we were unable to acknowledge that the right person in the form of a man had priority because we didn't know this other than instinctively and know it or not along with the whole culture we believed it and believing it we were hardly the best friends to our own relationship which for me at least was terrifyingly insecure and without support from any quarter other than our own guilty romance we were completely vulnerable to the claims of a particularly sexist society of male artists who sent one of their little knights to court my lover with the kind of overt persistence and determination that clearly held our relationship in such contempt that we were perhaps not regarded as being in a relationship at all and that briefly is the story of how two women in love were incapable of seriously objecting to the male prerogative in making our lives really miserable it was a miserable business. It would never have occurred to me to exclude the man altogether from our social life. It was unthinkable. The world of art that was ours in new york city was like every other world dominated by men and we needed the men to survive. It wasn't

survival however that kept us in the company of men but our belief in the men themselves and especially those of them that qualified as the good guys and that was all artists and we were all
artists or good guys together. In 1968 in london for the first time I
observed women tribally excluding the man and I didn't know
what to make of it, it seemed bizarre if not just unchristian. By
that winter of 69 I could appreciate it better out of that personal
urgency of my last trip to save myself and the world by living
happily ever after with my one true beloved who had the means
to buy up all the space we needed to establish the new lesbos on
the mainland. This attempt I was making to legitimize myself in
69 was the classic heterosexual or male method of making the
proper marriage. My male and female identities were extremely
confused. I mean who was I in the projected contract. I seemed to
be the dependent female traditionally in search of the rich male
who in this case was a female. I seemed to be the ambitious creative male falling in love with the ideal princess who admires the
older famous poet and wishes to help him and incorporate him
and make him into her mother and sister who wants the ideal
princess to be an aggressive boy to suit her female dependent
aspect which is basically in fact looking for the mother and so on.
Whatever it was I was certain I had to have it, and the male
population of the world was getting in my way. The trip was a
series of great escapes. We escaped our protector from canada
and finland who weighed over 200 and who was a jealous party
by sending him off at el paso texas. We escaped a bad man on a
hill in los angeles by sneaking out of his house in the early a m
and returning for our bags when we knew he wasn't there. We
escaped a bad family in the same city by feigning a terminal illness contracted from a disgusting piece of raw meat served by
their black maid and fleeing north to a motel in santa barbara.
We escaped the half breed skinhead indian in their jacked ass hot
rod all along the trail of route 66 out of l.a. through flagstaff
albuquerque santa fe etc. by changing into cowboy drag and pre-

tending we were custer or somebody. We escaped a bunch of refugee hippies in taos in a muddy shack serving up health shit leering lust and luftwaffe after me and polly but especially polly. We escaped every bad baboon and his wife in the holiday or other inns by just paying and leaving and not looking crosseyed. A veritable army of agents and spies were eternally on our trail. In ann arbor michigan the artist turned into the devil right before my eyes. These artists I knew were supposed to be my friends were not behaving any differently than ever before except that I was crazy and reading the mind of the barbaric amerikan psyche which included these creative alcoholic cigar smoking woman fucking husbands and artists whose attitude toward me and polly was no better than all the others I mentioned and so typically we fled to a holiday inn in detroit before driving on to pittsburgh the last stop before new york. Pittsburgh was a disaster too and for me there was no place left to go from new york we returned seven weeks and 12000 miles later no better off than before and no less sensitized to the environment. We did have someplace to go, we were supposed to get that little house out in the country, but I don't know if we even discussed it, within two days my lover had flipped out or in and fled to spain to her mother to seek her own level of legitimacy. Mine of course was still at stake and something had to be done. It was a desperate time. I had no credentials. Traditionally a poor male artist or a poor male something is acceptable to an heiresstocrat who legitimizes his claim to credibility through her own throne. If she falls in love with him. But now once again although love transcended all and was not partial to gender there was a moment when yr gender did make a crucial difference and that moment was when a male competitor of equal appeal made his appearance and established the priority of his sex or when this male competitor simply loomed in our social minds as the proper prospect, and that moment could occur when yr relationship with another woman became especially threatened under the pressure of durability in heterosexual terms called mar-

riage which traditionally involves family property and class and
any woman certainly of family property and class was tacitly required to hand same over to the male sex to insure its continuity.
So I had no claim to the throne except that of love which was by
then under siege from all these difficulties. Left in the big bad
city to my own disintegrating devices I involuntarily recalled my
delusions, the most embarrassing type of delusions, to come to my
aid. The effort of construction was well behind me, all I had to
do was recall them. It was in august 1966 that I had invented myself as a very important person. The christ trip of 1965 was
certainly something but I couldn't go around saying I was christ
or gabriel or any of those characters. Clearly I needed something
more credible, if not more impressive. Thus my psyche dredged
up a wonderful genealogy making me the daughter of various
royal families and families of great poets and mathematicians and
psychoanalysts and philosophers. A very rich complicated genealogy. The important figures of course were male, my father in
fact was a grand man of three wives and a number of high born
mistresses. Any dispossessed female had to have an impressive
father. How was I supposed to be legitimate anyway. I couldn't
marry a man and I couldn't devote my life to jesus and I wasn't
a successful writer yet. Obviously I wasn't legitimate just as a
woman. If I were I wouldn't have needed to marry anybody. Nor
would I have needed a giant fantasy in lieu of the religious life
or any real man or a questionable career. You do what you have
to do. The options for dispossessed females were always limited.
I thought my own solution was an amazing invention. Certainly
it was an interesting stopgap before the revolution. If the revolution hadn't begun I might still be crazy and off in a bin someplace
where my records would read paranoid schizophrenia with per-
secutory megalomaniac delusions of grandeur or something.
Actually I came down before the revolution. Just as I had previously after my trips in 1965 and 66. You do come down from these
things. And you become embarrassed remembering everything

you told people. But even down you have some consolation in the memory of your importance. It doesn't really leave you. Especially if you work at it and figure out what it all meant. Then you begin to realize it isn't the particulars of the story you created that are important or even that you created the story but that what you've done is to join some archetypal company of mythical heroes, the shadows of our heritage lurking behind the dramatis personae of the story. So if the delusions proper were a kind of holding tactic before the revolution began and concrete external social support was at last at hand, the transformation of the delusions into an evolved consciousness or into the invention of oneself as a creature of mythological destiny is an ultimate and permanent function which only interpretation can provide. In may 69 I wasn't interpreting a thing, I was in the middle of the delusions proper. In that state I packed the evidence in an attache case and flew to london and spain to present my credentials at court before the family of the princess. I don't know if they believed me or not or even found it interesting, they had only one wish and that was to be rid of me and find the suitable prince for their beautiful daughter. Another 12000 miles, this time by plane and in four days. They sent me back to new york via malaga barcelona and lisbon and that was virtually the end of the affair. In new york I sustained the delusions another few weeks just long enough it would seem to sign a couple of contracts that could be viewed as making me a more legitimate writer (at least), and flew back to europe for the summer to come down as it turned out in grand style, crying my way across the channel and south through france and along the riviera and across the french and spanish alps in a decrepit second hand british ford prefec going really nowhere except to lose myself in the classic despair of broken romances. I returned to new york much chastened and very sad in the old style. No doubt without the revolution of which I was not yet aware I would have done what we all used to do and that was to recover and eventually look for your real true beloved once again and go on with my life of adventure as a writer and my life of tragedy as a lover and at 60 or 70 with success be married to some devoted "companion" and go off to that little house in the country, something like that. Certainly my illusions about changing the world with one other person were over. I wasn't thinking about changing the world anyway. I was just a private victim again. That was one definite effect of coming down from the delusions. If my new sense of myself as a mythological hero was going to go anywhere it would go in the writing. I would become the traditional artist translating and expressing my social alienation culturally and not politically. Which means I still wouldn't have any identity as a dyke, unless it was as a literary creep. Those tokens of literature. The sad private creatures of fiction. Fortunately such was not to be my fate. The revolution was on and I was ready. I had come to the end of my real world as a busy person. I have come to the end of the stories of my traumatic confrontations alone against the male corporation. And to the end of the end of these stories in a melodramatic genealogical solution. I had tried absolutely everything there was to try and the only thing that sort of worked was writing. The new and unprecedented thing that was happening in the world was a political context for our difficulties. At last I could find out that I was an outcast because I was a woman, never mind being a lesbian, and that I didn't have to be personally responsible completely any more for whatever happened to me that seemed to be my personal fault, and that in recognizing myself as an outcast I could band together with the other outcasts, all of womankind, to legitimize ourselves as a political group in opposition to the group which made you an outcast, the group called men. That awful life of having to choose between being a criminal or going straight was over. We were going to legitimize ourselves as criminals!

SLOUCHING TOWARD CONSCIOUSNESS

often, we never meet, struggling with the "burden" of our homosexuality in isolated despair, committing suicide or dying as prisoners in mental hospitals.

guy nassberg

. . . a personal incident that was condemned to the oblivion of privacy is examined as a manifestation of the oppressed conditions women experience: the personal is seen to be a crucial aspect of the political. . . . by "speaking bitterness" the chinese peasants, subdued by violent coercion and abject poverty, took a step out of thinking their fate was natural by articulating it.

juliet mitchell

radical change in consciousness is the beginning, the first step in changing social existence.

marcuse

every important revolutionary movement produces its fearless catalysts prodding pushing probing challenging irritating power-tripping seducing all new comers and incurring much wrath on their own heads in this crucial sacrificial action and personal upheaval moving toward liberation through dramatic confrontation with others. lois hart is one of those. she's impossible and charismatic. the lois in these record book entries is her and she seemed to be a vigilante committee of one over my dormant political awareness.

RECORD BOOK ENTRIES, AND CURRENT COMMENTS

nov. 17, 1969—ann, washington, gay liberation front, gave me gay power button [*returning from europe i was homeless and stayed awhile with my friend ann wilson on the bowery. she kept feeding me religious literature, while suggesting i should be writing something political. this entry refers to some peace demonstration she attended in washington. somehow she found herself marching behind the gay liberation front banners and wearing a gay power button. i was astonished by the gift, didn't know what to make of it or do with it.*] somebody wrote an attack on me in a gay newspaper.

nov. 27—thanksgiving day. dinner at sheindi's last week. i mentioned i told a spade chick at macdowell i liked girls and she wouldn't speak to me after that. rosalyn (drexler) said can't you keep a secret jill and i should've said do you keep your marriage to your husband a secret? [*note use of spade, chick, and girls*]

nov. 30, sun.—thanksgiving last thurs. dinner at les's, after at glf, met lois and suzanne. like lois. maybe write for *come out*. [*"after at glf" actually just meant dinner at somebody's house where there were some "realesbians." ann brought me there, having told me for a couple of weeks that there were a couple of "nice lesbians" i should meet. she knew them through jim fouratt radical activist in glf and the lover of our friend peter hujar. i liked lois right off and typically also immediately crossed the thought of a "potential lifelong mate." —chauvinistically, i came*] *on, disregarding suzanne, who wasn't pleased. i had much to learn.*]

dec. 2 1969—glf meeting nov. 29 at church on 9th ave. talk about picketing vv for not printing an ad with "gay" in it. [*this was my first official "movement" encounter. i was amused and horrified at such a motley collection of "perverts" out in broad electric light complaining and proclaiming themselves. i felt aloof and remote. they were still the "other."*]

dec. 5—general despair (new hampshire) [*i was staying at macdowell, the artist colony, and driving in to new york frequently.*]

dec. 9—my complaints fill up the universe.

dec. 12—o daddy please don't cry—together we'll find a brand new mommy [*hit parade*]

dec. 15—how do you qualify as a hopeless case.

dec. 21—helen . . . blond baby hair, soft baby skin, laps me into terrific orgasm. ravenous mouth . . . return to farmhouse 4 a.m. sinking hazed over yellow moon—institutional sex? [*from this date til the end of january '71 i grappled off and on with l'affaire helen. i liked her. i liked the sex. i couldn't manage her tremendous need for me. she was literary and high wasp out of the south and sarah lawrence and very unhip. she was far more private even than me in her sensitivities and agonies and predilection for the "wrong" sex and histories of unrequited love. she was a wonderful natural lesbian having not even ever had a man but she drove people away out of a dreadful need and insecurity inherited from her straight puritan oppression manifested in a compulsion to envelop you and do absolutely everything for you. i've written of the end of the affair in* lois lane is a lesbian.]

this piece, in her altogether also, *written the middle of january and published the 29th conveys a brand of chauvinism (that is —the projected self-hatred of the lesbian pre-dating a feminist consciousness and ambivalence in both needing her and rejecting her suffocating demands)*]:

in her altogether also, january 29, 1970:

She stood up from a hot tub and passed out under the sink and broke a rib or two. I like to fall asleep myself in the middle of a story. Come again when you can't stay so long. And bring yr camera. My blood is thin, my heart is made of tin tonight. I didn't remember signaling with my foot my intention of dying with her and my foot isn't even stuck in the door. I'm stuck on the hi-way. Clapping my hands I am not singing joyfully in the moonlight. Frigid cold out as witches' tits. I stopped because of an interesting noise. flapflapflapflap . . . slowing down it does flap—flap—flap. Get out inspect the rear parts. It isn't the dis-lodged metal thing or any other hanging thing, it's a hunk of rub-ber on the wheel detaching itself from the parent body, so I stand some special helpless looking slouch leaning longingly in the direction of oncoming vehicles my Havid scarf arranged at some attractive chest spread. Wish the photographer was here. Whiz whiz. Nada nobody. Whiz whiz. Bastids. If I were dead praps all the problems that bothered her would be settled. What was the great catastrophe before the drying up of the oceans? The com-ing of the snows. I should be pacing back and forth looking like I have an appointment at the end of the world. Last year this time according to a Voice office index card I was "envolved in many strange and wondrous adventures. . . ." I should be leaning on my sword describing my defeat. I'm leaning on my car watching a bright red sports number slow down a few yards in front of my hood. Two smiling muscle boys are walking toward me. I hunch into my scarf and meet them halfway and stare at the snow and mumble about a disintegrating tire. Ye-s-s. And as they're into the jack and spare boy scout act I'm noting their massachusetts license plate. It reads S O S. Terriffic. I've been saved. I love being saved. Maybe while she was standing up from the hot tub and passing out under the sink I was backing into a snow bank stuck solid and gaily hacking away at the white stuff with a dust pan in order to find my way back to "grandmother's house" under the nothing night no stars even and falling into the embankments leaving the vehicle to be hauled out by the various rescue operation teams. I need photos of this business. No, I'm telling her, I'm not hiding my forehead, I'm showing my bangs. So she's clicking some pix of my bangs and other parts inside and outside but the ". . . strange and wondrous adventures" are not being recorded. Like looking out this window and seeing some abominable bird tracks and this leaning tower of silo and this deadduck apple orchard and many obscure but timeless traces of the great catastrophes before and after the drying up of the oceans. At that time according to certain prominent bioanalysts I became a female because another much stronger animal also anxious to return to the aquatic existence of which we had been deprived managed to bore a tube into me in order to create a passage to get into my puddle which became my uterus. Amazing. And I don't even have any callosities on my forward extremities to facilitate the clasping of any other weakling who got bored into. But I'm sitting in my vest and shirt and pants and pipe at a table looking at a chess set opposite my opponent in her altogether also staring at the chess pieces about level with a pair of great knockers before the separation of creation from nothing there was probably something. Flap. I'm leaning on my elbow describing a checkmate. The photographer is 5 yards away. This was my brilliant dephallible idea to get a shot like the original duchamp at chess with the chick in the buff a blubbler possibly detaching itself from the parent bodily situation to which the organization of the female accommodated itself in alternate projection apropobly. I make a move. Assault with intent to ravish. The set be-

*longed to the master and his widow themselves. She loaned me
the set. She didn't want me to make the picture. You don't play
chess, she said. It doesn't matter, I play lots of games. My opponent's hair is black like the original but five inches longer and
it's covering the profile. I don't care for my own. No, I'm showing
my bangs. My blood is thick, my heart is made of doodlebugs tonight. If she were dead praps all the problems that didn't bother
me would be unsettled. Let's shoot this one out in the snow she
said. Yeah let's do it on the way to the road. Now sit in the chair.
Now stand on the table. Now the hands. The bangs. The tie. The
dingle dangle. Now take off your clothes. No I don't do that. "He
looked at my naked body and found that it was perfect and
therefore destroyed his sketches." There's no padding interposed
any more between life and the word. This is not a strange and
wondrous adventure. I'm not terrible enough to be beautiful and
I'm not a streaming pillar of orange wax as a girl in a tangerine
dress rising up out of a hot tub and melting away under the sink
and I don't have an appointment at the end of the world. Either.
Where's the SOS car? She said she was available, she'd never
leave me, she has a beautiful soul too, and she's very good with
crazy people and how could I resist her. Come again when you
can't stay forever. I find myself suddenly within the unthinkable
itself. The lens is two yards away. Jesus she's foreshortening
some part of my bare extremities and possibly even boring another
tube into me somewhere and I don't need another puddle or any
other substitution for somebody else's aquatic existence. But it's
dramatically decadent. Capote on the couch. Just one frame, for
her she said. Sure, one frame. Then let's do it on the way to the
road. Then let's go up in that leaning tower of silo and make
some abominable bird tracks and find our way back to grandmother's house under the nothing night no stars even and break
a rib or two and wait for the SOS boys and the cameras to record
each small catastrophe each infinitely small thing is as large as
large things can be isn't it grand?*

dec. 31—the other night made trio scene with rosemary and a michael somebody, vinegar douche. only way to get rosemary, through a man.

ann: If i'm pregnant with larry poons' baby i'll call it an art event.

jan. 1, 1970—ti-grace. [*saw ti-grace atkinson at a new year's day party of artists and wives mostly. i'd known ti-grace for a few years but only in the context of the art world, when she wrote for art news, and headed the institute of contemporary art in phila-delphia. i hadn't seen her in awhile. i knew she was into the feminist movement. i was at this time contemptuous of the move-ment. i was a special woman. proud of my small accomplishment. if the first step in feminism is an admission of one's oppression as a woman, to read my disadvantage as anything other than the traditional trials and poverty of the artist in a materialistic society would be to concede much more than i was willing or able to the very oppressor who recognized and supported me in his own limited way. so i regarded ti-grace askance. and played the op-pressor myself. as is the wont of the oppressed. how can you ex-pect to emulate our miserable lives if you don't accept oppression. i challenged her outfit for openers. why was she wearing this peck&peck number. and the heels and stockings. and what did she do for sex and if she wasn't into men why wasn't she into women and so on until by some circuitous evening's up and down-town and up again rites of passage we ended at her apartment where i half seduced her through a bulky irish sweater and the fear of the return of a roommate and our mutual fear suspicion surprise embarrassment detached curiosity scientific experimenta-tion inadvertently i think i was witnessing the birth of a political or asexual lesbian and all i thought i was doing was seeing if i could enjoy myself that evening.*]

jan. 15—bob live with boy in new york. boy leave bob to live with girl on coast. bob subsequently visit girl and boy out on the coast. later girl leave boy and come to new york stay with bob. then bob leave girl and go join boy on coast. wants to leave girl with *me*.

jan. 16—tell gregory it's pointless to write for a gay paper. he should write gay stuff for a straight paper.

jan. 25—jj: if i was a man ann you'd jump to here and make me this goddam coffee, wouldn't you?—a: yeah, not for a cunt like you—i've got one of those. a: someday i'm gonna look like robert frost. j: you should be so lucky.

jan. 26—general despair.

lois told me on phone that the women have taken over rat—they thought of me as possible person to include but they said i have a very poor women's liberation consciousness. culture hero: jj: what the hell is a consuming desire. les: when you make the daily enquirer you've got it made. they don't put anything in there that isn't hot stuff. lois: stereotyped view of a lesbian imitating a man re duchamp photo. [*culture hero was a pig issue les levine put out with my cooperation about me, the cause of our permanent estrangement, and much embarrassment to me over his daily enquirer headlines (consuming desires etc.) and consternation in explaining myself to lois who rightly observed that my imitation of the famous duchamp photo taking the part of duchamp fully clothed playing chess with the naked woman was a lesbian chauvinist identification with the pig but who (lois) let me off the hook somewhat by compromising herself and allowing that i could've been posing with myself or my alter ego, me both clothed and naked as it were.*]

jan. 29—lots of ann and religion around this time.

jan. 30—woke up 5 a.m. nightmares over culture hero. it's all wrong or doesn't it matter—it does, today and tomorrow and how big is the ocean. ann: that a year ago i was popular because my writing was a turnon concurrent with a psychedelic and guru vogue and now the mood is political. —about women's lib: —how can i be part of a movement when i *am already* a liberated female. blah blah.

jan. 31—ann on bucky fuller: you'd talk a lot too if you didn't get to build anything.

feb. 2—thinking how to work up some coordinated rage.

feb. 3—a ship loaded to the gunwales with diminutive diseased chinese slaves.

feb. 4—somebody knocking on my door, it's lois and suzanne. coffee. give lois my rose crushed velvet pants now shrunken from the cleaner who saved them from the destruction of a malted milk spilt area of a year ago.

feb. 5—sent helen back to new hampshire.

feb. 8—glf meeting. very camp. much hilarity at expense of three straight dudes from princeton wanting to set up an "encounter" situation with straight and gay people. rowdy meeting. camp. but serious. and sometimes heated angry. all maybe? still fighting battle of identity of self respect or rather self sexual respect in society what don't like it. go afterward to hippodrome ave. and 10th st. gay bar dancing. go home with redheaded sandy, butch, i don't like it. barbara f: growing up with jill. general depression. guilty about sending helen away?

feb. 8—tv. ti-grace, david frost, dr. spock [*i think my sympathy was aroused here and with it a little crumb of potential feminist consciousness.*]

feb. 10—st. adrian's—attacked by l. poons—"you hate men" was his big idea. depressed [*being strictly verboten to "hate" the slave owner it had not yet occurred to me that it might be healthy to do so, and thus would one vigorously persist in a defense of one's own oppression.*]

feb. 11—breakfast at my place: ann, rosemary, lois, suzanne, ti-grace. [*lois enthusiastically announced that this breakfast was an "historical meeting between women's liberation and glf." not much later lois invited ti-grace and her red-stocking group to her place for a kind of encounter session which turned on at least two of the women to be gay. the meeting between lois and ti-grace i presume to be another critical step in the move ti-grace made toward affiliation with daughters of bilitis and the first bold affirmation of the lesbian as the advanced contingent of feminism by a well know feminist. ti-grace seemed hopelessly uptight to me physically. she wanted me to help her shop for more "suitable clothes."*]

feb. 17—visit a sharon with lois and suzanne. sharon: i'll see if i can continue to fuck and be a liberated woman.

feb. 19—ann: how can i be a lesbian if nobody will love me. jj: you should go to that consciousness raising group. [*i was always recommending a c r group to other people*] [*i thought ann had to be straight—in practice till then she was—since i wasn't attracted*] *to her. jane: well you don't have to sleep with everybody that's gay. it's not sexist to not sleep with them all, or, it's not necessarily sexist to sleep with them all*] jj, to ann: they don't have a sense of humor. a: revolutionaries don't, they want hellfirebrimstone and thunder and you're writing a serious philosophical tract on the human condition [*i was writing bullshit. my politics was union and happiness in the here and now.*] ann: to be a lesbian is a style now, it's like miniskirts or something.

feb. 22—rec'd valentine from charlotte moorman.

feb. 23—what d'you say to the naked lady.

feb. 24—suddenly classes of people whose styles of life had been practically invisible had the money to build monuments to their own styles.

feb. 25—general despair. . . . seduction by meredith . . . i didn't feel like it.

feb. 26—i thought i saw a black sun in an empty sky and a red ball of blood above the towers.

feb. 27—ann: we have a place for people like you who don't want to join the people's republic. it's called alaska.

feb. 28—dream: polly and two others(?), a couple maybe her sister and brother-in-law, and her mother and sidney. no contact between me and p. she sits around quiet. i begin getting nervous about food, like they're offering and withdrawing meat and i reach a peak of agitated frustrations and tantrumming—suddenly we're seated at a table for dinner. i notice polly wears wide gold (wedding) bands on all four fingers of left hand. somehow then i have choice of eating them and decide not to. i turn to her mother and say "i suppose you're . . ."—i was about to say something unsociable, and i smile, and she smiles, etc. i was going to say ". . . happy your daughter is no longer with me," or married, or something.

march 2—fantasy for yesterday of $ for a farm to make overground lesbian movie. make 15 thou on mexican pot gig, walking it across the rio grande.

march 3—joyce ". . . i'd like a language which is above all languages, a language to which all will do service . . ." at a time when others were questioning the liberties he took with english joyce was conscious only of its restraints upon him. party sunday last for rosemary at marjorie's. perrault assures me levine is certain i want to kill him. [*i think levine wanted me to play solanis to his warhol*] joyce ". . . my head is full of pebbles and rubbish and broken matches and lots of glass picked up most everywhere"

psychoanalysis is neither more nor less than blackmail.

march 7—day of total eclipse. lois and suzanne into women's lib for winnie [*my daughter*]. i tell them in effect to fuck off. p.m. marjorie hurls herself onto my bod and says does she have to rape me to get me over to her house. for what i want to know and i'm supposed to see when i get there.

march 8—she's very interested in protective coloration. at this the emperor could restrain himself no longer, but bade his soldiers drag her from the water, cut her body into pieces, and grind her bones to dust.

march 9—general despair.

wake up at ann's very angst and heavy on the loaded yellow pill.

rubin: the only exciting and meaningful thing to do in amerika today is to disrupt her institutions and build new ones [*dennis altman says jules feiffer was reported to've said that the love ethic went to chicago was polarized and came out as the fuck ethic*]

march 10—at dutton cy nelson gives me seven paperbacks. ellman on yeats. correspondence of miller and durrell. chute on chaucer. chute on shakespeare. magnus on gladstone. magnus on kitchener. woody guthrie on himself. [*almost all men, i didn't realize.*] albert fine: psychoanalysts are filthy hypocritical inquisitors.

march 12—the chinaman still won't (can't) locate my shirts.

march 16—awake under heaviest pall . . . existential vacuum . . . candle waxing down off a tuna fish can . . .
have to live at ice berg depth. . . .
ching: 1 and 10.

march 17—time is wrapping around us in a big iron band. a: i've got the key to my body in these clogs—3 hippies on w. b'way joking after laura dean with a long pole they're loading onto a truck. —gene wanted to build a parthenon in new york and for confusious to be president.

march 18—jim fouratt says i'm not involved in women's liberation because i'm crazy.

march 19—women's liberation becomes a thing to do.

march 20—when i say i'm a liberated woman they scoff at me.

march 21—i refuse to be cheered up.

march 22—dialogue with ann driving by judson church: —jj: i remember a time we were spending our lives in judson church. why don't we go there anymore? a: i don't know, all i know is we used to go there all the time, now we don't go there anymore. richard alpert (alias baba ram dass) at hunter: on his mother: she had no vehicle to manifest her high being, and every so often it would break out around the edges. no form in which to live it. lois: he (alpert) wasn't so holy then. lois says he's living a privileged existence and may not be aware of the hell we're all living in. [*lois refers to time she spent at the millbrook acid hangout as "one of the girls" when both leary and alpert were there, and to the sexism of all the men, including of course alpert, whom i viewed as a "religious person." indeed, as he said, his mother had no vehicle to manifest her high being, but alpert was thinking of his mother as another "person" not as a woman, who has no place in the historical religious pantheon of higher consciousness. at this time my own religious aspirations were holding me back from political consciousness. a little marx would've been a lot more helpful than the eastern stuff i was into. it's true i was becoming gayer, but to be gayer without developing a concomitant feminist consciousness was to merely consider yourself part of a special oppressed minority group without reference to the large political questions, the big picture, the overview of repressed female sexuality in relation to which your special oppression as a gay person was inextricably entwined. especially as a lesbian. anyway. i still didn't know that religion in all its forms is the twin agent with the legal apparatus of governments to maintain the patriarchal orientation of society and as such to continue the repression of women by the various appeals to our "higher natures" invoking the words and deeds of the exclusive male deity.*]

march 24—dear andrew sarris: why *don't* you belong to the happy-endings-for-homosexuals club?

ann: i'm 38 years old and i don't have an ironing board.

march 30—last night paul thek returned from europe. ann very happy. i wait for alpert to visit me.

march 31—look for the jaded ones, the jaded ones are the real innocents.

april 1—christopher says he's taking a greek freighter to london and sailing up the river thames for no reason at all.

ann: what did the temple priestess do when she didn't feel up to it.

april 2—(one liberated woman doesn't make any sense)

april 5—lee and lou went to the top of the empire state building and flew paper planes with poems on them—other night went to glf all girls dance. make date to go out with a cathy. [*i felt a bit guilty about going cruising to any glf function without being a "worker" in the movement—as though i was skimming a little cream off the bottle they were inventing with difficulty and shaping at the roots out of nothing*]

april 6—paul dividing ann and me.

april 11—E.—[*i had a black woman friend whose company i enjoyed who suddenly one day almost paralyzed me when i went into her bathroom and found a raspberry letter paper scotch-taped to the mirror saying "jill baby . . ." and continuing with an embarrassing proposition. i emerged and pretended i hadn't seen it but she wouldn't let me get away with that. i wasn't honest with her about how she was very overweight for me and instead pretended i couldn't on the basis of how i don't make it with my friends. it was the beginning of the end of our friendship. i*

thought later possibly she used my rejection of her as confirma-
tion of a racism she was beginning to attribute to all her white
friends as she developed a black consciousness and in my case she
was perhaps well justified insomuch as i was not then any more
sympathetic to the black cause than i was to my own, and con-
sistent with my entire individualistic approach to life thought of
our friendship as a "special" relationship transcending color class
and sex antagonisms by which the society at every level is
defined]

april 13—the day is beginning again, i suppose that'll have to be
alright.

april 16—two women were supposed to get married and i went but
they didn't. nobody was there.

april 17—what did i do today for humanity

april 20—dream: last night nightmare: arrive coast and helen is like
a 12 year old in long blond hair and mad in a storybook mad way
and we go on a boat like a roller coaster sort of a truck like the
trucks that transport cars—and i don't know where we were but
there was in the air how H. is hopelessly mad and finally she
burns up in the pages of a book.

april 22—visit segal's. me and polly in plaster.

april 24—public birth of a girl's baby on a dining room table at
stony point. stony point where i'm writing this at the waterfalls—
a jesus hippie spread this white canvas cloth robe arms at the
top where the water begins to fall and last may i made love to the
girl who just had her baby on the dining room table and the fall
before that i spaced out with polly into the trees and my kids here
once seemingly not concerned not interested particularly by the

naked swimmers and now here's peter on a rock in his jesus beard in one pink sock and one orange sock and me with a cherry soda down below where the second water begins to fall into the lower pool and ann now naked down even below that—"yahoo"—a white shaggy dog barking. [*truly this is where i was at in the spring of 1970*]

[*however—i was at the same time desultorily collecting the fragments of my additive gay consciousness and without knowing it the evidence of sexism for a future mental coalition of the gay and feminist consciousness.*]

april 19—there's a transcription of virginia woolf's suicide note to leonard. april 24—virginia's response to the death of jane harrison. and a note the same day reading strange activity copying from v. woolf's diary into mine. whatever day it was for virginia she was conceiving "a whole fantasy to be called 'the jessamy brides'—
. . . two women, poor, solitary, at the top of a house . . . sapphism is to be suggested . . . the ladies are to have constantinople in view. dreams of golden domes . . . for the truth is i feel the need of an escapade after these serious poetic experimental books whose form is always so closely considered. i want to kick up my own heels and be off." may 7—i was reading erikson on gandhi, still believing in the exclusive male divinity. ann: new york is hopeless, i'm going to newark. liberation is coming out the other end of any old tunnel. may 10—quoting the times on gide "never solving the problem of reconciling homosexual hedonism with conjugal platonism" and how he paid his wife "the compliment of putting her, in various guises, into his books, and killing her off symbolically no less than three times" and now when "he was most obsessed by it, he had not yet got to the point of publicly admitting his homosexuality." dream: last nite: my mother died and left me nothing in her will altho a number of us were eating at a table and from the head of the table seemed to ema-

nate pieces of her passed around to the company, in form of portions of creamed peas. arise to pee. times on floor—big black letters:—YOU TRUST YOUR MOTHER BUT YOU CUT THE CARDS.————! may 21—san francisco, dream: walking along shitting on people's lawns and some lady out, irate, yelling; i say back well you could have it for dessert. june 3—rereading freud on leonardo and identifying with leonardo and being irritated by freud's not altogether subtle defamation of leonardo's character. p.m. go to family dog auditorium to hear steve gaskin (more religion)—june 9—at dinner in pasadena i was notifying my companions of whom three were men and one a woman that i wasn't going to listen to an entire evening of male accomplishments. that was premature for me. my entree into women's liberation was through gay consciousness as i keep saying and i wasn't yet ready to concede that i was an oppressed woman or even a woman. i wasn't making all the connections. june 12—for example noting that a. ginsberg and j. genet were supporting the blacks and not the homosexuals, not realizing that the big obstacle for male homosexuals in coming out was the charge of womanliness by stereotyped social opinion and that successful men like ginsberg and genet were acceptable as freaks in the sanctity of fiction even though everybody knows they're homosexual they're artists first and that means they're recognized in a straight society defined by the ruling men who don't mind their fantasies in fiction but who don't want any outspoken women around. for a woman the reverse accusation has always been more of an advantage i suppose, and certainly my brief or too long deviation from a comfortable tomboyhood into a forced artificial lady image was a period of the worst oppression; in same words i got along quite well as a boy, especially since it was so much easier to pretend i wasn't a woman. the project of course was to become again as a child when i looked to myself from all the photos sunny and athletic and adorable and sexually indeterminate and that's how it came about to be again, but as a sort of overgrown little girl child woman and i feel comfortable once more why not. and that is all very well, but in realizing and coming to terms with the worldwisewicked prejudice against women i had to give up the conditional privilege accorded me thru the accusation of masculinity, a grudging backhanded concession to partial status as a person, by somehow affirming identity with my own sex. didn't gertrude Herself say "i always did thank god i wasn't born a woman"? june 17—arrive new york from san francisco. ann lois plus suzanne meet me at kennedy. lois straddling a railing at the gate shooting photos. i think she's putting me on over my famous person trip. june 18—find out what they mean by the myth of the vaginal orgasm. june 20—argument with lois. i said i was interested in common denominators in family constellations for female homosexuality. lois defensive aggressive that the cultural appraisal of homosexuality is the negative one of the bad relations between a little girl and her father instead of the positive with the mother. [*anyway i was still thinking like the culture myself just in questioning the origins of homosexuality. it is noteworthy, as dr. george weinberg said in his "society and the healthy homosexual" (p. 19) that we seldom hear the question: how did a person become heterosexual? we might well ask in my opinion, since our heterosexual world has seemed so determined for so long to annihilate all of us. (this is the subject of my chapter on orgasm and the new sexual woman.)—weinberg also says "the fact is that the combination of physiological readiness and social experience resulting in the development of* any *erotic preference—homosexual or heterosexual—is so intricate that science has not been able to fathom it as yet." and that the "ostensibly valid intellectual inquiry (of the heterosexual regarding homosexual origins) is frequently an expression of hostility or fears which become presented as if they were part of a serious intellectual exploration."*] june 21 (1970)—ann said the revolution stopped for the summer, they've all gone away. june 24—channel 13—7 homosexual activists. june 25—[*the 1970 gay week occurred in here somewhere,* and my third confrontation with ti-grace. ti-grace appeared to give a speech at daughters of bilitis. all the glf women went and so did i. the place was jammed. i think most of us shared the attitude that a feminist addressing a bunch of lesbians was like a roy wilkins going to oakland to talk to the black panthers. the lesbian was the true woman and a feminist was somebody who wants a better deal from her old man. but i underestimated ti-grace in my ignorance of her political fervor. she weren't no ordinary feminist. we may've been ahead of her with our bodies but she was a lot further along than the likes of me in her political comprehension. she even said that lesbianism was a practice and feminism was a theory. it was quite correct at that time to observe our situation thus dualistically. her militancy, in any event, was not compatible with my east west flower child beat hip psychedelic paradise now love peace do your own thing approach to the revolution. i still thought the men were divided into the bad guys and the good guys and the good guys like leary alpert ginsberg rubin hoffman etc. were on our side. ti-grace was standing up there saying the man was the enemy. the man, period. she said the man was the enemy and she went on about spikes and armor and militant tactics and ideological pitfalls and the murders of feminist revolutionaries in russia in 1919 and the vaginal orgasm as a mass hysterical survival response and frightening things like that. i was appalled. i actually thought she needed a good fuck. i was incredible. i had the gall to think as a man does that a woman wouldn't be talking like that if she wasn't frigid and didn't need a blitz trip to the bio-energetic reichian therapist. but at least to a realesbian. and i began to chastise myself for not having brought her out all the way that new year's day in january. as soon as she sat down i called out a proposition for bed. she countered the challenge by defining it and denouncing it as behavior belonging to the male psychology. "see" she said, "that's what i mean about male psychology." in her feminist rationale she had told us that the female dynamic is love and the male dynamic is sex. trans-

*lated: Man-Sex-Evil. versus Woman-Love-Good. to my surprise
and confusion arlene kisner of glf rose and defended me by saying
that any time a woman asserts her own desires and needs does not
mean she is showing male psychology. that was all very well, but
i wasn't asserting my needs and desires, i was putting ti-grace on.
possibly i had heard some elementary feminist theory for the first
time: i.e., women are a class by default, men by choice; all class
systems are dichotomous. but i didn't understand it and didn't
want to know from it. i thought i had the last word in feminism
and that was that i was an up front lesbian.]*

in that spirit of marvelous megalomania i came out officially july
1st (1970) in the Voice in a piece titled ambivalently from a line
by colette "of this pure but irregular passion." bravado and bu-
colic innocence. all gay and not much woman. embarrassing now
in its apology (i like men even if i am gay, or worse, i like men
even *better* now that i'm gay), its defense of celebration, its appeal for transcendence of real oppressive conditions, its plea for
acceptance and no challenge to the system which i failed to see
would hardly accept its most radical element which would represent the greatest potential threat to its preservation. so what was i
thinking of to send me out like that into such a silence all dressed
up in cymbals. i was doing something moderately terrible and i
was shocked by it. besides thinking i knew everything i was
shocked and embarrassed. and it was my mother's birthday. that
night i got smashed and lost my british passport and went to bed
with the first woman who seemed an unlikely prospect. july 5,
bought de beauvoir's second sex and notes from the 2nd year.
and ann gave me alice's adventures underground. july 12, explaining to somebody that unfortunately many feminists were probably
irremediably hung up on cock. i *still* thought *some* people were
straight. that *still* made me a freak. july 13, letter from a gay
woman: "do you know what i mean when i say i'm a human being
first and a woman by accident and a lesbian by preference?" —out

of notes from the 2nd year: "bitches are not only oppressed as women, they're oppressed for not being like women." july 14, jim says someone denounced me at a glf meeting. july 22, final horrendous argument with lois. she said "your politics are not sympathetic to the aims and aspirations of glf."

aug. 13—i was on my own. i had a camper and began to wander out my ponderously slow realization of the political truth. She was envolved as usual in many strange and wondrous adventures.

BASH IN THE SCULLS

East Hampton—One acre of love sun and sound at the Sculls. Drive along a Georgica road where the rich inherited the earth of East Hampton. An open sesame table at the head of the gravel driveway. Smiling women for equality. They say well look at list five other people called in to come for The Voice. Barbara Guest parries all checkshuns and leads me dancing and singing by the hand down the yellow brick road to the Crossbones. No she didn't but she was just charming and also flatterfull of good will too. This party I think Tom Wolfe would identifry it as Radical Chick for Women Striking for Equality, later on this month after reseiving the necessary funds from such parties as these that Bob and Ethel Scull sponstered at 25 grubs a poison to see their premises. That's not true but it's the way Bob himself now striding tord me cross his greeny lawn in his ducky white pants and candy striped shirt open at a mossy chest and his new Commander Whitehead beard under a rich smile did put it that people would be paying to see the place. He's happy to see me and so am I. Nice little bungalow you've got here Bob. Mmmm. I can't give you the style number and we're not allowed in, it's a lawn party, but it's a right angulated one story black and white and windowy modern mini-

mal everybody's building/Some are building monuments/Others
are jotting down notes. All my colleagues in the crime of report-
ing I never meant. Charlotte Curtis. Time. Newsday. Swiss Tele-
vision. United Press International Syndicated News Service. Once
I mingled in a group of five of which four of us were taking notes.
My editor (there too perchance) said it's the ultimate sort of
party where nobody shows up except the people who write about
it. I tried interviewing Charlotte Curtis who was interviewing two
men who might've been interviewing her while a lady was inter-
rupting to interview me about whatever went wrong between
Betty Friedan and me. What went wrong between Betty Friedan
and me was a lapse of sexual interest. I liked her below the chin
and was ready to talk at that level but she got super huffy when I
arsked if there shouldn't be a pub(l)ic conjunction between
Women's Liberation and the Gay Liberation Front. Her eyes went
big 'n bulgy and her lipstick leered crimson and she said crisply
enunciating each word that "it" is not an issue. What? She repeated. *And*, there's no relationship between the movements.
Well, and she softened a moment. I *am* against all oppression.
Good, but don't you think . . . — and she waved me off, excuse me I have other important things to do as she spun on her
maxi and I called out after her you mean "it" is embarrassing.
And Scull standing there looking at his feet his hands folded at
the duck white pants behind over the coccyx. He wanders me a
tour of the lawn garden fountain sculpture layout. Here's a
tomato red tube fabricated Alexander Lieberman. It matches your
napkin Bob. Mmmm. A stainless steel Walter de Maria cage. A
neon number. A gray minimal Morris he called a do-nut, it has a
square hole. A wood beam di Suvero faded weathering beautifully
into driftwood. A fountain of three di Suvero cast bronze hands,
and the story to go with it about how the one hand where the
water sprouts out of its palm was supposed to cost 400 and Mark
demanded 4 thou and got it and Scull says to me you know that
Mark insults me, calls me a robber baron and the worst names—

and I love him. He's beaming. Unhhuh, . . . you've changed
Bob. *Yeah* I feel *great*, just great. He looks yachtsman cocktails.
Tanned and supersuccessful. His wife Ethel is standing near the
mikes by the pool in a quilted maxi looking slim and Betsy Ross-
ish. He turns and smiles and says fondly you know we've been
married 26 years. By the pool. The pool! Don't Go Near the Water! The pool is the centerpiece here the perfect aqua rectangle
undisturbed by its peripheral human slow motion of cameras
cocktails interviews. Back in the bushes by a road bordering the
lawn sits a barefoot guerrilla. Why donchu come in I called out.
Because I don't have $25. I was near him and I turned and
scanned my sister and fellow guests and when I saw the host of
the Philistines I was afraid and my heart greatly trembled. No it
didn't. But *lo* a voice from heaven, saying, This is my beloved
Daughter in whom I am (not) so well pleased. It was time.
Something had to happen here. A new historical folks pass. In a
flash I turned into a One Eyed One Horned Flying Purple People
Eater. No I didn't. I continued interviewing and being inter-
viewed. I talk to Edith de Rham who wrote *her* book one year
after (in '64) Betty Friedan did and who saw that women didn't
have the freedom she had in being able to pay for a maid. I say
then you must've had an experience that wasn't so pleasant to
make you that sympathetic. Yes, she was married before her present marriage and with*out* the money for a maid and she wanted
to jump off a bridge from it. Right. It had eluded me that the
movement had so much to do with maids. We need a better dis-
tribution of maids. Maids for everybody. Maids for the MAIDS.
I decide to test her on the gay issue which Betty Friedan said is
not an issue. She isn't hysterical like Betty but torrentially defensive. You see we don't hate men and so forth. And a story
about a "queer" designer who was always describing his fabulous
mother. I register that she's had gay men figured out for some
time. Mother will never be duplicated. I change the subject and
suggest that the women who hate men the most (and vice versa)

are those who go to bed with them. She doesn't like any of it anyway and gives the old one-two about being normal or natural in
preferring her opposite. "I'm not narcissistic you see." St. John of
the Cross where are you:/ There is in every perfect love/ A law
to be accomplished too:/ That the lover should resemble/ The
belov'd: and be the same/ And the greater is the likeness/
Brighter will the rapture flame—Narcissime: qui consiste a se
choisir soi-meme comme objet erotique.—Our interview was being interrupted by another. Edith's book by the way was "The
Love Fraud" and I'm sorry I don't know what it's about a fraud
I guess. She said she's happily married now. Who can I seduce
here. Betty wears lipstick. Ethel is busy being hostess. Barbara
disappeared. Charlotte is taking notes. My editor is here with
her boyfriend. So I'm talking to Scull again over a manicured
hedge. Admiring his Commander Whitehead beard, just the right
dash of distinguished gray-white in a black brush as clipped as
the hedge. Schwebbers Electronics has that kind of beard now
too. Scull is expansive suddenly: I can't *wait* to see my depressions in Nevada. Your *What?*—My depressions.—Oh. My sculpture in the desert in Nevada, by Mike Heizer. Oh. Say Bob who's
that? I've spied my quarry across the pool. Pale blue cycle shades.
That's Gloria Steinem. Gloria! Terrific. I made haste round the
pool through the cameras cocktails interviews. She's in a bare-
back and just as pretty at eyeball distance. Our past and future is
settled immediately. Midwest-Smith-India-New York Magazine.
And I disclose my unscheduled pool event. Return in peace to the
ocean, my love; I too am part of that ocean, . . . we are not so
much separated. . . —We are instantly by an introduction from
Betty Friedan who's been giving a pep talk at the mikes about
Women for Equality. She introduces Gloria. I wander back the
other side of the pool, the hedge side. I was coming into that abnormal condition known as elation. I would cast my swine before
pearls and give that which is unholy to the daubs. I would return my body to the water (Gene before he died said he was re-

turning the earth to the land as he threw his flower pots from
fifth story to sidewalk). And I lectured my brethren: the proper
posture is to listen and to learn from lunatics as in former times.
No I didn't. I sat down to organize the explosion. Removal of
pants shoes socks hardware. I had to leave my notes behind. Too
bad. I walk quickly to the center of the shallow end. Almost fall
skidding on the slippery edge. Last Chance Balloon. Tarzana from
the trees at cocktails. I didn't cross myself. I didn't yell geronimo.
I dove in and did my lengths. I hoped my colleague reporters
would be noting my 10 point Australian crawl. I did a little exhibition breast stroke as well. The second time round I got rid of
the faded blue railroad shirt with a hole in the sleeve (Yes it was
a calculated costume). She's terrible, she's beautiful. She isn't
beautiful, she isn't terrible enough. Anyway I was alone in the
aquarium. Water lovely. No rubber ducky (in the tubby). I
emerge. Slippery edge. Jill tombe pour la seconde fois. Scull is
waiting eagerly with big yellow towel and so happily I think he's
my trainer and I just won the race. I go beyond the hedge into
the trees. A maxi lady is lurking in the bushes WHY DID YOU
DO THAT? I mean but extremely furious. I'm wiping the chlo-
rine out of my eyes. It isn't self-evident. Well . . . I was . . . uh
. . . hot—and drunk. HOT. And DRUNK.—God, where's my
notebook. The other notebooks are coming tord me fast now.
They're saying you were hot and drunk. *Were* you hot and drunk?
Yes. Were you protesting? Yes. Are you a woman . . . ? Yes.
Were you part of a Red Stocking Plot to Sabotage this Party?
Yes. Were you showing off? Yes. Are you a radical lesbian? Yes.
Do you like the Sculls? Sure. Did Mr. Scull put you up to it? No.
He neither endorsed nor discouraged the exhibition but I did get
permission from my editor. *WHY* did you do it? Well . . . I
think one should be serious in one's purposes but not necessarily
solemn. Well . . . Have gun, will travel. See pool, will swim.
Well . . . It was a Conceptual Swim. Well you see I have this
resportsibility to make my life interesting to my readers each

week. And then I stormed the mikes and lectured my brethren again: Except ye become as little children ye can in no vice exit the killdom of haven. No I didn't. I went behind a tree to write up my swim. Scull appeared. They're saying I put you up to it. Well just say I was hot and drunk. And offer me a dry shirt please. He gets another blue workshirt. Where's Gloria? They're not even thanking me for the awful time I gave them. No, it's getting all changed around. You were great. Terrific. Sensational. Verweile doch, du bist so schon. But Gloria won't dance. Betty is still put out. Ethel and Edith and Charlotte disappeared along with Barbara. A voice on the mikes is saying Ladies and gentlemen the party is over. Radical Chick is over. One acre of love sun and sound. Was there any perfecting of spirits here this afternoon? I'd like to leave my clothes impaled on a souvenir spear. Tell it all, brother and sisters. Dinner at the Silver Sea Horse. The Wheel of Wandering On.

> " 'I always say if you have a pool, you have a pool,' Mrs. Scull said, shaking her head."
>
> Charlotte Curtis
> *New York Times*, Aug. 10, 1970

> " 'All I see are the committed, their husbands and the press,' Mrs. Betty Friedan, author of *The Feminine Mystique*, said as she surveyed the crowd. 'I hope at least some of them are paying guests.' . . . Mrs. Friedan went to the microphone beside the Sculls' swimming pool and called the party to order. She thanked the Sculls for the use of their yard and said it was 'time to finish the unfinished revolution of American women. . . . They must be liberated from menial housework,' she cried, hitching up her plunging decolletage."
>
> C. Curtis
> *New York Times*, Aug. 10, 1970

"And then it happened; Jill Johnston, who writes a weekly monologue for the Village Voice called 'Dance

Journal,' dove into the swimming pool in her workshirt. After she swam a couple of laps she took off the shirt too and swam with bare bosom, but she did not swim the backstroke but the crawl. Everybody played it very cool and pretended not to notice what was going on, but Ethel and Bob Scull looked a little nervous, and Ethel gave Bob a towel, with which he stood at the shallow end, waiting for Jill to come out so he could give it to her. He had a smile on his face, a frozen smile, and then a male voice shouted from somewhere in the crowd, 'You're proving nothing, and we'd rather hear what the speaker's saying,' but in truth Jill Johnston swam gently and softly in the warm blue water."

Silvia Tennenbaum
Newsday, Aug. 15, 1970

" 'Enemy Within Surfaces'

Mrs. Friedan muttered something about 'One of the biggest enemies of this movement . . .' The rest was drowned out by the crowd. Miss Steinem tried to speak, too, but without success.

'It's a great pool,' Miss Johnston yelled, as she reached for a plastic surfboard, rolled over on her back and floated for a few seconds. 'We *are* going to be a big political issue,' Mrs. Friedan shrieked into the microphone. 'And now some of us will sing for you.'

The sounds of 'Liberation Now' came over the loud-speaker amid shouts of 'Right on!' Miss Johnston, who'd finished four laps, climbed out of the pool, accepted a towel Mr. Scull held for her and tripped off into a zinnia bed. Everybody was talking all at once."

Charlotte Curtis
New York Times, Aug. 10, 1970

by september (of '70) i was discussing or belaboring with g. segal the near total exclusion of women from henry's notorious met retrospective of american art. another note that same day concerning how jasper had told me for some reason last week how ages ago he vetoed a proposal to give me a grant—because i was a critic and i didn't ask myself at the time, and him, if that was because i was a woman, never mind the critic bit, or even why the hell he was informing me so belatedly of such an unpleasant rejection. a year later i commented on this: surely the relations between women and male homosexuals meaning all men ecce the homo could only improve when the latter come out and give up their own "straight" prejudice against themselves which is often doubly projected against women or the woman inside themselves against whom they are defending themselves, the woman they are supposed to despise by the straight injunction. sept. 20, picking up some second hand feminist rundown of marx and engels on the breakdown of women's original autonomy within communal collective systems under the institution of monogamy, private property, etc. it was to be close to another year before i read engels himself. sept. 29, visited ti-grace, she seemed very manic nervous infocused and angry at "sisterhood"—i thought to myself her bad scene in jail may have put her head in a precarious place. i was struck by the oval gilt frame on her wall of herself at 17 posing formally in white for her "wedding" picture behind a piece of cracked glass. a suitable memento. during october i was continuing to fool around with eastern tibetan transcendental trips mostly encountered at a meditation center in northern vermont gurued by the venerable trungpa rinpoche, the 13th and last reincarnation thereof. but in that month i was reading also eric neumann's *armor & psyche* which reminded me of some core facets of matriarchal psychology. the surrender of the bride. the death in marriage. the rape of kore. the primordial relation of identity between mother and daughter. the intrusion of the male. marriage as an abduction, an acquisition. like that. then oct. 14

noting from somewhere "a main theme of greek myth is the gradual reduction of women from sacred beings to chattel." and still
resisting admitting a personal relationship to such a dreary half
of the human species. —there it was. at that time i was writing
the most offensive antifeminist line in the form of some personal
snot about how i never considered myself the second sex. i had
apparently successfully convinced myself that i was not a woman.
or else i was a superwoman. not only did i not see myself as an
oppressed woman but i didn't know i was oppressed for not being
like a woman as well. whatever problems befell me it was an individual matter completely. this fall of '70 i bombed and bummed
around the east coast developing a gay head and reading a lot
and pursuing some interesting sex and being depressed, besides.
looking for salvation in the buddha or the lotus born padma.

THE KINGDOM OF HOLY INSECURITY

Dear Charlie, I'm sick today. I'm writing in G. Segal's studio of
white plaster pieces of bodies in Jersey. I can't breathe. I began
sneezing on 59th Street at "Five Easy Pieces." I received yr letter
that morning and had been in New York just two days. I woke up
wrecked from a hangover. The morning before I woke up in bed
with a girl who didn't understand why I said I should've slept in
my car. This trip I found sex in the provinces. The last trip I had
it good coming back to New York. I don't know if I need it or
not. After coming I wonder what I'm doing there if I'm not in
love. My night dreams are satisfying and my masturbation fantasies are virtuosic and interchangeable. Used to be I couldn't get
it off if it wasn't a single plot with a beginning a middle an end.
Then if you got stuck halfway you had to begin at the beginning
again. Peter and I discussed a lot of these matters over supper the
night I arrived. Girls don't talk much. Peter turned 36 two weeks

ago. He said I could say so. I sent him a Libra book with two fall leaves turning red and orange. Departing a remote place in Vermont I went searching on the road after the perfect dead leaf. I wonder if he minds if I say he's a virgin to women. I wonder if I should tell my James Taylor story. Or the dream I had making love with the girl I was in bed with. . . . Some female heavies were poking fun at me and reminding us of my history which made me say that most aspects of my life are common knowledge. The trouble with this girl was that she didn't have a cat. Every girl I shack in with has a cat. The two who married me gave their cats away. It doesn't work just to lock the cats out. Unless they're not psychotic and they usually are. If you define success sufficiently vaguely I'm doing all right. I don't manage in New York at all and I'm writing to you because your letter arrived in all its mythological splendor just as I was despairing of spending as much even as my recent limit of a few nights at a time on these battlegrounds of sex and business. Now I'm sick out at Segal's. Helen is away on an errant. George is talking into a tape recorder with Jan. Helen isn't sympathetic. George gives me aspirin and vitamin C. My glands are swollen. I'll never feel segzy again. I'll just talk about it with Peter. I tried explaining the sensation of anal orgasm and thought he should know more about it than me but he doesn't. I told him 36 is a significant age. Shakespeare changed dramatically at 36. Dante awoke to find himself alone in a dark wood (or at 35). So did Leary (at 35). The universe ultimately is a dream, isn't it, a product of the mind. It's raining today too. I had a rain dream in Sandgate. I was swimming in a lake of painted wooden statues like Egyptian effigies floating face up. Being afraid I woke, and saw myself as all the statues which I was, lying stiff asleep on my back in the van under the rain we were awash. I've not yet been given like Coleridge a page of undisputed splendor in a dream. I prefer what I'm doing to Kubla Khan however. And I relate to the difficult quotes you sent from Buber's "Daniel." I'm too sad in my

common cold to say more except I appreciate your message and
the knowledge that you too feel the necessity of the myth and
symbol. I was dissolving over the last quote when a neighbor
walked in and asked me what I was upset about. I said I only appeared to be upset. I mean I don't think I cry for myself personally these days. What do you think of events. Janis dead. Jimi
dead. Angela captured. Bernadette released. Trudeau in trouble.
Timothy in Algiers. In New York people look right through you
as though nothing had ever happened between all of us. And
you do the same so's not to be misunderstood. We behave like the
scattered fragments of the god that we are. (What greater glory
for a god than to be absolved of the world.) I'm not however
overly sentimental like some extravagant people who are overwhelmed by our own actions without knowing how to enjoy
themselves. Far north this last trip I enjoyed what Time described as the exuberant breasts of a Lachaise statue. On Sophia?
—The inventions of sex are no less fantastic than those of art. One
a. m. after orgasm I went to sleep again and dreamt I was walking with a friend down a childhood street in a black gauzy shirt
nothing else, an old recurring dream of embarrassment, and I
asked my friend to pull the shirt down in back while I tried but-
toning it in front and turning to her at the same time said you
know I used to have dreams like this.—The day before I'd been
reading some authority on the occurrence of a dream within a
dream (when one dreams that one is dreaming), which they
analyze as referring to a theme a person wishes were "only a
dream," i. e., not true.—I don't know. I don't think I'd be writing
like this if my letter was private. I'd be saying only the public
things we understand. At Goddard a couple of weeks ago a student flattered me by saying my writing was schizophrenic. The
students are quite advanced. That's where I found the exuberant
breasts. In New York Yvonne asked me if I liked that and I said
I think I prefer boobs like myself. She snorted I'm hopelessly
narcissistic. I stopped at Goddard to drop Sheindi and son Miles

whose older sister Laurie is a new student there. The girls and
boys share living quarters. I had the impression that contracep-
tives are supplied by coin and button next to the coke machines.
The youthful president is living in a dorm to see what it's like.
They have courses like Revolutionary Anarchism and Police Repression and the Justice Department and Women's Action Projects and Draft Counseling and Beyond and Politics and the Family and Radical Studies and Cain the Irreconcilable and Arthur
and the Need for a Hero and Existentialism and Zen Buddism
and Studies of Style and Temperatment in Pottery. I visited a
course in Homosexuality and hope to've stirred a homophile movement on campus, a possibility suggested in the catalog anyway.
In the cafeteria a student asked me if I was a girl or a lady. I said
I didn't know. I mean are you over 20 she pursued. I'll have to
ask my son whom I introduce as my father sometimes. We children went to see the Fortune Quackser movie where we were
embarrassed at the gooey parts. During a preview advertisement
for a movie of incestuous rape and murder and naked perversions
of every sort Winnie turned to me and said coolly this one will
be rated X. You'd like them I think. To Richard I said pleasant
dreams the rest of the week old man when I left them at home.
He had told me about a dream of gran'ma asking him to go someplace, but she appeared in my image. He's dealing with a small
problem of gran'ma taking his sister to the West Indies tomorrow.
His dream occurred *before* I told him I'd fly him down to Mexico
when I'm there if I have the bread, which I told him *before* he
related the dream to me. I want to remember to tell Peter that
Apollinaire was honored in Paris by a banquet when he was 36
and that last week I slept in a room containing exactly 36 horse
show ribbons. I don't think I'll tell the James Taylor story. I don't
think there's such a thing as fact on the one hand and fiction on
the other. Nor that we "condense" in our dream formations while
we "decompose" in our myth formations as some psychology people say. I think we condense (fuse, merge, superimpose) images

and ideas and also decompose (disunite, multiply, dissolve) in both dreams *and* myths, *and* art and fantasies we the undivided divinity that operates within us in all these forms of it are dreaming the world. Some nights I dream a procession of all my old lovers. They fuse and disunite endlessly. And I rejuvenate them and let them die and rejuvenate them again and they are me and I am them and we are together celebrating our collective miseries and splendors in our dissolving and merging images and identities. I feel better today. Even in New York. As you quoted: This is the kingdom of God: the kingdom of danger and of risk, of eternal beginning and of eternal becoming, of opened spirit and of deep realization, the kingdom of holy insecurity. Love, Jill.

Oct. 11, dream: virginia vita too tuo.—november i was preparing to drive to the coast. nearing time of departure i had two heavy and distressing scenes i would attribute in retrospect to my habit of barging in where lavender angels without any political allies and with an embryonic political consciousness would fear to tread. after the first i careened downtown very juiced and fixed myself up skimble scamble style and threw the incident in a column a month later: i see jill smashed one night before leaving hanging over the bathtub making soapwater sex, her sleeves sopping heavy above the hands caressing thighs and cunt juice and all that . . . WOMEN OF AMERICA, DO IT.

a devastating scene on cape cod the end of august the house of a rich young straight couple was no indication to me yet that it was impossible to appear without any supportive protection as an upfront lesbian—the world was on their side so what was wrong with me, and i converted my frustrated anger into a column setting the object of my fury in relief against my friend lee as the little prince and the doings of these strangers at the tibetan meditation center. these rich people were kids, like in their 20's and they were those weird grown-ups the little prince wonders about. i think their bread was ludens cough drops.

Another bad scene with straights nov. 14, dinner in new jersey, an engineer colleague of gerry's, i had mentioned visiting ginsberg at his farm upstate new york and he asked if ginsberg's "girlfriend" was there, alluding in this way and with further innuendoes to peter orlovsky. i hassled him on his prejudice, he kept bad mouthing me about "faggots," and the outcome was a standoff since our host and hostess were old friends of mine.

nov. 8 or 9 or thereabouts a heavy scene of another sort with kate millett. i was introduced to her at judson church the evening of the american flag opening. right off i asked her why she was posing as "straight" for the media. i guess other people had been hassling her and she was immediately aroused defensive and later at st. adrian's told me in effect i should go fuck myself at which i dissolved into my martinis and gregory who was there was no help at all. just before leaving for the coast i wrote a column called *for an improper person* in which i mentioned the incident but the voice wouldn't print kate's name and i was furious, having by this time apparently developed enough of a gay head to see that if everybody else came out i'd be in better shape too, knowing at the same time it was not my place to expose anybody else publicly. *for an improper person* is much about skeletons rattling in the closets: "i must sound like an extremely noisy skeleton." —"i'm forming a society of skeletons to clatter through the white house. we will speak mysteriously and grandiloquently of our ancestry, laying claim to high nobility and fortune." —"the mystery of the mystery is why these matters are kept a mystery." —"i presented noisily to one big women's lib leader the case for her falling out of the closet where she says she has to stay unless she jeopardize the success of the entire lady's movement which is depending upon her, somehow. she mentioned being bisexual several times. gregory was there. he said what's that? —she was quite angry at me. lak the rest (excepting ti-grace). a friend analyzes that i am a luxury which the women cannot yet afford." —"is it true that middle america would rather have its sons killed in vietnam than grow up to be homosexual?" —"do we have to go much further back and faster? where nothing is true, and everything is permitted? —the day goes by so strangely. for an improper person." —"the evidence which accumulates is the embarrassment caused by a rattle in the closet when the company is sitting down to tea."

a week later kate "came out" under pressure from an audience at a panel at columbia, declaring she was "bisexual" in answer to repeated challenges.

i felt very beleaguered myself at some other phase of gay consciousness and being attacked wherever i went, and happily split for the coast nov. 19th arriving san francisco thanksgiving day.

ranging up and down the california coast and one flying visit to mexico city i think i realized at last there was noplace to hide anymore and that i was not only gay but i was a gay woman. i had come out. i didn't have to say anything even. my attitude presence must have spoken for itself. the prejudice was everywhere. i was completely déclassé. i was on the beginning of my journey of refusing to adjust to my oppression. i was ready. a revolutionary consciousness is forged out of the fusion of experience and theory and accumulated information. by the time i drove east out of san diego early february i was a fuse box whose ignited wire was slowly crawling sizzling toward my center. i stayed with young gay women in tucson and houston and baton rouge and winston-salem and observed the compounded absurdity and anxiety of couples hiding out in their plastic homes pretending to be roommates and role playing the male-female game with each other and getting dressed up in drag femme unconsciously in the morning to go out and work for the man. i was angry and helpless. in new orleans my dynamite box blew up and i arrived new york after one last hairy scene in tuscaloosa with the straights of amerika fit to be tried and exploding with LOIS LANE IS A LESBIAN.

i preface the reprinting of this lois lane series with the retrospective remarks that although one could see how my *feminist* consciousness had emerged and developed and was in fact fusing with my gay head, that i was still unclear about the institutional source of our oppression. only out of a clear vision of the true historical source of our dilemma could a radical theory of gay/feminism be constructed. in such a theory would the personal and the political unite and dictate the revolutionary forms of action and behavior essential to the vision of a liberated society conceived in the collective experience of intolerable prejudice and discrimination. at the time of the writing of lois lane there was only one existent essay that properly expressed both the problems and the solutions of a nascent political ideology predicated on a gay/feminist consciousness. this was the *woman identified woman* written and printed underground collectively by Radicalesbians. and i hadn't studied it yet. sometime in april, after the three lois lane pieces had appeared, lois hart clued me in to that prime insight—the oppressive "heterosexual institution" around which the radicalesbian essay is mobilized—on a wild hilarious stormy weather drive from vermont to new york. lois lane borders tantalizingly on breaking through to that crucial political gazebo. that last step is a fatal point of no return and the last holdout in all of us brought up to believe in the ultimate unity of the two opposing sexes. i had held out with the best and the worst of us and when i gave in i felt both a tremendous relief and a sadness for my lost religious designs and not a small amount of terror for the revolutionary struggle ahead.

Lois Lane Is a Lesbian

I plotted this augmented "confession" driving out of New Orleans at 5 a.m. with a broken left shoulder feeling cosmically sorry for myself and the world. I could've been some river boat rake shot up in a gambling game and crawling off to die in a swamp, that's how bad it was. At midnight I fell down a flight of stairs in the unlit landing of a warehouse where some kids had been showing me how they manufacture water beds. At 12.10 out on the street there, after broadcasting my agony sprawled over a car hood, I heard this nice clean American male heterosexual hippie who had been my escort explain that we should sleep in my vehicle together. At 12.15 I figured I couldn't have been in worse shape if the concussion I had just sustained had been administered by the billy club of a cop who was now offering to rape me as a reward for being so attractively destroyed. At 12.20 I climbed over the frying pan into the fire where I signaled through the flames the message that we both liked the same sex. At 12.25 my ex-companion of the water bed company was in greater shock than me and I left him gaping and fuming there to go on and win a medal for driving or careening through enemy territory in critical condition to a hospital where for four hours I waited in vain for somebody to determine the extent of the damage. At 5 a. m., as I said, I was on the road. I didn't look back. New Orleans was a disaster area called Mardi Gras. At 2 p. m. when I arrived there the French Quarter I thought was the most exotic area every side of St. Mark's Place and Carnaby Street and Telegraph Avenue and Commercial Street in Provincetown. By 7 p. m. I had lost and/or been ripped off of eight bills, I hoped I would never see another peace emblem or insignia ever; I had paid $2.55 for a ginger ale in a low class strip joint, and 25 cents to pee in a normal restaurant; I had been inadvertently charged by a troupe of longhairs pouring out of a lavender bus demonstrating for more pay for their local police force; I had declined the advances of a

New Yorker who recognized me in a coffee shop, and passed up the subtler advances of a girl called Jill cruising me in a head-shop; the American eagle on my van had come loose and askew; and I had read in my own newspaper that I was part of a phony new industry of interpersonal technology of which my confessional gush is consecrated to the proposition that we must all abandon the privileged privacy of our most precious relationships or perish from emotional constipation and that these confessions are becoming increasingly profitable, both culturally and financially, and that I have been publicly exhorting every pretty girl in America to come out of the closet and into my bed (yeah) and that I want to look good so badly that I wind up making every else around me look bad.

If I hadn't been so upset over the new evidence that some of us are still finding it so difficult to celebrate all the things we are I would have been more astonished and flattered that a successful white American male heterosexual film critic had invested that much time and energy and rhetorical diligence to pay so much hostile attention to the meagre outpourings of the most oppressed and confused and unrecognized minority in every country of the world. It is as much your privilege to think I'm exaggerating as it is mine to believe I'm stating the case to fit the facts. Each of us is a barometer of social conditions which we observe through the perceptual screen of our needs. Reviewing and re-reviewing my experience of growing up and sort of surviving in a male dominated heterosexual world I am now prepared to say that a female who is a lesbian in this society is about as well off as a Sabine woman trapped in a camp of black corporals. I am, by the way, more in sympathy with the black cause than ever before, and in fact with all causes, for it has recently occurred to me that all causes are the same cause (as my critic said, we are all in the same boat) and that what we're doing here then is educating all the members of ourselves to certain needs which have gone unheeded or unrecognized or worse damned and vilified and thrust underground so that we can all coexist more happily together. My initial reaction to the women's movement was a classic. The line was "What's the matter with *them, I've* been doing it all these years." You can hear this same line from accomplished females all over the place. It's an elitist capitalistic attitude which blesses the fortunate and condemns the ignorant. My initial reaction to the black movement was hey wait a minute I didn't *choose* to be born white, and let me tell *you* about the problems of a white homosexual female in a . . . et cetera. Now I suggest you go up to a black person and say White People Have Problems Too and see what kind of response you get. I'm going on record here to notify every heterosexual male and female that every lesbian and every homosexual is all too aware of the problems of heterosexuals since they permeate every aspect of our social political economic and cultural lives. That we were in fact educated on these problems. That we were brought up and spoon fed or pitch forked on the crucible of the problems of thousands of Romeos and Juliets radiating outward from all our sublimely miserable and broken families into the movies and the funnies and the histories and the psychologies and the novels and our great Western classics. It is, in fact, the heterosexual problems which create a gay liberation movement or any movement to end the artificial social construction of sexual specialization which makes some of our members ill and confused. It is the heterosexual problem which creates this tremendous body of clinical literature to brand some aspect of sexuality perverse and abnormal. It is the heterosexual problem which creates the monstrosity of transsexualism, surely the most pitiful operation going, to "help" some gullible people *not* to be homosexual in a society far from convinced that all the equipment we are born with is perfectly beautiful. It is the heterosexual problem which creates therapies designed to "cure" people of their natural sexual interests. These therapies and those clinical studies belong to the same market of a disease called normalcy. A healthy society would enjoy and encourage all of its

perversions by which in fact the society would be defined. Polymorphous perversity is the norm. There is no norm. Unless it's
Mailer, who perfectly embodies the heterosexual problem. I think
all of us are authorities on the heterosexual problem. Knowledge
on the subject is instantly available, in case you've missed out, in
every daily newspaper with their front page accounts of the
Wars. We are bored with the news from the heterosexual fronts.
We want to hear from the lesbians and the homosexuals now. I
want homosexual movies and novels and funnies and histories
and songs and classics. Even problem stories. Certainly the songs.
Let all those gay rock artists come out from behind their phony
lyrics. But the movies! The big medium. I don't expect the next
batch of gay ones to show us nothing but the doomed clandestine
affair of Therese and Isabelle in boarding school, and the wrecked
life of Sister George whose girlfriend leaves her for a great white
witch of the west whose cold clawing sexual advances constitute
the only sexual revelation in the film, and the huge tree of D. H.
Lawrence's well equipped "Fox" falling on one of his two hero-
ines to effectively wipe out the contender to his hero's object, or
the girls in "Persona" never getting to the point, or the sisters in
"Silence," and the boys in anybody's band parading their stereotyped images to a public greedy for their distress and martyrdom.
—Andy Warhol could give us a few straight stories. Eight hours
of Nancy and Little Lulu in bed. Or Blondie and Lois Lane. I
don't care much about endings one way or another but the homosexual movies could begin by making up for all the years we
grew up watching Gary Cooper and Richard Greene ride glori-
ously into the purple sunset with Myrna Loy and Mrs. Miniver
etc. to live happily ever after. This film critic a few months ago
wrote in the context of some review that "although I don't belong
to the happy-endings-for-homosexuals club . . ." which made me
ask him when I saw him "why *don't* you belong to the happy-
endings-for-homosexuals club?" Exactly. The question is why we
don't all belong to the happy endings (and beginnings and

middles) for everybody club. Can you imagine me saying, in any context, "although I don't belong to the happy-endings-for-heterosexuals club"? Can you imagine anybody saying "although I don't belong to the happy-endings-for-black-people club"? Can you imagine any intelligent observer at this moment in history writing an article damning the blacks and their social agonies? Or suggesting that James Baldwin or Eldridge Cleaver or LeRoi Jones were something *more* or something *other* than their blackness—that they were not so much black people who happened to be fine writers as fine writers who happen to be black? We are not *any* of us something more (or less) or *other* than *any*thing that we are. We are the sum total of all we are and we are all of what we are in every thought and in every action we manifest.

The Western habit of separating everything and of constantly defining our own spaces by the creation of an enemy is the habit that projected a profession called criticism by which people glibly judge and assess the complications of the lives of others. I never woke up one morning to say Ah now I am going to write something culturally and financially profitable called a confession. I don't share our film critic's obsession with careerism in the forms he describes it as Looking For An Edge. Confession isn't a luxury, it's a necessity. By any American standards none of us is rich. When any artist in this crazy pragmatic country begins to survive by doing just what he wants to do, his art, it seems to me an occasion for rejoicing. That the artists themselves should be attacking each other for arriving at this precarious position of a tenuous security seems to me the height of insanity. In New Orleans that apocalyptic afternoon I picked up the James Taylor cover pix issue of Rolling Stone along with The Voice. Taylor is quoted: "It is very strange making a living out of being yourself." —and the writer goes on: "which neatly defines the personal confessional school of songwriting which promises to supplant much of the hard rock of the '60s." —Confessional literature in any form hardly needs an apology for its current expressions. One shouldn't have to refer to our honorable ancestors St. Augustine or Rousseau or de Quincey. The form is a misleading one in any case, for one might always ask what is *not* a confession? Still, there is a kind of religious consciousness, awakening, by fire and shock, which powers the necessity, an inner compulsion, to forge a confessional style. Nerval and Rimbaud and Artaud are such artists in the French tradition. The French historically have seemed especially susceptible. In any country the tradition can be related by a short mental jump to the religious ecstasies and confessions of a Theresa of Avila. At the present moment in America there's an activity we might call confessional journalism which is practiced along the whole gamut of profit at one end and revelation at the other. It's interesting to me that our film critic should express his distaste and displeasure over the medium while practicing it in the same breath. If I had anything to do with stimulating his interest in himself to the point of public display I'd be pleased since I believe the entire practice of criticism is a pathetic projection of personal terrors and inadequacies and suppressed ambition. The rhetorical expertise of some of its practitioners is the best educated refusal to deal with the central problem of the world—the Self. My "confessional gush" is consecrated to no other proposition than that of collecting all of my selves that I can raise to consciousness in the shape of current experiences into some form of literary energy at the moment I sit down most every week to write that damn column. Sometimes I get a masterpiece seizure and work very hard for a structural coup. Sometimes I'm unsuccessfully trying to merge my literary ambition with my cause concerns. It's *always* a dilemma. What to say and how to say it. And you have to perpetuate the illusion that it means something to somebody besides yourself. Otherwise why the hell would you be publishing it? Why the hell am I bothering *here* to regress to an old academic style to answer a person who feels that his own myths and feelings are being ridiculed when he sees an exhibition of another way of life? Because that's the way I feel *right now*. I have straight friends whose lives I honor and respect and *they* don't feel ridiculed by the difference they discern in *me*. If it's anybody's turn to feel ridiculed, and by the massive heterosexual culture, you know who it is, and that's what the gay liberation is all about—to end this ridiculous posturing about anybody else's sexuality. My first and final line if I had only one on the subject would be that if you can't walk out your door and down the street and into the park in any familiar embrace with the one you love the whole society is in trouble. Men will have to give up the idea that every female is their potential mate. And women will have to abandon their designs on every male. Gay people are now expecting and demanding the same sanctified regard for *their* sexual interests and unions as they have rendered for as long as they can remember to the weird forces that endowed them with life in the first place. Now there is only one way for this social change to take place. And that is for all gay people, those who know it and accept it, to stand up and speak for themselves. There is no other way. The laws and discriminatory practices will alter according as the attitude does, and the attitude continues absurd as long as the society tolerates its aberrations by successfully pretending that it doesn't know what it already suspects. Ask any gay person about their traumatic confrontations with their families. Everybody *knows* everything. That is, we are in constant telepathic communication. But society is an iceberg. Most of it is under water. Knowledge which would reveal our most ancient archetypal terrors and taboos, our collective sins and guilts, is rigorously repressed. When this unconscious material erupts and surfaces we become the animal I can only imagine we once were—an animal all of whose parts were in mutual and open-ended communication. The human animal is, perhaps, in the tragic position of having to surface all the way up in order to go all the way back down, or vice versa. Total conscious knowledge means clear traffic from the depths of the unconscious to the rational parts of the functional forebrain. If the iceberg of society surfaced completely we'd be living in a painful but compassionate utopia. I believe with Freud and Brown and Reich etc. that sexual polymorphous perversity (you *can,* by the way, reconcile Reich with the others) and all its social consequences is the paradise we most profoundly wish to recover. Specialization (sexual, technological, etc.) is the monster that civilization visited on itself to sustain its material needs. We're working now for an aerial view. We need to know what we already know. Not enough can be said to inform people of what they already know. A secret is an archaic hoarded treasure. Secrets mean borders and barriers and codes and passports and thick walls and frontiers between people. Just a year ago I permitted Rosalyn Drexler at a small dinner party to convince me I'd been a dope for revealing myself at an artists' colony where I'd been I was not being self protective as Rosalyn pointed out "Oh Jill, can't you keep a secret" and I was not yet able to reply immediately "Do you keep your marriage to Sherman a secret?" —But if you think I'm having fun being a blabber mouth lesbian you're mistaken. The field is thick with clashing swords. The ground is already drenched in blood. If you think I'm feeling sorry for myself you're right. But I'm greatly in favor of people feeling that particular emotion. It's against the grain of the fearless Protestant ethic. Yet you don't know you're a human being until you feel sorry for yourself in a very grand way. Then you look around you and see possibly for the first time how we're all in it together and then you'll feel that big cosmic emotion and that's how you discover with a certain shock that you're religious even though you've read the French existentialists on the death of God.

I know the media thrives on our petty intramural battles but we really want something bigger for ourselves don't we? Why, in any event, would a quarterback want to tackle his own center? I've got enough trouble. I'm persona non grata with every "group" in the country, just for openers. The women's lib people don't like the way I swim. The Gay Liberation Front says I wouldn't get any support from *them*. Both organizations think I'm a male chauvinist pig, probably because I take more girls to bed (or want to or pretend to) than I have a right to—as though nobody was ever luring *me* to bed. —A black man once told me that Le-Roi Jones and the like wanted my head on a platter. The artists were never pleased that I began to find their lives more interesting than their work. The religious groups accuse me of grubbing around on a fame and art trip. The artists coalition types begrudge my sudden minimal independence in my old age. All radicals dismiss me as an idle dreamer. Gay newspaper says I'm an exhibitionist. And I suppose the Aubudon society has it in for me too. Anyway I'm on everybody's list as number one menace to the universe. I have a case of the most exquisite paranoia. It's a wonderful feeling. For a female lesbian bastard writer mental case I'm doing awfully well. The only movement I'm dedicated to myself is finding out what anybody is calling me so I can say yeah that's me. For example: Co-opting the names in the name-calling dictionaries called psychoanalytical textbooks would finish a profession which defines its existence by an occult terminology of names branding whatever it isn't—that is, the enemy. Schizophrenics, Unite!

POST SCRIPT

My agitation on behalf of Lois Lane dates most specifically back to last November in San Francisco. That afternoon a few weeks ago in New Orleans was just the detonation of the fuse that was lit back in California where I had driven away from a melodrama dinner party and a busted affair feeling more like a Joan in armor than I know it's wise or safe to. But the incident convinced me I would no longer tolerate an innuendo which sounded like an assault on a sexual identity which is fragile enough in the present social circumstances. Moving away from a more detached Ti-

betany trip I had to justify my sudden militancy so I just said
well you have to go along with it until it's over, you can't deny
that rage you experienced, you don't even know where it's going,
you just keep a watch on it and see if you can explode it where
it'll hurt the most to mean as much to the peoples you imagine
who share the same or similar vulnerability as it meant to you
when you thought you were experiencing the entire social prejudice in hurricane form in the microcosm of a dinner party. A
black person these days has a certain advantage in being clearly
black. I'm not keen about walking across any threshold and an-
nouncing my sexual preference over a hello and a handshake.
But we might have to alter the etiquettes to suit the new consciousness of the awakened and confirmed lesbian and homosexual who no longer wish to participate in the prejudice against
her/himself by permitting any host or hostess or companion to
assume a sexuality not clearly defined one way or another by look
or style. I don't know how it should work. Lots of radical lesbians
are currently in isolation to enjoy only their own company. One
told me that the straight friends I've alluded to must be unique
in transcending their programming with their humanity. Maybe
so. Or else I'm kidding myself. These straight people in San Francisco were strangers to me and friends of a girl who was a quasi-
romance of mine for a year, meaning in the worst sense of literary
male chauvinism someone you have possessed but from whom
you have remained nevertheless detached. I had arrived in November with ideas of being more involved if possible but I think
she was eager to make me pay for my old detachment which she
considered a cruelty. The prices of interesting sex. And I wasn't
completely immune to the unexpected revenge since after all I did
care you know, in some way, so I felt bad enough for a couple of
days and even returned after I got my head together to see if she
really meant it and she didn't after a sloppy dinner at a water-
front restaurant where I got smashed enough to pretend that the
interesting bed scene we ended up in would be emotionally more

substantial than the way it always was when I was partly not there. —Such a business. So the next day there I was again trying to feel more involved but clutching the same old way wanting to run from the clinging which was partly responsible or the original detachment which was clearly the mode of my involvement in this particular relationship. We then permitted, so far as I could see, this tenuous affair to be shattered by straight society in an incident that was potent enough apparently to make me feel the way LeRoi must have when the black power thing hit him. Anyway I began to understand the meaning of a true social rage. It happened on this evening about 8 p. m. over a tableau of the Mr. and Mrs. and my lover and her roommate and me uncomfortable enough trying to tolerate the barking cheesecake friendliness of the Mr. while relating to the slightly hysterical but not unnatural warmth of the Mrs. who began to insist on a therapy rap which somehow evolved into the dreadful moment when she referred to a male friend, or acquaintance, in tones of slow heavy import as an "in-cur-a-ble hom-o-sex u-al." The place got hung purply apoplex there for a few seconds during which I flashed a number of thoughts and decisions while the Mr. who had been reclining on the couch ogling the roommate got ready to clinch the opener and close the case for straight America with a ponderous gutteral back-up "We-l-l, *honey,* we don't rea-ll-y *know*"—which had the effect of turning my body inside my skin into an armored tank smoking at the joints and hanging over a precipice. I became an instant revolutionary. But I had to hold on and hang in there for the evening with my old fashioned decorum because in the few seconds between her remark and his I had flashed the awful knowledge that I was stranded between the necessity of responding to an intolerable assault and my responsibility to a lover whom I couldn't betray in her closet relation to these people who knew the truth anyway I presume and were playing on the ambivalence of their friend in the normal acceptable fashion of stressing the secret to render it socially impotent. Now I could see for the first time the full import and impact of the closet game. The whole secret-shame-sorry syndrome. I was raging like 20 titans inside my skin unable to act. I went mute but nothing was right. A slaughter was in order and the lady moved in for the kill. The victim became the roommate whom we eventually carried off to cry and scream the rest of it out at home. Now can you dig also that my girlfriend had become angry at *me* for all this? Yeah, these are the wages of sin in our cockeyed society whose collective guilt is denied by the pretense of secrecy. The reverberations of this scene must've traveled down the coast to the Los Angeles fault that made the earthquake. I arose that a. m. in a pure white fury and yelled myself blue in the eyeballs. That was the end of the relationship and the end of my own equivocation as to my sexual identity in any social circumstances and the identity of anyone else with whom I was going to be involved.

POST POST SCRIPT

My two grand passions of the last six years (one before and one after London) were not advantageously arranged. Besides remaining exposed in the shark infested New York art world I had the nerve to be married to a couple of Cassandras, or Cleopatras, as well. One had the kind of eyes that drive Kings mad and cause Empires to fall. The other had the kind of somnolent seductive athletic grace and classic aristocratic features that drives *every-body* mad. Both were very intelligent people too. The first was in mortal fear of her blue chip family whose house she dutifully visited once a week for dinner, an occasion that neither of us thought for a moment should include yours truly confused. She was also the object of probably the most determined and persistent courting in the history of that sort of assault (by a third party on a couple) which was launched by a macho male boy wonder artist assisted with the greatest zeal in the enterprise by his dealer who even followed us to provincial cities to continue their blandishments in a nearby house or in the same hotel! —The second was no improvement for me in these respects because she was not only a beauty and a bacchante but an heiress as well. She moved in with me and spent the money I didn't have and met my famous comrades and tried to seduce my best friend and sucked me into oblivion and threw my Village Voices in the fire and introduced me to her mother who consulted the psychiatrists and became ill, and angry ("I buried that long ago, dear") and called her husband in from Spain and just generally mobilized all her powerful resources to save her wayward daughter from the corruptions of real love until she wisely gave up and retreated in refined resignation to Europe to brood I suppose and to wait for the inevitable. I had an authentic princess and the royal family was furious. I believe they were better off than the Rockefellers and Kennedys combined. And don't think I didn't have designs on every bit of their bread. My plan was a modern Lesbos on the mainland. Whole cities of pleasure palaces for girls. Whole paradises of Daphnes in bunches of elegant chateaux catered by beautiful eunuchs and liveried flowers. Why the hell not. Well, alas, as you know my scheme aborted because the heroine, whom I really loved by the way, disappeared, and although I tumbled after like a good Jill by flying to Spain to rescue the princess from the big bad witch, they were waiting with the psychiatric machinery and the shut-up money and a bottle of whisky on a hot Moorish hilltop to wipe me out and of course I obliged. After all, who was I but an impoverished American female posing as an important British bastard. Anyway we weren't the proper story book couple. I returned home and began screwing around right away. I refused even to be a Snow White for another Snow White any more. I'm urging all Snow Whites to get up out of their caskets and mobilize and claim their own sexuality.

♀ LESBIAN FEMINISM

1. THE MAKING OF A LESBIAN CHAUVINIST

At a time when many feminists are considering the alternative or possibility of another woman as a lover the struggles of those who came to the feminist movement as lesbians and call themselves Gay or Lesbian/Feminists are more often than not conceived and projected by the feminists per se as the female equivalent of the male chauvinist whose behavior defined by that term indicates the oppression of sex roles the feminist movement is dedicated to eliminating. Lesbian chauvinism was the new phrase by spring 1971 if not earlier. I think the phrase naturally emerged out of the old stereotyped ideas of gay women being either butch or femme in imitation of the heterosexual role dichotomies. Although my own lesbian relationships never conformed to these role playing types, I too had some preconceived notions about lesbianism along these lines. And often tried to explain myself in passive and/or aggressive terms. As though I had to be either one or the other. Mainly the phrase was an easy invention by association to further discredit the lesbian as the upsetting gadfly of the feminist movement. Possibly a few feminists had the experience of being pressured to "come out" on ideological grounds by a political lesbian. Certainly the pressure from lesbians in general as a tacit force naturally accompanying their personal persuasion projected into a political framework could not have been overlooked. "Woman Identified Woman" is a powerful document.

148

The new political feminist lesbian who was especially clamorous coming from the angry aggressive positioning of the Gay Liberation Front—an unprecedented uprising of both gay women and gay men to assert pride in homosexual identity. The conjunction of the Gay Liberation Front with the Feminist Movement produced this amazing phenomenon of the sexually straight woman confronted with the challenge of their straight identification at the embarrassing bullseye center of their problem with the man—the sexual foundation of the social institutions. Many feminists could see the instant logic of sex with another woman as the basic affirmation of a powerful sisterhood. Most however were committed at the outset to "reform" of the institutions of oppression—leaving intact the staple nuclear unit of oppression: heterosexual sex. Most were terrified of the implications of their own radical politics and remained firmly entrenched behind barricades of conditioned attitudes toward homosexuality. Knowing perhaps full well that an illness is created by an attitude and not by the intrinsic nature of the sexuality. Suspecting perhaps that in that very taboo against their own homosexuality lay the key to their oppression. It was a jubilant historical moment for the confirmed lesbian. The militant gays had moved very fast from the conservative 60's homophile organizations seeking civil libertarian reform and other appeals for integration into society as an "oppressed minority group." The militant Gay now was conceived that Gay Liberation was the axis for revolutionary change. This was a momentous series of steps from self hatred in guilt and secrecy to apologetic pleas for greater acceptance and legal sanctions to affirmation of identity to aggressive redefinition in the context of revolution. Thus the ideological pressure from the politically advanced articulate lesbians on their straight sisters constituted a state of continuous psychic siege to which the feminists have responded or retaliated according to their various capacities or limitations for change and sexual liberation. The lesbian denounced as chauvinist was a neat way of delaying the issue. I picked the phrase out of the air spring of '71 just when a certain amplified notoriety resulting from the town hall affair and the exposure of Lois Lane as lesbian made me suddenly the object of attentions that could be said to qualify me as a score for a certain type of groupie. Hero to lesbian groupies, far out! Or put another way: token lesbian to the curious and succumbing straights. Sex was available! Lesbian chauvinism was a reality! It isn't easy to convey the great import of the availability of sex to a woman who was a secret unacknowledged lesbian for any amount of time before the gay revolution. The significance of such a fugitive life is integral to the tone and message of my travel and despair piece "Love at First Sex" in the still dark ages of my unawakened political consciousness. The significance of that life as I reiterated over and over was its hopeless apposition to the codes of the heterosexual institution. The sexual deprivation of the woman in relation to man has been well established, but the double deprivation of the woman whose orientation was toward her own sex in relation to whom she was much more severely circumscribed by compulsive secrecy is an intolerable de profundis and derangement of destiny that few women were lucky enough to transcend. Looking back from the precarious standpoint of 1968 I could say I was fortunate to have had three consummated relationships with women. Within his oppression the male homosexual has always moved more freely in the extensive underground urban network of bars and baths and highly developed cruising techniques and designated places to cruise. By comparison the lesbian meeting grounds have been nonexistent to singular. Woman has *always* been defined sexually in relation to man and many people even now never *heard* of a lesbian. During my life in New York consistently I knew male homosexual couples and observed male homosexual flirtations and seductions and phallocentric groupings at parties conveying ineluctably the impression of an exclusive male sexual fraternity which we know very well to be inherited from at least the Greek tradition of acceptable male pleasure apart from their secluded and sequestered women. From this perspective the claim of the militant male gay activist to greater persecution than the lesbian from straight society is a truth which continues to obscure the unrecognized sexuality of the woman who is naturally not persecuted for a condition she is barely exhibiting and following which she is not even imputed to possess. The male gay activist pursues the enlargement of his already recognized sexuality by protesting the loudest against his own persecution which is the social affirmation however negative of that acknowledged sexuality. During my life in New York I never knew a lesbian couple other than my own arrangement except by hearsay and I never observed in any social situations whatever the phenomenon of women paying prime attention to each other the way the men did. The woman was invariably hanging on the privilege of the man. The lesbianism of all these women was inaccessible to them in direct proportion to the social definition of themselves exclusively in relation to the sexual needs of the man, whose pre-emption of the woman as sexual functionary has never deterred him from the enjoyment of his own sex as well. Not only has the sexuality of the woman been thus circumscribed but we know too that the woman has been profoundly conditioned to orient herself toward accepting a single partner around whom her life would center in a "marriage for life" and for whom she waits in suspended animation as for the storybook prince who will arouse her love and sexuality simultaneously. Love and sex. Sex without love was the condition of prostitution. For the woman there was no inbetween. The historical origins of that organ of the psychic life called romantic love are highly conjectural but a number of educated suppositions place the evolution of the emotion in direct relation to the evolution of the family. This is the way I comprehend it. The cultivation of such an emotion would naturally be encouraged as a coercive tool in the development of the family. The family organically perpetuates the emotional apparatus for its own duplication or continuation in the prolonged dependency of the children in the exclusive oedipally focused two-parent ménage. In primitive societies in which child-rearing is communally diffused the bonds between parents and children are more casual and the children grow up realizing there exist many alternative suppliers of love. Philip Slater deftly and briefly deals with the oedipal backward looking fantasy image of romantic love so characteristic of the isolated nuclear western family in his "Pursuit of Loneliness." Slater analyzes the "scarcity mechanism" upon which romantic love is based. He says the intensification of the parent-child relationship creates scarcity by inculcating a pattern of concentrating one's search for love onto a single object and by focusing one's erotic interest on an object with whom consummation is forbidden. "The magnification of the emotionality and exclusiveness of the parent-child bond, combined with the incest taboo, is the prototypical scarcity mechanism." He doesn't indicate the far greater effects of the process on females, but everywhere in civilized societies the adult male moves with a relatively much more extensive mobility and success in the variety and quantity of sexual encounter. The political rhetoric of the feminist movement directed toward economic and representative equality I think obscures perhaps even to the feminists themselves the fundamental drive of feminism which is sexual liberation. I don't think the feminists, generally, envision their liberation in this form. I think their orientation basically is toward the material male superstructure within which they want parity. All the feminist issues—abortion, child care, prostitution, political representation, equal pay—are in relation to the man. In other words in relation to reproductive sexuality. Within which the woman remains trapped as a sexual nonentity. The function of the woman as reproductive agent and her isolated situation in the family and her oedipal orientation toward the single sex-love partner are inseparable components comprising her sexual deprivation. The so-called liberation of the male-oriented woman in the "sexual revolution" has been exposed for what it is and I've made my own remarks here and there in this book, including key quotes on hippiedom by Valerie Solanis. Here's Juliet Mitchell on the subject. "Women are enjoying a new sexual freedom (changing moral attitudes and availability of reliable contraception) but this is often only for their greater exploitation as 'sexual objects' within it." Women will have little or nothing to gain from these up-dated forms of tribal "group marriages" until their matrilineal honor is reestablished and the male privilege has disappeared. That eventuality is something the Gay/Feminist perceives as a possibility only through instant revolutionary withdrawal of women from the man or the system (Man and system being synonymous) whose privilege remains impregnable while the woman persists in accommodating herself to it either of course by convention and tradition or even by the new standard of feminists in revolt for all the items I mentioned by which women will remain in definitive conjunction to the system after the minor and major concessions have been made. The lesbian/feminist is the woman who defines herself independently of the man. "The lesbian's refusal to be an inferior to man is absolute, while with 'normal' woman the rejection of man's superiority remains relative" (Charlotte Wolff). The woman in sexual and social relation to herself who retains the tragic oedipal and monogamous and role playing solutions of the straight heterosexual institution (defined by the domination of one sex over another, modelled after the original authoritative parent-child relationship) is not necessarily any more liberated into her sexual autonomy than the straight feminist, as the feminists keep pointing out in their objections to the lesbian alternative. Many lesbians like myself can testify to the terrible oppression we experienced waiting in long draughts for a "true beloved" in the form of a woman instead of a man. Although as I said my own lesbian relationships never conformed to the role playing models of heterosexuality I was just as hopelessly addicted to the ultimate oedipal for life romantic fantasy stuff as any straight girl. Moreover, conditioned to be a "passive female"—to wait and die politely—made the prospects of the appearance of your savior grimly unlikely in the scheme of things whereby *all* women are more or less similarly passive. A woman could thus easily wait forever for another without suspecting that the other was also waiting for her and this is the tale of many unrequited and unconsummated "friendships" between women. The question being which passive woman is going to make the first verboten aggressive gesture. Passivity is *the* accommodation of the woman to her oppression at every level of the straight male defined society. Passivity is *the* index to a woman's proper behavior as a role playing feminine counterpart to the aggressor. Passivity is *the* dragon that every woman has to murder in her quest for independence. Independence means autonomy means aggressive control of one's own destiny. Lesbian chauvinism defined very simplistically as the aggressive assertion of your sexual and sensual needs and interests is a good phrase. If all women were lesbian chauvinists we would all be aggressive equals and the phrase would be meaningless in its negative aspect as associated with the male whose chauvinism as aggressor implies his entire privilege in which his biological function is united with his social authority. Chauvinism as a pejorative is only meaningful in reference to the role dichotomies which the feminists oppose and out of which the word was revived to describe the superior half of the dichotomy. Considering the social position of the lesbian— the woman who refuses any participation in the male privilege except to rip it off if possible (I mean the man is paying me to write this book)—the allegation of lesbian chauvinism as the female equivalent of the male of that description seems to me quite grandly ironic. There is however a sense in which lesbian chauvinism as pejorative is appreciable and that is when applied to indicate a lesbian still held up in her male identification—a lesbian not yet turned feminist. The woman in this extraordinarily oppressed place of herself naturally tends to oppress other women in the male determination of property and possessiveness, persuading and coercing by involving all the emotions of greed envy fear guilt anger jealousy and so on all the defensive aggressive equipment attending the onset of romantic love. Playing the aggressive or passive roles at their extremes. The butch and femme. Aggressive as I always was in the pursuit of my accomplishments I was a lesbian femme par excellence and was ready to oppress any potential lover with the most excessive monogamous demands. Any potential lover always being of course a remote possibility. The remoteness and the oedipal need being features of each other. It may seem contradictory to say I was a lesbian femme and at the same time that my relationships never conformed to the role playing types of the heterosexual model. But that is true. There was never any conventional division of labor in or out of bed or command and submission program; yet I would characterize myself as femme (conventionally socialized female) in my inability to make a move to satisfy my needs either by regarding a woman as a potential lover or by doing anything about it once a potentiality was established. And further, once a contact had actually been made, strict monogamous expectations and a terrifying dependency were common to both butch and femme. The elimination of butch and femme as we realize our true androgynous nature must inevitably mean the collapse of the heterosexual institution with its role playing dualities which are defined as the domination of one sex over another and with it all enclaves of sexuality such as love between women which have aped the normative institution. My personal liberation began with a rebellion against passivity. Dennis Altman has said, "most male homosexuals . . . pass through a period during which we seek to protect ourselves by refusing any contact other than the purely physical one." This was a phase I had never experienced and I'd venture to say *most* gay women had never experienced. As Altman also emphatically noted: "gay women are after all doubly oppressed and suffer particularly from the social norms that expect women to repress not only their homosexual but even to a considerable extent their heterosexual urges." In similar words, if the oppression of homosexuals is part of the general repression of sexuality and women especially suffer from this repression then the repression of the lesbian woman or the "woman identified woman" will be doubly severe. I said I was fortunate to have had three consummated lesbian relationships—within such a suffocating system—but they were plagued by guilt and secrecy and the great fear of loss or abandonment, and it was necessary for me to plunge through the fires at the gates of the forbidden *twice*—to come out *twice*—with an intervening period of a decade!—in order to establish my sexual identity. My indictment of society rests on the revelation of the degree to which I obliterated my true sexual nature or identity by internalizing the social hatred of women as woman and as gay/woman (which means the same thing to me) and conforming to the heterosexual ideal. During that intervening decade I even sacrificed myself totally in the feudal agonies of marriage and two infants for four years. An aberration of nature! A perversion of narcissus! A lapse of moral instinct. A serious deviation of destiny! For if the phrase biology is destiny has any meaning for a woman right now it has to be the urgent project of woman reclaiming her self, her own biology in her own image, and this is why the lesbian is *the* revolutionary feminist and every other feminist is a woman who wants a better deal from her old man. At a time when many feminists are considering the alternative or possibility of another woman as a lover the struggles of those who came to feminism as lesbians and call themselves Gay or Lesbian/Feminists are more often than not conceived and projected by the feminists per se as the female equivalent of the male chauvinist whose behavior defined by that term indicates the oppression of sex roles the feminist movement is dedicated to eliminating. No woman is in a better position to comprehend a state of existence in which these roles have actually been elimi-

nated than the lesbian. For all her posturing and stylistic imita-
tions of the heterosexual models and her longing for monogamous
security or stability the lesbian is the woman who has experienced real equality in relationships in which no party has the biological or social advantage which characterizes heterosexual
coupling. It's the liberation of the lesbian from this very projected idea from her prefeminist past into her natural polymor-
phic state of identification with other women at multiple levels
of the physical intellectual and spiritual which should constitute
the new ideal for any feminist aspiring to equality and self realization *or* reintegration with her own female principle. The light-
handed use of the phrase lesbian chauvinism as pejorative by
feminists shows little understanding of the incredible wasteland
most of us have come from. The use of the phrase by lesbians
themselves is something else. It isn't easy to convey the great import of the availability of sex and affection to a woman who was
a secret (unacknowledged) lesbian before the gay revolution.
You were either of three things: an embittered angry bar dyke;
a eunuch by default; or a partner in a fearfully tenacious dependent isolated remote déclassé illegal and paranoid marriage. Or
any sequential or simultaneous combination of these impossibilities. In so much as to many feminists chauvinism has meant the
aggressive attention of any male in relation to which she felt like
a sex object the term would naturally apply to any woman who
behaved the same. Yet it was this very aggressive behavior that
has been a key expression in the initial liberation of many lesbians. Speaking for myself certainly. And whether the new assertion was undertaken before or after the dawning of a feminist
consciousness could account for the type of chauvinism involved.
For myself some of my behavior before acquiring a Gay/Femin-
ist head may have been deplorable from any standard of sisterhood. But there was no other way. Just before my last fierce
monogamy the summer of '68 the door opened to my sexual
liberation. In Lois Lane I mentioned that my momentous visit to

London that summer prompted my return to America as "a roaring lesbian." I meant that I discovered I could sleep with a woman and not feel like it was the beginning or the end of the world. Meaning it was possible to just go to bed and have a good time and get up and share a cup of coffee or not and say goodbye and thank you quite amicably like any self respecting male chauvinist for whom the pleasures of the body are not necessarily complicated and constrained by the emotions of greed envy fear guilt anger jealousy etcetera all the defensive aggressive equipment attending the onset of romantic love. The British taught me this lesson. They were very hard on me. I arrived a gaping tourist and left a hardened sexist. Not really. I cried all the way home. I don't remember why. But I remained as mushy as ever which was pretty mushy. Possibly I hadn't grasped yet that it wasn't a crime to fall in love with every British princess who seemed as interested as I was in the mere pleasures of the body. Actually, there were only three, I think. That was enough. For a three week visit the average was outstanding. For a pure innocent virginal american it was lurid and licentious. For a victim of lesbian monogamy it was a revelation. Having dutifully tramped through Westminster and St. Paul's and Charing Cross and the National Museum and Trafalgar Square and Piccadilly Circus and the Tube System and Soho and the Tower and around the Palace and so forth one day I decided impulsively I had to visit a Gay Bar. I had never done this in my life before. Except once as a very young lesbian naturally not connecting my thinking into my activities or fantasies, therefore imagining I was a nice normal person, I went slumming with a friend to a Village place to be a tourist and watch the freaks and get excitedly aghast at *members of the same sex dancing together!* By this summer of '68 I was still disconnected in such a way my thinking or my attitudes or prejudices and my true nature were distinctly and neurotically separate from each other. I was a walking contradiction in turns. I just couldn't see myself as a freak. It was bad enough I was too tall for my age and wore my freckles when the sun came out. I was even strolling around in those fashionable gabardine culottes or leather miniskirts. I must've looked ridiculous. A lesbian still pretending to be available for invasion. Anyway, I went all out there in London and learned about a place called the Gates or Gateways Club. George Brecht located it for me. Very reluctantly. He said he was disappointed in me. I guess he thought he had an exclusive patent on chauvinism, not that I knew at the time that's what he was. I assumed all men had the right to drink a lot and insult womankind and drag as many as possible off by the hair to their caves. So naturally he was not enthusiastic about being an accomplice to my initiation as a rival chauvinist of the lesbian variety. Not that either of us realized the ultimate significance of his innocent investigation. The Gates, by the way, was the bar that figured as the freak joint in "The Killing of Sister George" which I saw a few months later in New York. The entrance had a speakeasy feeling about it. You'd never see it if you didn't know where it was exactly. The door opened directly on a flight of stairs leading down to I imagined a dark den of sin. It was just a smallish well lit rather cheery basement room with comfortable round booths, a bar, a jukebox. The woman at a cash register at the bottom of the stairs was a hardened something or other. Dressed high femme lipstick earrings stockings heels etc. with an incongruously low dark voice and garish features. The bartenders were handsome heavy set butch, a type that always repelled bewildered and frightened me. I sat down and waited. Eventually the only other customer addressed me sort of like over her shoulder from her position turned three quarters away from me. I could appreciate her bleached blond straight short hair and middling cockney accent. Hearing my own american she warmed up and even not too much later turned round to face me. She introduced herself as Maureen. She got so warm in fact she was inviting me to her place to meet her roommate who "likes american girls" and her own lover who was an ex-patriot american. I said I'd like to do that but later on if possible after I found out what this bar was all about. Soon I found out. It seemed the entire gay woman population of London must have decided this was the place to be that night. I had no idea there were so many gay people in the world, never mind London. I was very embarrassed. I didn't know what to do. I didn't do anything. I think I just sat there transfixed with horrified curiosity. I had a very snobbish attitude. I'm sure I didn't think I was a lesbian too. Yet I was rigged out to conform to one of the two stereotyped roles obtaining in conventional old line gay society. Excepting my long hair. But they overlooked the hair because of my tie. The tie seemed to guarantee my role as a female who would play the part of a male. In my three lesbian marriages I had never played any part whatsoever unless it was all parts, so I regarded the attitude with amused toleration, thankful to be attractive to one half of the jam-packed room for inadvertently wearing the right thing. I became friendly and adventurous. I asked someone the time and was threatened with murder by her girlfriend. I supposed she was desperate. It was a good thing I just asked the time. I realized right then I'd better not make a move to talk or dance or anything or they'd be flying me home as a corpse. So I waited. I didn't wait too long. I was pretty popular as I said. Thus there were a succession of sidewise or bizarre approaches. All femmes. I was a butch! The most exciting proposition was a note pressed into my hand by the femme I thought to be the most beautiful in the place; she was so expert in her treachery, passing the message on the run as it were and no doubt while her "steady" was collecting their coats and momentarily out of sight. It was very dramatic. A sequence in a spy movie. I repaired to the ladies right away to read it and find her name and a telephone no. scrawled in pencil. I took the names and numbers of two others who weren't as spectacular in their looks or approach and left to go to Maureen's flat to see about her roommate who "likes american girls." I felt saturated by London lesbiana. I felt I had learned something. I didn't know what exactly. Probably my unconscious was fast at work transforming me overnight into a raging chauvinist. One thing was certain. It no longer seemed bizarre for two members of the same sex to be dancing together. One other thing was certain. There were lots of lesbians in the world. Maybe half the world were lesbians. And I suppose I left with the faint suspicion that I too might be one of them.

At Maureen's house I met her ex-patriot american lover and her roommate Sammy who had me on the floor within minutes. I had sex with Sammy all night and left in the morning thinking I was supposed to see her again immediately and possibly get married for life. Sammy was an Experienced young bar dyke and she didn't care to see me again. She thought I was an american tourist and I was. The second one thought so too and I had to give her up right away as well. She was the "beautiful femme" and I didn't understand her anyway. She came on very butch once you got inside the door. The third had a name out of Ivanhoe—Roxanne or Rowena or something—and I had to give her up immediately too. She was 20 and beautiful and voluptuous and she appeared at a pub one late evening out by the Tower where I was drinking with George Brecht and some English friends of his. One of the friends was a raunchy lowdown art student kid from up north who was coming on to the Ivanhoe princess. All pissed somehow the three of us became involved necking at the bar and we closed the place down tottering out on the deserted street looking for a taxi to go to my flat which was big and empty or so I thought. There was no taxi at that hour out around the Tower so we piled up like a totem in a phone booth still groping each other and called for one. The princess was all over me inside my pants exclaiming she'd never done it with a woman before. We fell into the taxi and she turned into a herd of cows in heat. Sprawling agape and wet and panting in between me and the art student, whose attitude leering at me suggested what was supposed to happen was that both of us do the princess somehow. It was a new kind of scene and a half for me. I don't think I was properly piggish at all. I was still ready to "fall in love" as soon as I put my hands on her. Anyway we staggered into my flat and concluded the orgy to the best of my imagination, taking advantage of Roxanne or Rowena, who probably wanted to be tied up and beaten, whose appetite at any rate for assault and ravishment seemed enormous and unappeasable.

Back in New York I looked round at the world with new interested eyes. As though I was noticing for the first time a certain kind of bird or tree that had always been in the neighborhood and I had until then overlooked. One evening outside Max's I caught a glimpse of two women necking in a VW bug and I went right up and rapped on the window. They jumped apart and looked out at me frightened. I said I'd just returned from London and things were very good over there. They invited me in and drove me up to 47th St. and a mafia bar on floor thirty something of the ———— Hotel. They wanted to know why I'd never been to a bar before. I didn't know what to say. And I didn't begin going to them either. But I *was* giving off a new air of poised bait for the sex I wanted. One night at Max's a Nancy sat down cross from me in a booth and transfixed herself into my eyes and followed me out and home and into my bed and some excellent sex until she realized a week or two later we were both women. I was still a fall dyke for a romance. So such encounters the end of that summer of '68 or the beginning of the fall were just preliminary skirmishes for the real awful thing again. The real awful thing I've described in "Love at First Sex." I met Polly that October. The following spring I made my true leap into chauvinism. "Most male homosexuals . . . pass through a period during which we seek to protect ourselves by refusing any contact other than the purely physical one." The way I explained it

to myself and with great anger aforethought was what the hell
was I supposed to do now wait around for another couple of
years pining after an old princess while waiting for a new one
and rotting in my skin from sexual death and my mind from the
sentimental malaise over yer lost love and all that and I rebelled
in earnest at last against my own ancient passivity. I took command of my sexual destiny. The results could be brutally or bale-
fully bizarre. I have to remind anyone my feminist consciousness
was so underground as to be close to the center of the earth on
the other side of China. One afternoon shortly after P. flew off to
Spain a British woman called me to interview me for a British
magazine. We talked for two hours. Then she called back and
wanted to fall by. After ten minutes and a drink her questions
shifted gear into the provocatively personal and within another
few minutes I got the message and said brusquely if she wanted
an "experience" I had fifteen minutes before an appointment
and we could try to do something in that time and I went and
lay down on the bed and waited for her to wrestle out of her
dress and a cumbersome difficult bra and made some halfhearted
love to the poor woman whom I then briskly bundled into a taxi
as I went on my way to the aforementioned appointment. Not
much later I found myself upstairs in the bedroom of a huge
rambling house in Pittsburgh coming on the stomach of a skinny
pretty girl and casually saying goodbye as I turned over to sleep
and she left the party to go home. Back in New York I was on
stage at the finish of a panel I'd arranged about myself called
"The Disintegration of a Critic" at Loeb Student Center of NYU
telling the panel and the auditorium in answer to the moderator's question about where I'd just come from and what I'd been
doing that I'd just seduced a woman at my place and as soon as
the panel was over I left with another woman collecting on my
way out my wallet from the first woman who had come with me
and was sitting in the audience I went back home to seduce the
second woman. Also around that time I remember a movie type

hustler set me up with his "beautiful mistress" who met me on a sort of blind date basis at Penn Station and went with me to the Chelsea Hotel to register for a room for the night on the hustler's donated bread. The desk man recognized me and referred to me as a "famous writer" which seemed to fit the general design. But the "mistress" was so "beautiful" in some dead or deadpan dumb movie queen sense that we lay in bed like corpses and I couldn't do much on a very dry mouth and a shaky hand and her apathetic posture and anticlimactic question "don't you like men" to which I think I gave up completely and wasn't sorry. What could I say then that was not the story of so many others. Such were the chances and corruptions and concupiscent precipitations of my new life as a liberated lesbian chauvinist. I was delighted and startled. I hoped I would never perish over another woman again. The only thing wrong with it was that I was still a male identified lesbian. Later on, that fall of '69, returning from Europe I met the women of Gay Liberation Front and I've documented my alterations and growth of consciousness in this book. At least I found out that some one night stands can be rewarding just as some lasting relations can be disastrous. But whatever a lesbian does if she does it out loud she'll be condemned by some new twist of the language. More than anything else the phrase lesbian chauvinism as pejorative is another way of negating the sexuality of woman by impugning any move by the woman to take charge of her own sexual destiny.

II.   THE MYTH OF THE MYTH OF THE VAGINAL ORGASM

Should the hypothesis be true that one of the requisite cornerstones upon which all modern civilizations were founded was coercive suppression of women's inordinate sexuality, one looks back over the long history of women and their relationships to men, children and society since the Neolithic revolution with a deeper, almost awesome, sense of the ironic tragedy in the triumph of the human condition.

Mary Jane Sherfey, M.D.

The process of physical and psychic self-affirmation requires full relation with those like oneself, namely women.

Ecstasy, a paper written by
a gay revolutionary party

Many of the new theories and descriptions of woman's basic equipment and orgasm may sound right to a lot of women. They don't sound bad to me, but they're almost exclusively written in relation to the man with the implicit instruction that the man had better shape up and recognize this "inordinate" sexuality of women and learn the more effective means of stimulating and satisfying his partner. Although many women can satisfy themselves in relation to the man it's not well known at all that the woman can satisfy herself just as well if not better in relation to herself or to other women. The sexual satisfaction of the woman independently of the man is the *sine qua non* of the feminist revolution. This is why Gay/Feminism expresses the proper sexual-political stance for the revolutionary woman. Sexual dependence on the man is inextricably entangled in the interdependence of man and woman at all levels of the social structures by which the woman is oppressed. It is in any case difficult to conceive of an "equal" sexual relationship between two people in which one member is the "biological aggressor." Although a hole also moves forward to enclose a sword it is the sword in all known personal-political forms of life thruout history which has assumed initiative to invade and conquer. The man retains the prime organ of invasion. Sexual congress between man and woman is an invasion of the woman, the woman doesn't get anything up to participate in this congress, and although a woman may be conditioned to believe that she enjoys this invasion and may in fact grow to like it if her male partner makes rare sacrifices of consideration in technical know-how, she remains the passive receptive hopeful half of a situation that was unequal from the start. The fate that woman has to resign herself to is the *knowledge* of this biological inequity. A fate that was not originally the occasion for the *social* inequities elaborated out of the biological situation. From this knowledge the woman can now alter her destiny or at least reclaim certain ancient historical solutions, namely the self sufficient tribes of amazons, to a physical problem in relation to men. Some Marxist-Socialist thinkers envision the solution in our technological advancement whereby the test-tube baby will relieve the woman of her reproductive function and release her to the wideranging sexual pleasures traditionally arrogated by the man. But *no* technological solution will be the answer to the spiritual needs of the woman deprived of herself in relation to the man. Feminism at heart is a massive complaint. Lesbianism is the solution. Which is another way of putting what Ti-Grace Atkinson once described as Feminism being a theory and lesbianism the practice. When theory and practice come together we'll have the revolution. Until all women are lesbians there will be no true political revolution. No feminist per se has advanced a solution outside of accommodation to the man. The complaints are substantial and articulate and historically sound and they contain by implication their own answers but the feminists refuse to acknowledge what's implicit in their own complaint or analysis. To wit: that the object of their attack is not going to make anything better than a *material* adjustment to the demands of their enslaved sex. There's no conceivable equality between two species in a relation in which one of the two has been considerably weakened in all aspects of her being over so long a period of historical time. The blacks in America were the first to understand that an oppressed group must withdraw into itself to establish its own identity and rebuild its strength through mutual support and recognition. The first unpublicized action of many feminists *was* in fact to withdraw from the man sexually. Feminists who still sleep with the man are delivering their most vital energies to the oppressor. Most feminists understood this immediately but were con-- founded in their realization by the taboo against the obvious solution of sex with another woman. Not only is the psychic-emotional potential for satisfaction with another woman far greater than that with a man, insomuch as every woman like every man was originally most profoundly attached to herself as her mother, but there is more likelihood of sexual fulfillment with another woman as well since all organisms best understand the basic equipment of another organism which most closely resembles themselves. The erotic potential between like organisms consists in the enhancement of self through narcissistic identification. Narcissism is the ideal appreciation of self. Women who love their own sex love the sameness in the other. They become both subject and object to each other. That makes two subjects and two objects. Narcissism is the totality of subject-object unity within the self extended to another. "When a heterosexual woman loves a man she is confronted with otherness, and so is a man who loves a woman. Otherness implies something completely different from oneself, something one has to learn to understand and live with . . . At one time or another, the 'normal' (heterosexual) woman will always be put back into the place of being an object." (Charlotte Wolff, *Love Between Women*, p. 70) Normalcy for women is the adaptation to their own oppression. Or to the male standard for perpetuating his privilege in unequal relationships. Normalcy is the fucked up condition of woman. Normalcy is the unsuccessful attempt to overcome the obstacle of otherness by resigning oneself to one's own deprivation of self. Normalcy is an appeal to numbers in the form of majorities to justify coercion in plans to cooperate for the benefit of "mankind." Normalcy is the disease of maladjusted coupling by different or hetero or otherness species. Normalcy is achieved by puritan ethical appeals to the moral correctness of doing things that are worthwhile by their difficulty and hard labor through delayed gratification of real instincts, or uniting with self. True normalcy would mean the return of all women to themselves. Majority behavior, which defines civilized schizophrenia, is pseudo-normalcy. The first order of business for a woman is the redefinition of herself through assertion of her sexuality in relation to herself or her own equal, in other words, independently of the man. Early feminist writings project the suggestion of lesbianism as an alternative to the widespread sexual dissatisfaction of women in relation to men. There was, in these early manifestos, both fortunately and not so fortunately, a concentration on that aspect of the basic equipment in which orgastic satisfaction originates. I thought everybody knew the clitoris was the doorway to orgasm, the way a certain type of jill-in-the-box might pop open after sufficient rhythmic friction against its trap door. Apparently this glorification of the clitoris was a revelation to women who remained frigid in intercourse through neglect of prior stimulation of the external or clitoral part of the organ. Or who remained frigid in intercourse regardless of said prior stimulation, this actually being the true situation, according to early pronouncement, based on the total absence of feeling or orgastic potential within the vagina itself. I have a record entry June 18, 1970: "find out what they mean by the myth of the vaginal orgasm." Subsequently I asked a few "feminists." They informed me, in effect, that I don't experience what I say I feel or feel what I say I experience or any combined way of being a liar. And their chief authority was Masters & Johnson. Studying the feminist literature I decided that the feminists had found the perfect rationale for their frustration and excuse for not being required to fuck with the man any more. They didn't actually say this. They were mainly contesting the "myth of the liberated woman and her vaginal orgasm." The refutation of Freud's thesis of sexual maturity in the woman consisting of her transference to the father as proper love object developing parallel to the shifting of orgasmic location in the clitoris to the "mature" vagina. Wherever these feminists obtained their "evidence" for an insensitive vagina, if not in themselves, it seemed not to matter either about the source or the (in)sensitivity if the issue constituted a rebellion against being defined sexually in terms of what pleases the man. It seems actually amazing that what they were asserting was a stubborn refusal to submit to conventional intercourse on grounds of an insensitive vagina. *Equating* intercourse with vaginal orgasm as it were. (No mention of hands or bananas or dildoes.) Really as though one was unthinkable without the other. As though the case for an insensitive vagina provided women with their first legal brief for the indictment of phallic imperialism. This rather misguided attempt of women to dissociate themselves from the suppression of their pleasure in "reproductive sexuality" was nonetheless a crucial rudimentary step in establishing sexual independence from the man and leading to the fuller dimension of womanhood in Gay/Feminism. In fact within two years or so after the appearance of these papers the feminist line includes more overt accommodation to and recognition of lesbians, as well as lesbianism itself within the ranks. I said "misguided" because the feminist equation along the old standard of "reproductive sexuality" or penis-in-vagina as proper model or primal scene, and their "discovering" of the insensitive female half of the bargain, important as it was, left them with only one operable part of the basic equipment—the clitoris—and the ignorance of a solution involving all the equipment with their sisters. I always agreed with one half of Freud's equation. That a woman moves from clitoral to vaginal orgasm. And that the latter *is* more mature in the sense that the activation of the inner walls brings about a more profound intensification of orgasm. I would add that this shift occurs in two kinds of time—over a period of months or years as a "discovery" of the orgastic potential of the internal walls, and as a transition in every sexual encounter, moving from initial stimulation of clitoris (as the seat of sensation, the *origin* of satisfaction) to full orgasm experienced in the total organ which includes the "deep" vaginal wall. I take issue like the feminists with Freud's postulation of "heterosexual maturity." Since a woman can achieve vaginal orgasm herself or with another woman clearly his case for maturity was in the interests of the continuation of phallic imperialism. The rights of the father to the mother. The Gay/Feminist revolution involves the rights of the mother to the mother. Woman's thighs are the gateways to infinity for women as well as for men. For women give birth to themselves as well as to boys. I was struck particularly by these remarks in the Masters & Johnson book on female orgasm: "During the first stage of subjective progression in orgasm, the sensation of intense clitoral-pelvic awareness has been described by a number of women as occurring concomitantly with a sense of bearing down or expelling. This last sensation was reported only by parous study subjects, a small number of whom expressed some concept of having an actual fluid emission or of expending in some concrete fashion." And: "Twelve women, all of whom have delivered babies on at least one occasion without anesthesia or analgesia, reported that during the second stage of labor they experienced a grossly intensified version of the sensations identified with this first stage of subjective progression through orgasm." These reports seemed to confirm my long suspicion that orgasm itself originated in the parthenogenetic birth of our unicellular beginnings. The daughter cells. The immaculate conception is the female fantasy of her own birth without the aid of the male. I can personally testify to the aboriginal reality of this state of being through having experienced a "psychic parthenogenesis" in certain hallucinatory symptoms of childbirth—psychosomatic labor pains—attending the birth of myself during a critical period of cosmic consciousness more commonly called insanity. Women of course do the same for each other in any intense relationship. I should also remark that my "rebirth" was accompanied by a great expansion of sexuality in the realms of both sensual awareness and orgastic potential. During this time for instance I began to experience the intensification or deepening of orgasm that I could only describe as "inner" or "internal." The feminists claimed Masters & Johnson as an authority in their case for an insensitive vagina. Yet Masters & Johnson say "The physiologic onset of orgasm is signaled by contractions of the target organs, starting with the *orgasmic platform in the outer third of the vagina.* This platform, created involuntarily by localized vasocongestion and myotonia, contracts with recordable rhythmicity as the tension increment is released" (italics mine). And "Vaginal spasm and penile grasping reactions have been described many times in the clinical and non-professional literature." And "Regularly recurring orgasmic-platform contractions were appreciated subjectively as pulsating or throbbing sensations of the vagina." And "Finally, as the third stage of subjective progression, a feeling of involuntary contraction with a specific focus in the vagina or lower pelvis was mentioned consistently." The Masters & Johnson team remain loyal to the standard of heterosexual coupling but they've presented the most impressive physiological findings to date of the extensive orgasmic response of the woman. I really think the feminists basically were making a common complaint in the new terminological context of feminism. That the man was no good in bed. That he was insensitive to the essential clitoris. That he just didn't know how to do it. And as an added fillip the new challenge that a woman or feminist anyway would henceforth refuse to accept responsibility for a frigidity that wasn't her own fault. The solution has still not been posed within feminist theory. It can't be because feminism is not a solution. It's the complaint that got the movement going. When the feminists have a solution they'll be Gay/Feminists. Until then, they've got the best problem around and that's the man. Feminism is a struggle terminology. Concerning women at odds with the man. Since women have always been at odds with the man feminism is the collectivized articulated expression of women's demeaned status. Feminism will no longer need itself when women cease to think of themselves as the "other" in relation to the "other" and unite with their own kind or species. Being male and female is, above all, defined in terms of the other. Feminists could begin by realizing that not only do they not need a penis to achieve their supreme satisfaction but they could easily do better without one since the timing involving the essential stimulation of the outer tissues prior to and/or concomitant with penetration requires a penis that can be erect for entry at a more or less precise moment in the progress toward climax. Some women and men work this thing out, or in, but most women, as the feminists observed, consistently receive a penis into a dead or dying chamber from which the penis eventually emerges as the savior in the form of a child. In any case the question many peoples are asking now is if "reproductive sexuality" is no longer the standard for sexual approach—for men it never was completely—what is keeping women from their total pleasure with other women. We know why. "Women far more than men are trapped in a social view that suggests that their ultimate worth is derived from a suitable heterosexual attachment and the result of this is that they come to despise both themselves and other women." (Altman, 79) In order for a girl to achieve an adequate motherhood, she must to some degree relinquish her libidinal attachment to her own mother. The acculturation of women to believe most exclusively in "reproductive sexuality" remains pervasive and powerful. Altman (p. 60) again: "As a consequence of the utilitarian view of sex there is an extremely strong negative attitude toward all sexual urges other than those that are genital and heterosexual." Or: "Sex has been firmly linked, and nowhere more clearly than in Christian theology, with the institution of the family and with child bearing. Sex is thus legitimized for its utilitarian principles, rather than as an end in itself . . . even where sexual pleasure is accepted as a complementary goal, the connection between marriage and sex still remains." As a complementary goal women have no need to stay in relation to the aggravation caused by the "biological aggressor." If the male fears absorption and the female penetration, and both fears represent the disturbance of a static equilibrium—in which nothing is either gained or lost— (Slater, 103) it seems clear that the various global disturbances now accelerated by technological expansion are material visible extensions of the primal antagonism between men and women in some evolutionary distortion of destiny. (Not that there is such a thing as an evolutionary distortion.) Marcuse commented on Norman O. Brown: "If I understand his mysticism correctly it includes abolition of the distinction between male and female and creation of an androgynous person. He seems to see the distinction between male and female as the product of repression. I do not. It is the last difference I want to see abolished." Speaking of sexism in high places! If I understand Marcuse correctly. Since I too would not like to see the distinction abolished, but not I think for the same reasons. Agreeing with Brown, I'm not sure that he would envision the solution in the withdrawal of women from participation in that repression by which the distinction was created and sustained. Or even that he would define it that way. The fall was from some primeval division into two sexes. I think any bio-analytically oriented person knows we were originally one sex. The fall is a constant reoccurrence through birth or separation. "The sin is not between the lover and the beloved, but in parentage." The project in our cycle toward species extinction should be clear enough. The present revolution of women is a clamorous reminder of that destiny and the proper organic means of achieving it. Many male intellects hope to see the abortion of this destiny. Not necessarily specifically identifying the agent of that abortion in the potential technological disasters of the male power problem. The key to survival in the interests of a natural death is the gradual extinction of the reproductive function as·it is now still known and practiced. For it is by this function that the woman is so desperately deprived of herself. Lesbian or woman prime is *the* factor in advance of every projected solution for our embattled world. In her realization of herself both sensually polymorphously and genitally orgasmically she experiences her original self reproductive or parthenogenetic recreation of herself apart from the intruding and disturbing and subjugating male. Genitalorgasmic sex between women is absolutely consistent with our total sensual and emotional mutually reflecting relations with each other. The lesbian woman is not properly equipped to oppress her own kind. But she *is* equipped to give herself pleasure, and she doesn't need any artificial substitute for the instrument of oppression to give herself that pleasure.

III. THE SECOND SUCKS & THE FEMININE MYSTAKE

A lesbian's best friend is an upside down cake. The feminist issue is an instruction sheet for getting on better in the system. There is no feminist issue. After there are proper child care centers and free abortions and easy contraception and equal pay and representation and job opportunities—then what? There'll still be a man. And biology is definitely destiny. The woman in relation to man historically has always been defeated. Every woman who remains in sexual relation to man is defeated every time she does it with the man because each single experience for every woman is a reenactment of the primal one in which she was invaded and separated and fashioned into a receptacle for the passage of the invader and that's why every woman is a reluctant and a fearful bride throughout all time the woman has capitulated by custom and custom alone to an invasion that was originally the outcome of a biological warfare and is now sanctioned by those very social structures that the feminists somehow keep insisting are merely learned behaviors as though the social structures were a diabolical invention of no consequence in relation to a difference of clear disadvantage in mobility to the female. Role playing is the elaboration of that (dis)advantage into the various passive-aggressive or sado-masochistic dualities. The role-behavior of the man which entitles him to power and prestige is the expression of an original biological advantage accrued in some primeval victory and defined as brute strength in surviving a hazardous environment. The female was the original test of that strength. The female became a separate species subdued and subsumed like the other animals in the competition for survival. The female is a separate species. The female in relation to herself is not *naturally* a role playing animal. The female in relation to the man is only half a woman and a disadvantaged one at that. The man in relation to woman is an advantaged half of a man. The message of learned behavior is that a woman fulfills herself by uniting with her opposite but in reality she becomes lost to herself in service to a foreign species. You are who you sleep with. Thus the lesbian rightfully says she is the woman par excellence. "I *know* I'm a woman, I'm the most woman that can *be* a woman." The only radical feminists around here worthy of the name that I know of are Ti-Grace Atkinson and Valerie Solanis and they don't have to use the word lesbian to define the man as the enemy we can take instruction from the pathological purity of their fury. The lesbian has no quarrel with them unless it be personal. One could suppose them to be beyond the necessities of erotic gratification. The woman in relation to herself is beset with the inherited bull of the heterosexual institution in its hype of ownership and romantic love and role playing or the guilt resentment syndrome reassurance tenacity confluence principle fear anxiety loss cancellation escape mechanism all equaling marriage for life. The woman in relation to herself is at the beginning of a prolonged struggle to purge herself of all that manmade shit. The projected accusation of sexism and chauvinism and oppression by many feminists onto the lesbian is their own expectation based on all they know in relation to the man. The lesbian herself is emerging from these expectations in a new identification of her own womanhood. The butch or diesel dyke is fast disappearing. The butch or diesel dyke is a stylistic imitation of the male whose structures she thought she had to transpose in relation to herself to obtain gratification. Likewise the femme. The woman in relation to herself is not a butch or a femme but a woman. She is not *naturally* a role playing animal. Role playing occurs through differences in which one different animal can't tolerate the difference of another in some restless sense of insecurity and incompletion. Identity achieved by superiority and submission. If radical feminism is addressing itself to the "total elimination of sex roles" while still talking sex in relation to the man who defines these roles in the sex act by a certain historical biological-cultural imperative they are going in circles of unadulterated contradictory bullshit. Seeking a "better" place beside the man in his own system moreover is to perpetuate the same authoritative hierarchical oppressive ordering of things by which the woman would remain subjugated by class, if not caste. Attaining a better place beside the man the woman would remain still half a woman while resting secure in the *apparent* privilege of some greater material advantage. A spiritually dead woman beside the spiritually dead man. The feminists are now asserting the possibility or alternative of sex with another woman under conditions learned from the very male power structure they claim to be oppressed by. The straight woman can't yet *think* of relating to another person sexually as an equal. Her sexual situation has always been defined as passive and invisible. The puritanism of the feminists is rooted in sexism—sexism being synonymous with the repression of her sexuality as the passive invisible partner. Thus she projects her experience of the straight world onto the lesbian with a preconceived opinion of role playing or sexism. She thinks for sample that any woman who expresses an interest in her sexually is being oppressive (oppressive equals aggressive equals male equals sexist) and so she converts this interest into the sex-seductive game maneuvering of the straight world in which the lesbian is objectified as desirable for an "Experience" or for a "Relationship" if the lesbian plays the game correctly by pretending that the straight woman is a special prize difficult to obtain or to be treated as a delicate passive instrument of exceptional concern. The lesbian is thus oppressed by being considered an aggressor in the manner of the man. In mutual aggression where equals all express their sexual needs and interests there is no aggression in the sense of mastery and control. The most effective means of control and mastery in the straight world is the cultivation of attachment by love and romance. The love object is a special instance. And as such a private one. Nobody else's business. A personal matter. The lesbian relationship has been a personal matter for so long that many lesbians are practicing lesbians without thinking they are lesbians. Women actually live together without acknowledging they are doing so. The woman they are with is a "special case." The more unusual overt looking lesbian who is now a militant one in the context of the feminist revolution was very often a woman who endured a major disappointment or two or more in relation to another "special" woman and was thus forced to consider her sexuality in broader social terms and define herself as a woman who loved women or not—a hard choice in a world in which the personal is not yet a political issue. Now you can hear many experienced lesbians saying of these reform type feminists gingerly considering another woman as a lover "well maybe they need to fall in love to make it happen" and that's precisely the way many feminists hope it will happen and we hope so too that they bring each other out that way if it has to be that way because no self respecting lesbian can tolerate the oppression of even pretending to be the total end of the world oedipal answer to another woman's straight fantasy. It's quite true that such lesbian relationships are little threat to the male in his structure since they remain "isolated lesbian examples" and as in the movie "The Fox" the first guy who steps into a limbo of consciousness gets one or both of the girls. Otherwise known as arrested development by the straights (O'Wyatt). The lesbians many feminists consider oppressive—the self-confident, swinging thrill-seeking female females (who) have contempt for men and for the pandering male females as Solanis said—are oppressed by the reactionary puritan attempt of these feminists to bait them and solicit them or condemn them according to the very sexist definitions the lesbians are struggling in their peer relalationships with each other to transcend and leave behind in the heap of personal isolated solutions to a vast political problem. Dig this exchange in an *anonymous* interview with a woman: Q: What made you fall in love with a woman? A: I didn't fall in love with "a woman"—I fell in love with Jen (or Jan)—which is not exactly the same thing. A better way to ask the question is: How were you able to *overcome* the fact that it was a woman?—(Italics mine)—Dig she didn't fall in love with a *woman*. I think the way you translate that is that she fell in love with a *person*. A special person. Who just *happens* to be a woman. Meaning love is indiscriminate and it could as well be a woman as a man or vice versa. It's great that this woman is getting it on with another woman. I'm not disparaging the relationship. Which may be her primer step in gay-feminist consciousness. But for such an approach to be put forth as an official definition of acceptable lesbianism *within* feminism is a whole bunch of backward reactionary crap that seriously retards the revolution. It belongs to the baggage of bisexual excuse and delay formation that characterizes the best part of adjustment and compromise or don't worry to the wondering male who won't mind a lesbian turn-on if it doesn't interfere with his own prerogative. Bisexuality is an intermediary solution for women on the way to relating completely with their sisters. Bisexuality is not so much a cop-out as a fearful compromise. Many women pride themselves on their bisexuality, claiming they happily have it both ways. But one half of those both ways is a continued service to the oppressor, whose energies are thus reinforced to perpetuate the oppression of that part of the woman who would make it with another woman. For as Wendy Wonderful said at a Columbia panel in 1970 "I'm bisexual, and when I say I'm having an affair with a man it's groovy, but when I'm having an affair with a woman not only is it not so groovy but it's not acceptable, thus the oppressed part of me is the lesbian and therefore I say I'm a lesbian!" Bisexuality is staying safe by claiming allegiance to heterosexuality. Everybody assumes you are heterosexual so bisexuality is a cop-out because if I say to you I'm a bisexual you would assume I was a heterosexual who sometimes has sex with a woman rather than I am a lesbian who occasionally indulges in sex with a man. She's still on the right side of the fence but occasionally strays to the wrong side. Bisexuality is still heterosexuality. In the gay revolution the lesbian most jealously guards her exclusive relations to women, for the male privilege is rampant and ubiquitous. The gay male can talk and behave bisexually without relinquishing his privilege. The gay woman has nothing to gain in sexual relations to the man except the illusion of a momentary status by association with male privilege and the illusion perhaps of a "total" sexual life. Bisexuality is a condition *within,* and not a condition to achieve *outside* oneself by running from one sex to another with the idea of uniting the two sexes in oneself in this fashion. In fact in that half of the transaction with the opposing sex the woman upsets the bisexual balance within herself by surrendering some part of that "internal" totality to the totality of the other who doesn't *feel* so total, who feels historically and so notoriously incomplete without mother or woman. Bisexuality for women in the revolution in any case is collaboration with the enemy. Bisexuality is a state of political oblivion and unconsciousness. "The claim to bisexuality is commonly heard within the movement, and while bisexuality is not physiologically impossible, the term cannot be used to characterize a stable socio-sexual orientation. Because no heterosexual relationship is free of power politics and other masculine mystifications, women who assert that they are bisexual retain their definition by men and the social advantages accruing from this. Bisexuality is a transitional stage, a middle ground, through which women pass from oppressive relationships to those of equality and mutuality. It is a struggle with privilege and fear, and not all women come through it to their sisters on the other side." (Ecstasy. A paper of a Gay Revolution Party.) The new hysteria of feminism is a second wave of accommodation to the lesbian element that was originally considered a side or nonexistent issue or an annoying embarrassment. The hysteria obscures their advanced analysis to which many lesbians are indebted and which the feminists are still refusing to make explicit by obvious inference in their own lives. And denying their social analysis by reverting to individual solutions. If you're not part of the solution you're part of the problem. Many women are dedicated to working for the "reconstructed man"—or any translation into movement rhetoric of the old saw of a woman with clout in the home who gently prods her provider and protector into being a more thoughtful oppressor. The energy expended in convincing or persuading or working on the man and at length at its most exhausting in the creative strategies employed to defend new positions against the aroused opposition is energy best directed toward the building and refining of new interactive structures among the very people, namely women, who form the subject of this new offensive revolution. Feminists who still sleep with the man are delivering their most vital energies to the oppressor. To work out a suitable compromise or *apparent* equality, at any private level, is an exceptional

solution between exceptional people, and although not a solution
to disregard or denounce in a disjunctive culture, it remains an
effort in isolation from the ground thrust of the most fundamental
social revolution in the world. Out of the interactive energies of
women at all levels of physical mental emotional chemical spiritual will arise the new autonomous identities or aristocracy of
women whose mutual energies and identities will define the new
social structures. If you're not part of the solution you're part
of the problem. A personal solution or exceptional adjustment to
a political problem is a collusion with the enemy. The solution is
getting it together with women. Or separatism. The non-separa-
tist woman who is not included in the common conception of the
feminist solution may be viewed as a co-opted part of the problem. At this time all women are a co-opted part of the problem
insomuch as every sphere of government and influence is con-
trolled at the top by the man; thus the essential separatist solution is operative at present in theory and in consciousness and
at the local manifest levels of communal fugitive enterprises.
The lesbian feminist's withdrawal as far as possible from the
source of her oppression can in no way be construed as a political cop-out. On the contrary it is at this point that the confluence
of the personal/political (articulated but not significantly ex-
plored by feminists as a whole) attains the dimension of imperative reality to the lesbian. With her consciousness that she alone
has no vested interest in prevailing cultural forms she finds that
she must struggle within her sexual peer group to create wholly
new nonhierarchical modes of interactive behavior. She *must*
face her acculturated alienation from herself and other women
and for her very survival she must learn to tap the source of her
erotic energy, i.e., reclaim her sexuality. Radical lesbians know
that men will not soon "get better" through the efforts of women
to reeducate them. They envision the process of gay feminist
revolution as an extended struggle. Tribal groupings of such
women, the fugitive Lesbian Nation, have begun and will con-

tinue to serve as sustaining support and psychic power bases within the movement. The woman in relation to herself is not *naturally* a role playing animal.

IV.   WOMAN PRIME

The continuing emergence of the insurgent gay liberation literature may soon make it apparent that the gay revolutionary movement constitutes the first significant challenge to the existing social structures. The counter culture has produced its most important bastard. The counter culture itself is being exposed as an integral part of the system challenged by the gay revolution. The culture of hippie gangbang or folk and hard rock groupie sex. The true counter culture may now be defined as the gay revolution. The overthrow of the system implicit in counter culture theory and activities clearly belongs to the solutions of historical revolutionary change in which the grounds for the necessities of change have remained unacknowledged and unchallenged. Revolutionary social change in the past has occurred within systems characterized by institutionalized heterosexuality and oppression of the female. Historically, revolution has meant the overthrow of one class by another, leaving the oppressive institution itself intact. Such revolutions result in new class systems or a return to a previous social order in a new disguise. Gay revolution addresses itself to the total elimination of the sexual caste system around which our oppressive society is organized and through which distinctions of class and race are reinforced and maintained. The target remains the same—the ruling class male, and the ruling class aspirations of every other male, but not by the old definition of that target as simply economically oppressive. It is now recognized that any Marxist-Socialist analysis must acknowledge the sexist underpinnings of every political economic power base. Gay liberation cannot be considered apart from women's liberation. Gay liberation *is* in reality a feminist movement. The oppression of women is pivotal in the strategy and goals of the gay sexual revolution. The more overt discrimination and persecution of the male homosexual makes this point clear. I mean that the hatred of the gay male is rooted in the fear of the loss of male power and prestige. Since society accords many special benefits to men it is considered worse for a man to "act like a woman" than the reverse. The upfront gay male surrenders his prestige in a sense by acknowledging he is not participating in the system by oppressing the woman where her oppression begins—in bed. Gay liberation emerged out of women's liberation and through the critically intermediate figure of the lesbian the two liberation fronts unite as a Gay/Feminist movement. The mere feminist is an incipient revolutionary. She is a woman in revolt against her prescribed and confined feminine role but she has not yet envisioned the solution to her dilemma for she persists in recognizing the brute sexual prerogative of the male while seeking reforms to alter her condition *within* the male defined structures *dictated* by that sexual prerogative. The rights of the father to the mother. She has forgotten her own rights to the mother as she once experienced the same erotic and nutritive dependency on the mother as did her son and brother. Her conditioning has been so complete that she has forgotten. The lesbian is the woman who somehow never lost the link or who remembered by some accident of love or contact in an environment that was conducive to remembrance (i.e., jail, boarding school, camp, the wacs, etc.). The lesbian is the key figure in the social revolution to end the sexual caste system, or heterosexual institution, for she is the clearly disenfranchised of the four sexes. She has abdicated her inherited right, or rather command, to participate in the male privilege by association, through bed and marriage and even friendship. From the consciousness of this remoteness from the sources of real power and her corresponding social ineffectuality or position without sanction the lesbian is the figure at this moment in history in the proper place to seize the initiative for change by affirming her own or woman's identity through tactics of mutual support right down at the very level of her social impotence—where she consciously abandons the male system to build her own. The lesbian has experienced male prejudice within gay liberation and heterosexual fear within women's liberation. Both fear/prejudice phenomena are blood kin to the oppressor: the straight ruling class male. The angry lesbian naturally at first joined forces with gay men in the camaraderie of the shared interest of loving one's own sex and the illusion of an "outside" oppressor common to both. That oppressor of course being the conventionally straight woman (as well as her male keeper) who also turned out to be many a fearful feminist. In the fast realization of the sexism of her gay brothers, who, after all, partake in the general male privilege, the lesbians made the correct and inevitable withdrawal from organizational and personal alliance with gay men to align themselves with the feminists, who were ill prepared to accept their most rebellious element. It's one thing for a man to be homosexual. Quite another for a woman. The issue keeps turning back over and over to the oppression of women. And then again to the lesbian, who is the most oppressed of women for being most like a woman. Here again is the key to revolution through the lesbian woman. The logic is by now devastatingly clear. The least oppressed woman is the woman most like a man; that is, the straight identified woman who has been called the "real woman" and has been fooled by this definition of herself into thinking her womanhood *depends* on her relation to the straight man who defines her and has called her this "real woman" according as how she suits his needs and remains at his service. This is the ultimate hype for all women. And from this superior cultural vantage point of participation in the male privilege the straight woman (and the straight femin-

ist) see, ironically, the lesbian as the "male identified woman."
It should not be so amazing that the most oppressed women will
be those who are most womanly (the same principle by the way
operating within distinctions of class and race). The woman
whose *imitation* of the style of the man, if such it is—and this I
resent from the point of view of comfort, men's clothes being far
more comfortable and easier to get around in than women's
wear—has given people the impression that she is somehow the
most manly of women. It seems important right now to make the
distinction between imitation and connection. The lesbian may
affect a stylistic imitation, but her connection to the actual life
and mystique of the male is minimal to nonexistent. The lesbian
as practicing woman is now reversing the cultural appraisal of
womanhood. The lesbian is woman prime. The woman who main-
tains or regains her integrity as a woman. By (re)uniting with
her feminine principle. The reunion of the mother and the daughter into the true sister principle. The straight woman will discover how she has been colossally duped by being robbed of her
womanhood. The irony of this reversal is the crux of the revolution. Its outrageousness is the measure of its truth. The test case
of the oppressed woman is the woman who is the most woman.
Since it is the nature of woman to be oppressed by societies organized around the heterosexual institution which is defined
by the domination of one sex over another the woman who is
most oppressed will be the one who refuses to be oppressed by
acting independently of the oppressor. And thus not being recognized. And as such being severely oppressed through extreme
identity confusion. The liberated political lesbian by this reason-
ing is of course no longer a woman. Woman being defined as an
oppressed person. Defined in other words by man. The language
is no longer adequate to signify the liberated sex. The woman
identified woman was an excellent phrase to help define the lesbian in her prime womanhood in distinction to all women who
still partake of male privilege through bed, marriage, and frater-

nization, but "woman" is too overwhelmingly the name of the sex so called and thus checked and retained by the man. My own use of the word here was convenient to expose the fraud of the "real woman" and establish the is-ness of the lesbian as the sex with the organs commonly referred to as woman. It is not so confusing if we remember that the author always creates her own definitions. Woman creates herself and she can refuse to call herself the name she is oppressed by. Or she can use the name by which she was the *most* oppressed before she recognized that her very oppression was the key to her liberation. The Lesbian. Being so most completely outside the straight system even as a secret lesbian pretending to be straight in certain aspects of her life being thus so being most ideally positioned to seize her own destiny as total woman long pre-dating culturally defined woman once the gay revolution released her consciousness to recognize the institution of oppression and unite with her more truly oppressed "male identified" sisters. All but the most radical of feminists remain the oppressor of both themselves and the lesbian or the lesbian within them waiting to be liberated. As the lesbian sees it the feminist movement is still basically a "reform" movement directed toward bigger and better participation in the male privilege through equality in his system and thus a further denial of her own identity in the wages of power in the same sexual caste system which she claims to be the source of her deprivation. Even so, the lesbian is now dedicated to the true radicalization of feminism by weaning her straight sisters away from their efforts to reform the institution of oppression itself. The constant identification of the media of the lesbian with the male homosexual movement is a clever device to separate women from each other, as though woman are not already separated enough, and to continue the negation of the sexuality of women by the subtle (if unconscious) co-option of the most upfront sexual woman (the political lesbian) by the already overwhelmingly recognized sexuality of the male, whether straight or gay, and perhaps especially the gay in his well known pursuit of variety and quantity. The woman is again a token—this time in the context of the gay revolution. By media pronouncement at least. For in reality the lesbian feminists constitute the revolutionary core of the feminist movement. Gay/Feminism advocates an end to the oppressive heterosexual institution. The lesbian and the gay male by their very existence are a threat to the program of marriage/family/home that every child is conditioned to believe is "the true way." For gay is roleless, or consists of relations of equality naturally obtaining between members of the same sex. Biological equals. The feminist rhetoric is steeped in a denial of biological destiny. For if they can deny the biological forces that created the cultural conditions of oppression, they can start with the culture and work from the top as it were to reform things where they appeared to go amiss, and thus retain the man with whom they consider themselves originally (that is, biologically) parous. But biology is not simply ancient or primeval history. Biology is right now. One can observe the constant renewal of biological imperatives creating their novel if always patriarchal forms of cultural oppression. It is impossible to disentangle biology and culture. The cultural takeover of the male is biologically motivated. All systems of inequity are rooted in some biological imperative of the male. The female was originally the self sufficient self recreating creature. The male one of her offspring. The male could recreate himself only through the female. Herein lies the desperation of man and culture. Or: all systems of inequity. Family, church, state, racism, despotism, feudalism, capitalism, nationalism, imperialism, communism, etc. The primary creature was parthenogenetic whether you call her a female or not. The cultural repression of woman is rooted in womb envy. If you can do it and I can't, that's *all* you can do. Man and culture are synonymous. The theory Engels developed to account for the transition from matriarchy to patriarchy remains as good as any to describe the simultaneous evolution of culture and the captivity of woman. If the woman had in some transient sense needed the male to recreate herself by impregnation she nonetheless was never in any doubt as to her self recreation or the identity of her offspring. The domination of the female by which the sexual caste system was effected must have occurred in prolonged periods of great historical change during which the male in his restless quest for identity somehow invented the concrete means of imposing parental primacy through the secondary phenomenon of culture—the institutions of control and submission. The ownership of tools property, etc. Then the law to safeguard that ownership. Then the institutions of learning to transmit the law. And so forth. The ultimate property always being women and children. The female was gradually weakened in all her powers, except for periodic outbursts of insanity, by her captivity enforced around her "reproductive sexuality" and related role playing evolving over centuries into the rigid structures of correctness by which she eagerly embraces her own coercion in the mores of forgetfulness. The female has forgotten her freedom and her struggle to resist the moment of her coercion. Gay revolution is the first significant challenge to the existing social structures which are characterized by oppression of the female. The contemporary gay revolutionary male is the first homosexual male in history to relinquish some crucial aspect of his male privilege by not leading the double life by which he had it both ways in the sense of maintaining a straight pretense thus oppressing women and of participating in the gay underworld. This is not to underestimate the problems of identity for gay males in all societies rigidly defined as straight. Some of these revolutionary types remain straight identified males who oppress each other in the manner of role playing heterosexuality, rejecting the woman without consciousness of woman's oppression. This is the gay male with a gay head in rebellion against the suppression of his gay identity, without a feminist consciousness or an active struggle with his own sexism. There are very few Gay/Feminist males. In some sense there can't be. A gay male might come closest to experiencing woman's oppression by appearing at large, not as a transvestite or passing for female, but as an obvious male who is surrendering privilege by overt female dress and behavior. A beard and a skirt and stockings, say. Even so, the gay revolutionary male has withdrawn support from the nuclear weapon of the sexual caste system by which he is damned and curtailed in his freedom to love his own sex: the family. Home, church and state are the enemies of sexual revolution. The most virulent outspoken enemy of homosexuality before the advent of the psychiatric profession was the church. As the chief agent of the patriarchal judeo-christian tradition the church sustained the task of legitimizing oppression to safeguard the system of its own profit and continuation in collaboration with the state or man, or culture, however you have it. Gay liberation has moved so far in a decade beyond the conventional notions of deviancy and abnormalcy imposed by these agencies that it seems a commonplace now to remind anyone who may not know that the gay revolutionary is no longer interested in being tolerated or accepted by a society we consider to be sick in its straightness. During the 60's homosexuals were still seeking integration into society—agreeing that homosexuality was deviant while pleading to be given a chance to show society how square—if not straight —they could be. Gay militancy is defined by its refusal to conform to an oppressive culture by submitting to therapy or by pretending to be straight. Psychiatry favors individual solutions rather than social change. The emphasis is on conformity and adjustment rather than liberation. As Dennis Altman said "no longer is the claim made that gay people can fit into american society, that they are as decent, as patriotic, as clean living as anyone else. Rather, it is argued, it is american society itself that needs to change." The axis of gay revolution is the shift from apology to affirmation and from affirmation to aggressive redefinition. The aim is an end to the organization of society around the sexual polarities of "male" and "female." An end, in other words, to sexual duality or the two-sex system and a gradual evolutionary movement through the massive liberation of homosexuality back to the true parthenogenetic species. All men start off as women and that's the way they'll end up if they don't destroy us all first. All forms of civilized culture are expressions of the profound conflict between man and woman. The congealed institutions of oppression at every level reflect the outcome of a struggle for parental primacy which the woman lost. Yet the woman is parent prime, and the man in his anxiety and desperation to become the master of himself has pitched himself against "nature" (woman) in his creation of culture as a kind of monstrous compensation for a real or at least felt inadequacy. The world in the 20th century is a spectacle of the gross amplification of the insecure man. Certain of his own immortality only through the subjugation of woman. Man is completely out of phase with nature. Nature is woman. Man is the intruder. The man who re-attunes himself with nature is the man who de-mans himself or eliminates himself as man. The man correctly attempts to do this in his wars against himself but he carries too much of nature along with him as he does it. Gay revolution or the reassertion of the female principle is the peaceful means of de-manning society by reintegration with the polymorphous sexuality of perverse equalities. "Heterosexual men are driven to abuse women because they can't directly express the love they have for each other. They literally fuck their friends' women because they are unable to fuck their friends." (Steve Dansky, "Hey, Man," in *Gay Flames Collective*) Or Altman: "The argument that men fight each other because they are unable to love each other is a version of Marcuse's formulation that aggression results from a failure to give sexuality free reign." Revolutionary social change in the past has occurred within systems characterized by institutionalized heterosexuality and oppression of the female. Historically, revolution has meant the overthrow of one class by another, leaving the oppressive institution itself intact. Such revolutions result in new class systems or a return to a previous social order in a new disguise. Gay revolution means an end to the sexist underpinnings of every political-economic power base extant which have remained unchallenged in the successive waves of class and racial disorder leading to novel forms of oppression.

A gazebo is a structure commanding an extensive project.

By the end of March '71 I felt confirmed in the Gay/Feminist design for revolution and straightened out into a new fusion of the personal and political. I was then catching up on some standard required feminist reading. This is my version of the trashing of the Viennese patriarch of pathology, here presented without the original long preamble indicting an old friend of mine who had been a patron sugar daddy in the tradition of my surrogate protectors.

SIGMUND: AN ANALYSIS OF A CASE OF HIS-TERIA

As for Freud, I've never made a secret of my admiration for the old man, having even claimed him for a shady ancestor, and I disagree as well with many of the feminists in the great clitoris and/or vagina controversy which begins with a full scale attack on the pronouncements of vaginal maturity by the Viennese patriarch; still, I admit to having been oblivious to Freud's misogyny simply by conveniently unconsciously accepting the patriarchal

192

order of things (always of course excepting myself as some freak of nature) and reading chiefly Freud's male dominated studies like "Moses and Monotheism" and "Totem and Taboo" (even the Leonardo study!) in which I presume he was ever rooting out the prototypes for his own identity as a primal father, with whom I too could identify in my own labyrinthine search for a paternal heritage. A neat coincidence is that two days before I saw the Richard Gilman piece in *The New York Times* on Freud and women, I was reading or rather whooping and hollering my way through Freud's classic study of "Dora: An Analysis of a Case of Hysteria," which I've been carrying around for months. Apparently I was experiencing the feminist romp. Ah hah this and ah hah that. Ferociously underlining the key incriminating passages and copying some of them in my best huge excited script and stopping now and again to raise a clenched fist and shout and quote and run at the mouth at a mildly bemused audience of three who never heard of Dora and care much more about anything than her dead psychoanalyst. Anyway I offer to whom it could concern a few choice bits from the evidence: ". . . the behavior of this child of 14" (Dora was a very attractive intelligent 18 when Freud engaged her as a patient) "was already entirely and completely hysterical. I should without question consider a person hysterical in whom an occasion for sexual excitement elicited feelings that were preponderantly or exclusively unpleasurable."—". . . I believe that during the man's (Herr K.'s) passionate embrace she felt not merely his kiss upon her lips but also the pressure of his erect member against her body." (Dora never *said* that).—"I let her go on talking, and she suddenly recollected that it was Herr K.'s birthday too . . . a fact which I did not neglect to use against her."—". . . I came to the conclusion that the idea had probably occurred to her one day during a sitting that she would like to have a kiss from me. This would have been the exciting cause. . . ."—"I looked upon her having told her parents of the episode as an action which she had taken when she was already under the influence of a morbid craving for revenge. A normal girl, I am inclined to think, will deal with a situation of this kind by herself."—"Her breaking off so unexpectedly, just when my hopes of a successful termination of the treatment were at their highest and her thus bringing those hopes to nothing—this was an unmistakable act of vengeance on her part."—"Incapacity for meeting a real erotic demand is one of the most essential features of a neurosis . . ."— "It is possible for a man to talk to girls and women upon sexual matters of every kind without doing them harm and without bringing suspicion upon himself, so long as, in the first place, he adopts a particular way of doing it, and in the second place can make them feel convinced that it is unavoidable. A gynaecologist, after all under the same conditions, does not hesitate to make them submit to uncovering every possible part of the body."— "For how could the patient take a more effective revenge than by demonstrating upon her own person the helplessness and incapacity of the physician."—"I do not know what kind of help she wanted from me, but I promised to forgive her for having deprived me of the satisfaction of affording her a far more radical cure for her troubles."—Guess what Freud's radical cure would have been and guess what his own revenge was upon a naturally pretty confused adolescent girl whom he could see for himself was a pawn in the marital troubles of her parents, even saying that "she had been handed over to Herr K. as the price of his tolerating the relations between her father and his wife . . . the two men of course never made a formal agreement in which she was treated as an object for barter" and that he was further compounding Dora's difficulties by adding a third handsome middle-aged man (Freud was 43 at the time) to her sexual confusion. Although he did some justice to the girl's repressed homosexual needs by recognizing her deep affection for Herr K.'s wife whom she "used to praise for her 'adorable white body' in accents more appropriate to a lover than a defeated rival" he bore down relentlessly on his patient's resistance to his "cure" which would be her total acquiescence in his first and final judgment of her unequivocal love for a trinity of daddys to whom presumably she must yield (in what way he never specified exactly) or sacrifice her health in hysterical symptoms of sexual displacements. Freud's analysis of the "transference" phenomenon as central to the therapeutic techniques he developed is a thin disguise as a rationale to cover his own problematic designs on his vulnerable patients. Freud's elaborately refined and original mindfucking became the giant respectable industry called psychoanalysis. Although he also recognized the "counter-transference" phenomenon he never stopped in his Dora study to seriously question his own motivation in such an intensive battle of wits with a keen young girl already struggling to survive the attentions of a lech whose wife was the mistress of her father whose guilt was a prime cause of his daughter's distress which her therapeutic daddy insisted was due to her inability to accept her "real sexual longing" for the guys who were frightening her. Some story. Freud's dismay over the aborted treatment (Dora broke it off after three months) was a kind of coitus interruptus which he resolved by the proxy completion of his study on the subject which might also be viewed as his own revenge. The entire book in its unmistakable terminology of depreciation (hysteria, neurosis, illness, symptoms, aphonia, perversion, psychosis, etc.) is a model for a future science of aggression and submission in the name of health. Freud's own model for the study was another famous case of Anna O. who was a patient (in 1880-82) of his first medical hero Dr. Joseph Breuer whose patient was also highly intelligent and "extremely attractive in physique and personality"—a worthy opponent you might say. The Breuer case more dramatically illustrated the (in)direct erotic involvement of the analyst. Ernest Jones reports in his biography of Freud: ". . . Breuer was so engrossed that his wife became bored at listening to no other topic and before long she became jealous.

She did not display this openly, but became unhappy and morose. . . . Breuer terminated the treatment, and Anna O., who was by now much better, relapsed, and went into throes of an hysterical childbirth—the logical termination of a phantom pregnancy that had been invisibly developing in response to Breuer's ministrations. Though profoundly shocked, he managed to calm her down by hypnotizing her, and then fled the house in a cold sweat. The next day he and his wife left for Venice to spend a second honeymoon, which resulted in the conception of a daughter. . . . The girl born in these curious circumstances was nearly 60 years later to commit suicide in New York." Anna O. eventually recovered and became the first social worker in Germany, founding a periodical and several institutes and devoting a major part of her life to women's causes and emancipation. *"She never married, and she remained devoted to God."* My hasty conclusion is that by accident of association with Breuer Anna O. experienced a religious conversion in an extreme symptom (simulated pregnancy) called by other names in the sanctified environments of convent and monastery (i.e., the stigmata of St. Francis, the convulsions of Theresa of Avila, even the constipation of Martin Luther). It's interesting, in fact, that one of Freud's favorite expressions was "hysterical conversion symptoms." Religion and hysteria (i.e., ecstasy) have always been two of a kind. Freud could easily have been one of those turn-of-the-century investigators branding the symptoms of Christ Himself as historical incidents of a hysterical psychosis. These studies are buried in the archives. Albert Schweitzer once indignantly defended Christ in a counter study. Anyway, I'm merely indicating here the great social ironies of the valuation or depreciation of the same psychic-physical phenomena according to time context, location, etc. And of course sex. For hysteria (from Hysteron—Greek for womb) was deemed to be most specifically female, who has fared no better in her new role as patient-subject to the investigating father and his inquisition machinery than she did as witch or a demon possessed and on the loose in a society not yet equipped with the sophisticated intellectual apparatus for justifying the same judgments and incarcerations. The stake and the hospital or the prison were (are) not necessarily the dramatic termini of the paternal investigation of the female. I have a classic case story of today which brings Breuer and Freud up to date in their modern incarnations as less inhibited in the pursuit of "the proper conclusion" to their treatment. A girl I loved not too long ago was perhaps not unlike Dora and Anna O. in her class and attributes and she certainly had a daddy problem for her real daddy had put a bullet through his head when she was nine; but in the contemporary spirit she was actively pursuing her sexual interests, which her therapeutic daddy, who had, like his predecessors, encouraged, found increasingly interesting in whatever graphic detail he could manage to elicit from his precocious patient. This analyst, by the way, was a middle-aged Gary Cooperish recently divorced ivy league Park Avenue $40-a-visit man. My appearance on the scene was a bit much for him apparently because although he *seemed* to approve of the relationship, and of course listened, as I said, with great interest to the detailed developments, his covert feeling for the patient quickly asserted itself in maneuvers worthy of a jealous husband or father for their frontal clarity. He sensed a real rival after two years of her harmless fooling around (with boys she had sex but no love, and I was her second girl) and before long moved in with extra-therapeutic suggestions like coffee and snacks or luncheon after the session followed quickly by a theatrical third act climax right in his backstage inner sanctum which was his bachelor apartment from which I received a kind of SOS phone call from his patient my lover who was being plied with drinks and proposals the man had totally blown his cool and seemed set on a kind of elopement or something. It was a real scene and a half. She left with me after many understandably odd maneuvers of extrication and the next day took her own Dora-like revenge by terminating her "treatment" in a formal office visit. If you can believe it the man kept sending her the $40 bill for her last visit and called her several times as well to see if she was really serious about not finding him the most dashing white knight in the world. A few months later I did my best to get him on the panel I had arranged at NYU called "The Disintegration of a Critic: An Analysis of Jill Johnston." He agreed at first but then must have realized what I was up to. I was up to no good. It wasn't him personally I was after really but the entire profession he represented. It's always been Freud the intellect who interested me and I must say until reading the Dora book I had never linked him directly with the modern profession which he inspired after all and which has been my personal Goliath ever since observing first hand its victims and martyrs in extremis.

March 30, Vermont, copying passages from de Beauvoir's chapter on lesbianism in her Second Sex. Amazed or not so amazed by her completely ambivalent presentation of the subject. Apparent acceptance of Freud's notion of the linear development of sexuality towards the "mature vaginal heterosexual type." Equation of clitoral fixation with "Sapphic love." Wholesale Freud. —"The homosexual affair represents a stage . . . an apprenticeship; and a girl who engages in it most ardently may well become tomorrow the most ardent of wives, mistresses or mothers." *Phase.* Very disappointing. Yet considering when she wrote the book . . . And for all that she appears to contradict herself by celebrating lesbianism almost as though after dutifully paying respects to the old man of Vienna. —". . . Between women love is contemplative; caresses are intended less to gain possession of the other than gradually to re-create the self through her; separateness is abolished, there is no struggle, no victory, no defeat; in exact reciprocity each is at once subject and object, sovereign and slave; duality becomes mutuality." She too, like many american feminists, thought "reproductive sexuality" and pleasure ("there is a great deal of anatomic and clinical evidence that most of the

interior of the vagina is without nerves") were mutually exclusive, thus arguing that "in woman there is a choice of two systems, one of which perpetuates juvenile independence (she
means lesbianism I guess) while the other consigns woman to
man and childbearing."

April 3, Vermont, Jung: We are all wrapped as her children in the
mantle of this great Isis.
Reading Jung's Four Archetypes.
Those who cannot be reborn must be content with moral conduct,
that is.
Mephistopheles materialized out of a black poodle.

April 6, Vermont, Lois: Constant effort to de-program myself in
terms of words—the psychic institutions (of oppression). From
Masculine/Feminine: Readings in Sexual Mythology and the
Liberation of Women. Edited by Betty and Theodore Roszak: "An
especially interesting aspect of the story (Strindberg's A Mad-
man's Defense) is the husband's jealous fantasy that his wife is
enjoying a lesbian love-life (this fantasy still appears as a common male reaction to the phenomenon of feminism)"—right on.
. . . Strindberg's domestic struggle to dominate the assertive
women in his life . . .

April 10: A judy somebody said to me on the phone: People ask
her if Gloria (Steinem) is a lesbian and I say 'of course not'—
she's living an independent life, like a man.

Letter from Liz Smith: quoting Gloria: "you know, no lesbian
has ever made a pass at me except at that party (she means the
Sculls in Easthampton) Jill Johnston asked me to dance. It sort
of threw me. But on the other hand I really liked her and she was
the only person there I was interested in talking to." Liz comments, "this was before you burst like a bombshell on the public
eye—right after the swimming episode."

April 15: Meet another Polly

April 16: The Book of the Hopi

April 22: Behan on Wilde: My life on you Oscar—Yourself had it both ways.

April 25, Vermont. Chez Robyn. Preparing Town Hall speech. Robyn wants to participate in the action. She told me a dream: They were eating some dignitary that night for dinner and that was the purpose of the dinner although nobody admitted it. It was very elegant.

April 27: I'm having difficulty being an exception.

April 29: At Hofstra with SK yesterday. Read the Town Hall piece in progress. Afterwards a sort of lesbian workshop. Students intimidated by Jacqueline Ceballos and the school woman psychologist both doctrinaire heterosexists.

April 30: Day of Town Hall. (See "Tarzana from the Trees at Cocktails") Is this not an evening to be unremembered.
Ann: Better you should march on Delphi.

May 2: The aftermath of Town Hall was gathering its bizarre and kinky heroic momentum. A woman was calling me every day and hour and at last I met her someplace to be told she wanted me as her "second woman." My mail was funky and outrageous. And mythological. I was receiving far out messages and invitations from people like raindance & orange or snowshoe No. 22 or lake circumspect. I was sleeping around to the best of my time and inclination. I could appreciate Jerry Rubin's comments on his life as image: It's weird getting recognized by strangers on the street. I dig it. Being a celebrity . . . people listen to you and tell other people stories about you.

You are myth.

You are media.

Usually by the time a story moves it has little if anything to do with you as a person, but deals with other people's fears, prejudices and fantasies. Everybody sees me as JERRY RUBIN but I know I'm just jerry rubin. I have trouble dealing with people's expectations of me . . . to keep my sanity I must remember the difference between me and my image. Image is a powerful political weapon. Images battle—not people.

Right after Town Hall at the party downtown at Westbeth a "Truth Group" approached me and a young attractive woman said she'd like to go to bed with me. I said I'd call her sometime and I did on a lazy afternoon and she said she'd meet me at Max's with her roommate where I said I was going to be to see an editor and she did but she brought this entire "Truth Group" including its "leader"—some 15 people maybe—mostly very blooming young women (the leader a male)—and they held a rather scary impromptu kangaroo court by the window at the round table, from which I extricated myself by agreeing with whatever they said.

A German journalist called me for an interview. We met at her hotel, then dinner at Max's. Halfway her tone turned personal and I said possibly she'd like to go back to her hotel and make love so we did after she called me a Don Juan and tried to rearrange my outfit to suit her taste. In a piece published June 3 called *16 More Women, Each for a Night*, I wrote "I enjoyed a German journalist between appointments of which she was one although she said it was too intimate to kiss on the mouth and there was one other thing she wouldn't do but she hopes I come to Munich soon."

May 3: Leaving this loft a week ago today to go to the Voice with my copy in and having just scribbled the title *On a Clear Day You Can See Your Mother* a friend handed me a folder out of a file cabinet saying oh here's some mail for you it was mail from a year ago I stayed in this loft a month or so that time the mail arrived after I left it was a few announcements and a letter from my mother dated April 21, 1970, since which we have been incommunicado thinking I suppose it must've been for the best since I didn't receive the answer to mine I had written asking please could she remember the precise moment of my birth for someone interested in my horoscope I was interested myself as always in whether I had actually been born or not she doesn't remember too well as it turns out I keep making it up anyway saying pretty lines like On a Clear Day You Can See Your Mother walking out the door with the letter and the title and then and I didn't believe this a block down the street on Spring Street with my friend on the way as I said to the Voice a big bang smack noise brought us up short we looked down it was a brandnew paperback edition of Marmalade Me a foot in front of our feet. Mother! Eyes up and scan the building. No sign of a soul. Maybe out of my own nabsack, nope I'm not carrying it around. The damn thing really came from somebody up there is watching you. SK picked it up and put it in her own bag saying well that was nice since she'd given her own copy away. I've got a new title for my autobiograffiti. My Mother Was a Vestal. SK says hers is Up To No Good On Bicycles. Being a legend in your own time causes a lotta wild talk. Who is Humphry Clinker? How is Betty Shabazz? Whatever happened to Lisa Lieberman? Is Ida Rubinstein lipstick?

May 12: Dinner and bed with a Jewish princess. A.m. she got up and planted a rosebush in her backyard.

May 14: Enroute TWA to St. Louis. Escapes were in order. May 28 enroute Swans Island, Maine.

June 5 Reading V. Woolf's *Room of One's Own.* Interview by french photographer Chantal

June 7 dream: Twins born into a jar as a little omelette

June 9 Reading Woolf's Three Guineas

June 12 Reading Engels

Still catching up with feminist stuff. This piece includes my version of the Engels revelation and its significance for feminism.

WHO IS THE FATHER OF HER CHILD?

After a ridiculous weak I waked up to write the making of a lesbian monogamist and decided instead on the celebration of a lesbian celibate. Certainly 1 no longer qualify as a chauvinist. I declined a weekend country invitation because it sounded too complicated sexually. Just chickened out. And it was me all along who was saying we should share the same lovers. As for monogamy, Frederick Engels may still have the last word on this archaic form of bondage: "And if strict monogamy is the height of all virtue, then the palm must go to the tapeworm, which has a complete set of male and female sexual organs in each of its 50-200 proglottides, or sections, and spends its whole life copulating in all its sections with itself."—This is ideal, but it isn't monogamy, it's super auto erotic interfuckulating parthenogenesis. Anyway, Engels goes on: "Confining ourselves to mammals, however, we find all forms of sexual life—promiscuity, indications of group marriage, polygyny, monogamy, and polyandry." Please read the Engels ("The Origin of the Family, Private Property, and the State"). All women must read this outdated masterpiece of fanciful anthropology. The reason I never read it before is that I'm an uneducated female. I was encouraged to read "Black Beauty" and Nancy Drew and "The Snow Queen" when I could have been finding out about the Decline and Fall of the Roving Empire of My Own Sex. And other tidbits. Recently someone reminded me it's weird to spend four years reading plato, sappho, sophocles and like that and never mention homosexuality. I studied philosophy with an old man who mistook me for Alcibiades. A boy disguised as a girl, or vice reversa. As a 20th century Platonist out of Manchester, Heidelberg, and Harvard the old man has long forgotten the true sexual origins of his own discipline. By now the histories of the glorious ages of Greece are a disgrace to the proper understanding of our extravagantly beautiful perversities and the nowhere nothing of women. As for Sappho the only woman who was something more or less than all the raving Delphic priestesses, how could I really get to her when all that survives are the fragments altered over the centuries to conform to such as some early victorian scholars who went around changing the case endings of her lovers from feminine to masculine. I didn't know Sappho and Socrates and all the rest were gay until it was much too late to destroy the educational systems perpetrating all that trash and omission. What do you think Socrates was *really* on trial for? Who do you think Plato was *really* in love with? Why did I have to spend so much time studying the love affairs of boys and men? Imagine what Norman O. Brown is doing right now to the heads of his women students by not even so subtly invoking the exclusive male tradition, saying "It is all one book (he means the literature of the world), which includes the gospel according to Ovid, Saint Ovid the Martyr; and Petrarch, and Marvell, and Keats, and Andre Gide, and Pound. Also the ravings of every poor Crazy Jane. Every poor schizophrenic girl is a Delphic priestess; or a Daphne, saying 'I am that tree.' 'That's the rain—I could be the rain. That chair—that wall.' It's a terrible thing for a girl to be a Delphic priestess. In the cave the priestess raves: she still resists the brutal god, to shake from her hapless breast his breast; all the more his pressure subjugates her wild heart, wears down her rabid mouth, shapes her mouth into his mouthpiece." He's right of course. But he's wrong too. We do have a real live tradition of women with names and great works and everything, but at women's colleges like Bennington the President is a man and the faculty is 80 per cent male and they now have 110 male students and the catalog of courses reads like an inventory of male histories and almost all the women become the wives or mistresses of the faculty before or after a short interim of freedom and adventure working as a secretary or messenger girl to a male corporation in the big city. Engels has satisfactorily explained this odd situation to me. I suppose anyone reading it now understands that he was talking down to the "savages" and "barbarians" by analyzing the origins of the modern family as a civilized advance over the more primitive forms. Yet occasionally he glimmers the contradictory insight that every step forward was relatively a step backward, "in which prosperity and development for some is won through the misery and frustration of others." Every clear thinker now realizes that a return to the savage conditions of the various types of "group marriage" is the sine qua non of a bewildered new world. The two contemporary expressions of our childhood awaiting us out of the debris of civilization's autodestruct are the longhair communes and the unsettling withdrawal of both men and women from the institutions of male-female patterns of domination-submission that thrive even in the communes, for the true equality of the sexes can only reoccur through a massive social upheaval involving customs and consciousness brought about by the revolt of women combining tactics of withdrawal and that reassertion of mother-right by which the woman maintained an honorable position in relation to her own sex and to her brothers and fathers in the certainties of maternal parentage. The withdrawal of both men and women mentioned above is of course what the gay revolution is all about. The promiscuity in the gay world is the natural expression of all peoples pre- and post-dating the legal binds of property rights that resulted in our abnormal closed monogamous family structures. The far greater activity and promiscuity of gay men is merely the outstanding expression of the advanced sexual mobility of *all* men, who have retained their rights of promiscuousness within the same institution of monogamy by which their sisters are deprived. The married man is polygamous. The married woman is monogamous. Engels clarified for me the single absurdly simple historical reason for this repression of women. I never saw it myself because I'm too much a product of the very situation that made me too outrageous to believe that my strange birth was actually a condition for something much better than the social psychosis they had laid out for me in the textbooks. I was supposed to be a deprived child. As it turns out I was that marvelous anomaly of a female relieved of the tyranny of paternal preeminence. As such I grew up in an unreal world of self revolving maternal identities and never properly understood the submission that was expected of me when I met the male corporation. Thus I had a precocious sense of my divinity. Given five years or so in the shadow of the greatest phallic masterpieces of urban civilized accomplishment I became the pathetic female of the textbooks. Five more years and I confirmed all their expectations. An official mental case! It was a perfect history. But in 1964 or is it '65 we were moving into the Aquarian Age. We were dying and being reborn in droves. New tapeworms all over the place. The fugitive invisible second city of the psychic outlaws arising from the ashes of the atomic bomb destruction of shattered minds. I saw the beards and flowers and lollipops and the resurrected heroes of Howl and I didn't foresee the revolution of the women and the explosion of the homosexuals. History is now the Everlasting Present. The repressive social structures belong to the real histories of recorded time and monuments and these are the paternal histories. The revelation I just lugged out of Engels is the simplistic explanation of the origin of history to be found in the transition from the "group marriage" in which whole groups of men and whole groups of women mutually possessed each other, living together indiscriminately in many large families, to the emergence of the patriarchal family and the establishment of the exclusive supremacy of the man in order to secure the fidelity of the wife to insure the clear and legal paternal identity of the children. It's so silly, but you've heard it a lot in the past few years. How many a woman in a longhair commune is uncertain who is the father of her child. It was this situation in savage and barbarian communities that naturally made mother-right (matrilineal descent) the order of inherited identity and substantiated the honor of the women in an otherwise historically always difficult position of relative physiological immobility in her child-bearing capacity. As the daughter of a Virgin I am now happy to assert my normal birthright as a barbarian. "Among all savages and all barbarians of the lower and middle stages, and to a certain extent of the upper stage also, the position of women is not only free, but honorable." The overthrow of mother-right was *the world historical defeat of the female sex*. It was apparently the elaboration of the means and tools of production that created this momentous shift in the relation of the sexes; for since the man was in charge of obtaining the food and the instruments of labor necessary for survival and he *owned* these instruments and eventually also the new sources of subsistence in the form of cattle and slaves, it followed that the man would at least insist on the undisputed claim of paternal identity to stabilize the inheritance of wealth and property in his own image. The confined woman is merely the woman to whom access is limited or guaranteed to the expectant father. All the Danaes in the Towers. We're moving backward now. We can't go back fast enough. I'm going to England to buy my maternal birth certificate again. I have my father's name in my mother's country and my mother's name in my father's. I am now a citizen of my mother's country in my father's equally phony name. My mother was precociously independent. From the present vantage circle even the incestuous barbarian group marriage would be a form of bondage for the women. The woman bought her way out of the fearful chaos of belonging to every man by sacrificing her sexuality her mobility in the *apparent* securities of monogamy— the situation that made her *either* the Virgin Goddess *or* the Bitch Whore, both of them impoverished in mind and spirit and deprived of material autonomy. Woman now has the supreme task of withdrawing her services to wrap them unto herself. To reclaim her identity, her sexuality. The lesbian woman and the homosexual man are the frightening vanguard of the disruption and ultimate collapse of all modern archaic forms of bondage and warfare through the purchase and captivity of the woman who no longer remembers, unless she goes on a huge acid bender, how she got into this state which she has been conditioned to believe is desirable, especially in its current hypes of token liberties and promises. Please read the Engels and then read Virginia Woolf's "A Room of One's Own" and "Three Guineas." I suppose you have already. It's another measure of my ignorance as a woman that I read all of Woolf as a young tapeworm who just enjoyed reading through her novels and stopped short at her two feminist masterpieces. Nor did I ever hear of Harriet Taylor Mill. Or Mary Wollstonecraft. The women in the country will soon be pressing for their own education, for by and about themselves, in order to learn a new history of the world. All over the country the women are still being educated for by and about men in preparation for being more intelligent helpmates and companions. For the reason that I assume the absurd position of righteous confusion over my polygamy and my monogamy and my polyandry and my celibacy all prefaced by my essential natural and political lesbianism I refer anybody to another masterwork of sexual politics and revelation: Sandor Ferenczi's "Thalassa" subtitled "A Theory of Genitality." From this book I acquired a healthy sense of depression and tragedy in regard to the weird evolutionary adjustments our forespecies made to certain global calamities like the drying up of the oceans. Ferenczi's fabulous bio-analytical speculations leave no doubt that the ongoing warfare between the sexes is a perennial reenactment of the primeval warfare in which the animal divided itself by attacking itself and by constant obtrusion and recession creating an instrument of aggression whereby one half was forced to submit and be worn away into a cloaca for the eventual deposit of the other half in its frantic and successful efforts to evolve an aquatic substitute in the form of a womb. Where we are headed from there is perfectly clear to me. N. O. Brown's "Silence" in "Love's Body" brings us full circle. I'm disillusioned with Brown because I located his inherited misogyny and actually saw it in person in his house in California over his dining table his wife was the silent obedient mistress occupying one fourth of the space in remote and isolated control while her brilliant husband held forth and Robert Duncan and me were polite contributors and admirers. But N. O. B. can't help it. Nobody can. We're evolving back to our tapeworm selves and then over and out into our primeval slime and eventual silence so we might as well relax and enjoy, enjoy, in our beautiful journey to extinction. Anyway this is the week of the new worldwide celebration of being Gay!

June 13–24. Some unexplained time spent with Yoko and John, who sent me long stem roses and books and patches and bought me shoes and socks and luncheons & such it wasn't clear why although I was flattered amused and involved. The 24th, wild scene all day on Queen Elizabeth the boat and later at Bici Hendrick's divorce party.

Bici invited me at the boat. In between the boat and the divorce I got laid at Ann Wilson's house. Ann is in Europe. Ann's ex old man came to the divorce. Bici is married 10 years to Geoff. Yoko thought they were really divorcing. I think they really were. A ritual of renewal on their 10th anniversary. Yoko told me she cried a little. I was moved myself when Bici informed me that she and Geoff came out recently. So that's why there were so many gay people there. Gay women, actually. And old Flux people. George Macunias. Jackson Maclow. Ray Johnson. Barbara and Peter Moore. Like that. And Kate Millett. It was a beautiful event. They made it difficult at first to get to the kitchen to the beer and cheese. Obstacles of tires and barbed wire. But no piano tuner to interrupt my resumed concert. Bici sang soprano or contralto. Bici looks great. So does Geoff. They had a tug of war and other ceremonies of Separation. I saw the tugging only. I know that marriage and divorce are all the same. To have and to harm till death duty part. There's a spiderweb grow acrossing these old flowers. And birth and death. The tires to worm through. The barbed wire to get stuck on. The wine and beer to celebrate. And Yoko writing in my book "the past that I remember is the past that I create now because of the necessity of the present." I forgot to tell her she was divorced that day too. "Apotheosis" on the Queen and "Fly" on the Lafayette.

June 23, Went to a "meeting" of "uptown feminists"—invited by lawyer Brenda Feigen Fasteau. I wrote about it a month or so later in a piece mostly about visiting Yoko and John in Ascot outside London.

I had never been invited before to a meeting of women up or down town, they spent an hour or so deliberating whether they should send me away, this was an interesting modification of the pattern, to be sent away before I got a chance not to be invited back. They were quite right of course. Until everybody writes their own column we'll be oppressed by our present limited available distortions. But I was impressed by the women there and wanted to stay. Gloria Steinem was helpful. She said she didn't think they should worry because I write fiction anyway. Gloria! —I invited Yoko to that meeting thinking that if I can no longer assist in vindicating her career as artist I could expose her to some advanced women of America who might throw her paranoia into a new dimension—the shared world of women in the same bateau. Yoko is a woman now in an extraordinary predicament. Although it's reasonable to assume that if she were not with John she would be as (un)recognized as other artists who have worked in the same genre as herself, all of whom have remained relatively obscure, not only in respect to the world at large but to the art world itself, excepting a Walter de Maria, who had his day with what might be called the minimal immaculate conceptual stuff of which Yoko's examples are as tough and as good as Walter's or anybody's, and that Yoko would be in the greater traditional twilight of obscurity accorded a woman, it is another terrible fact of the present that no amount of recognition now granted her could convince anyone much less herself and she's a very smart person that the attention she receives is not because of John but for the work itself. The power base is John's. That's the ultimate steel-trap issue of women's liberation. She brought John to the women's meeting. I told her she couldn't. She said she had to. It's like they're Siamese or something. That must be because they are their selves only with them selves since everybody else has the ulterior motives that could obviously be ascribed to them in their relation to everybody who can and does assist in making them even more inaccessible to ordinary everyday human people contact. . . .

June 24, Collect ticket at Air France for Monday the 28th to Paris.

June 25, Kate on Gloria: She's so glamorous, and *nice*, too! Germaine on Kate: She blew it.

June 27, Gay Celebration Week. I suppose typical enough of the week was a scene the day of the march a woman attached herself to me for most of the hot walk up avenue of the americas to central park and arriving at sheeps meadow we were standing around when the young woman I'd made it with the night before came over and I stumbled over her name couldn't remember it there trying to introduce her to my marching companion. As it turned out I saw her that night and we had a good time again. I wanted to write a piece called *Claire's Thigh*. I'd never come on a thigh before. It was very nice. —I went to only one dance on Wooster street, DOB. Almost everybody was waving their breasts around and I stayed in all my clothes.

June 29, arrive Paris. I stayed in Europe three and a half weeks.

Late July and August heavy reading in Jung, Laing, Nancy Milford's biography of Zelda, Philip Slater's Glory of Hera. Bought two Joan of Arc books & some Marx and Gilbert Murray's Rise of the Greek Epic and Slater's Pursuit of Loneliness and Adam Smith's Wealth of Nations and the Diary of Alice James and a new Ching.

Visit Richard and Winnie in camp in northern vermont.
Playing tennis and softball.

TEACH YOUR ANGELS KARATE

Once I had a boyfriend who signed his yearbook graduation picture to me love and all the other indoor sports and we thought that was a clever joke. We were both sports crazies and we imagined the whole world was a sport which it was although we knew very little about the indoor love variety so the autograph really was more of a joke than a boast and besides what love we made I think as I remember was hardly ever indoors but outside since we attended these interesting prisons called prep schools. Guy was on the Kent crew or baseball team or both and I was on the St. Mary's everything. We were the sister school to Kent but we didn't play Kent or any other sister school whereas Kent naturally played its brother schools Choate Groton Hotchkiss Deerfield Andover etcetra and nobody wondered why they did as opposed to why we didn't or rather why we were restricted to competing amongst ourselves consisting of the two teams the Defenders and Invincibles just like camp where it was blue and white or green and purple whatever it was exclusively intramural and viciously competitive. The future wives of all the Jonathan Winters Edwards the IVth or XXIVth were no slouches on the courts and fields of the schools preparatory to becoming the better educated companions and tennis partners to their future ruling class husbands. My hero in my first year was a tall tan lean athletic curly headed junior called Marty Whitcomb. If Marty became a mother I'd swallow all the bats and balls she knocked us out with. I had another hero called Stuie short for Mary Stuart who was plumpish and maternal but she was the captain of the Defenders before Marty succeeded her I think Stuie became captain because she kicked a mean soccer ball and yelled louder than anybody for our team to win and maybe also she was just a nice allaround popular girl I think so anyway I was crazy about her and appointed myself her mascot along with the stuffed monkey that was passed on every year from captain to captain to transport from game to game when it wasn't sitting on their window silly in its bright ochre cardigan and beanie. When I came of age I acquired the monkey by election to the office of my first heroes and my blazer was just as decorated from shoulder to cuff the length of my sleeve with the bars and chevrons meaning first and second teams and tournament championships in singles and doubles of all your years. If ever you were to meet a St. Mary's schoolmate of mine she'd go on about how I was a hero of the courts and fields and that was what it was all about. Our big fall game was soccer and I played right wing. Our winter game was basketball and I played center forward. Our spring game was softball and I was fine in the field but rather lousy at bat. I played with The Voice last week in Sheeps Meadow and Ross assigned me third base of which there were two—two bald spots a few yards apart and I didn't care myself but Howard designated one as legitimate by putting a paperback in the center of it in case anybody could see it over and through the clumps of grass weed jungling the diamond. Nobody ever did find out where second base was exactly. We were playing against ourselves so it wasn't supposed to matter. Once I was assisting the opposition who happened to be my editor Diane find her way from second to third base instead of preparing to receive the ball from the field to put her out. Since St. Mary's I've become pretty casual about the sort of competition that makes you a winner or a loser until the next game war game. In the weird professional world of culture you can pretend you're winning even if the scorekeepers are calling you out or foul or benched or home sick or unseeded or not calling you period. My best sports truly were the racket sports and I won't do more than volley now even I know I can win unless I'm badgered like last year at a camp my son was ping pong champ taking after his mother and he insisted on a game and I wouldn't let him win just because he's a boy or my son or anything but I don't like to play a game and he's beginning to feel that way too this year at his same camp we were into a volley ball game the kids were kind of clowning around about it but one parent was extremely gung ho and even flattering his own son every time he got the ball over the net this father is a regular fellow after all but the kids many of them now are standing back to observe our winning and losing culture and making fun of it I wish I could remember all the remarks but naturally the one I do remember is my son's which was a loud cheerful accusation across the net "you're disqualified if you win" addressed I suppose to anybody who seriously cared about it. The Voice softball game was an 8-8 tie although I objected saying our team actually won because the time they called me out at the plate I was safe home is a good place to be safe I was home safe I was certain of it but they only laughed at me and I said it myself just to be funny. Ross told somebody he understands more about me now that we've played softball together. I wonder what that is. Maybe it's that I don't mind falling on my face striking out. My swing carries me into a stagger toward the arms of the pitcher. Maybe it's the noise I make. My friend M. says tennis is a very quiet game and I make loud samurai grunts and other types of embarrassingly audible sounds of, say, appreciation over my own good shots. I'm cheering myself on, hell I'm not winning silver cups any more and I can't put two weeks together to play every day and get my game back. I drove Richard 10 miles away from his camp to the one I went to at his age he was appalled to see this absolutely straight square place where the daughters of our founding fathers are still wearing white shirts and blue shorts and marching in to assemblies and changing activities by the bugle and signing up for them and winning prizes for being super best at anything there was the old silver cup for tennis sitting on the table set for the banquet that very night and our guide a very proud accomplished young athlete her hair up in curlers for the banquet for the blessings they are about to receive may the lord be truly thankful concerning the fitness of women for sports there can be no question even in their curlers I urge all women not to worry about your demons but to teach your angels karate for the new future sexually politically intellectually creative woman will also be an athlete a whole person trained in body and mind and not necessarily a terrified competitor modeled on the male idea de-

rived from the Greek contest system or zero-sum game in which
someone wins only if someone else loses making a redistribution
of assets without any increase in their total. I mean did we have
to be motivated by the prospect of a prize at the expense of somebody else's loss. I dunno. The last time recently I played a game
really seriously to win was two years ago my lover challenged me
to ping pong and hardly gave me a chance to warm up before ini-
tiating the game we played was tight but somewhat casual until
the score of 20-20 deuce at the end I got fierce and calm and determined and edged her out after many deuce and game points
after which I said now you can fuck me which she did it was a
peculiar thing to say but I think I meant it as a way of evening up
the score in the sense we use fucking to mean taking somebody
and doing them even when it's mutually pleasurable which it was
I believe or maybe as another thought I was in reality demanding
my own pleasure as an award for victory it could have been both
if you feel rewarded and vanquished at once by the attentions of
a lover who slays you forever in sinking white blinding blah blah
beautiful orgasm works both ways especially when you get it on
together in the synch sense sports and sex could be a universal
and eternal tie they are because any victory is only apparent in the
vanity of temporal illusion. Sex and sports. The true prize is historically the woman the princess we know that. For what purpose
would I be wanting to impress a man except a man pass on his
approval to a woman who then wants to save me from the fu-
tility of such exertions by loving me to death. A victory of moon
over banana. At St. Mary's my careers as clown and athlete were
mutually exclusive and now I put them together and fool at the
parody of playing superbly at being ridiculous but stylish and
excellent although absurd and foolish and relaxed and highly
concentrated caricature superimpositions like swimming exqui-
sitely in a forbidden place to please one woman who appreciates
style and one woman who likes your naked body and outrage all
the others who might shake your hand a year later and say they

met you around a swimming pool. Renatus in novam infantiam.
It matters not. A year later you might make it in bed with an old
friend who never saw you swim or kick or bat or catch or bounce
or run or even dance who shudders an opulent orgasm and asks
you casually if you want to go on or go back to sleep or get up for
breakfast so what the hell. And the little ones could care less too.
I visited B. & O. whose small daughter M. was peering at me from
inside this huge raspberry then trespassing onto the cushion I
was in a sunken fruit of my own she snuggled one whole side of
my bod and pretended to play with my dangle is a kind of a third
breast in the center like the better known third eye a half a year
ago I dreamt of such a breast having two nipples and shaded the
coloring of a birth mark. To run at Sheeps Meadow or tennis or
just to run I wear the woman's jock strap or bra and let the third
breast fly around at will. It did hit me in the face once. I'm still sore
from using my lapsed softball muscles. My best play was flat on
my back after fielding the ball by falling on it I threw it from that
position to second where it rolled right on since nobody was there
except the approaching runner whom I mistook for the second-
baseman. My next best play was yelling mine for a fly and then
ducking at the last moment to let the rushing footsteps behind
me do something about it. Almost all the men, anyway Paul and
Ross and Howard and Carman and Alan and Mike consistently
swatted magnificent home runs. Paul grins broadly, very annoying, while he's doing it. Howard is kind of serious and apologized
to me a lot after he came directly into my territory to take a throw
from the outfield. Also, when he was the pitcher he didn't want to
pitch to our interloper and I thought he should but possibly he
was right since the interloper wouldn't go away and he was far
too talkative and enthusiastic and obnoxious and I almost used
the bat on his balls when I was up and he was the catcher and he
said he'd like to see me in a bikini. Our side had a wonderful
catcher Pam was catching and taking photographs at the same
time. It was a fine game. Diane brought a bag of beer and hit a

line drive triple past first and theorized that women can't throw the way men can because of our elbows. She had a couple of us inverting our arms afterward to prove the point. It's true the sexual disparity at a mixed game is quite apparent but I insist I went to school with women whose only deficiency in relation to men would be brute strength. It's conditioning it's conditioning it's conditioning. Two or three months ago I was at a place where a black woman in her 30s (I think) was playing catch with a 10 year old Kirk Douglas or Steve McQueen who was so floored by his partner's skill he kept repeating "I never *saw* a girl could throw like that" and she engaged him in a heavy rap raising his consciousness concerning the expectations of little girls vis-a-vis little boys in places he knows best like his own schoolyard and what each sex does at recess and the attitudes of his sex to the other and vise reversa his own already are set in a superior aggressive chauvinism. Last year my daughter who runs very fast was quite furious for a week or two because a track meet at her school was arranged for the boys and not the girls. I told her she should demonstrate and cause a revolution or at least complain to the principal and she said with disgusted resignation "the principal is *superior* to the children." So much for the principal but what about the invisible forces of discrimination. A young girl is not usually hip to the culture at large. Nor is a grown woman necessarily. I have a fine lesbian chauvinist (ex) friend who says she feels discriminated against only when she sees she can't drive down the West Side Highway topless in a convertible. Well that's cool but anyhow she's an athlete too and the difference between her and the black woman I mentioned who was playing catch with the 10 year old is one of consciousness, that my (ex) friend made it as a kid across the barrier to sexsportual mobility and doesn't basically question her position as an exception. Or didn't. Or does and thinks it was all her fault. I mean it's a fault either way. What's in it for a woman to go out and play with the men and feel like a dope for being no good. Or to go out and play with the women and receive no cultural feedback mirror action in every media across the land the men can see themselves playing all their sports while the women can see only a fragment of themselves occasionally occupying a small space as a strange exception is not enough to motivate a growing girl to become an accomplished athlete or consider a sport as an option professionally since the media virtually excludes her own sex she will by the same token be unaware that there are, and there are, many organizations of women who play incredible lacrosse and field hockey and softball & such now really this has to change and the female sex has to begin doing something about her atrophied muscles. I was playing tennis a few weeks back and witnessed a classic scene of a young woman maybe 17 idling by the wire on a bike outside the courts watching her father and brother very strong welldefined proficient fellows playing up a smooth storm quite a while when the sister daughter got ready to leave and asked her father and brother if she should tell "mother" they'd be home soon and I don't need to mention her undeveloped musculature and what mother was doing at home and what she probably looked like by now and what her daughter will look like later on. A society which derogates women produces envious mothers who produce narcissistic males who derogate women in such a society female exhibitionism will be prohibited and the men must perform and must perform the prejudice I have to say at the risk of offending somebody whose four excellent photos of athletes in Central Park marked the front page of The Voice two weeks ago that the three men were naturally in action and the one woman was standing still at the plate talking (or yelling) at the pitcher. Yelling. Hurricane Doria. Hurricanes Edith and Irene. And Hurricane Fern was no longer a hurricane but a tropical storm said the radio. The Greek males as a group were terrified of any female who was a whole woman. The Greeks were terrified of the statuesque passionate women they portrayed so effectively—Medea, Clytemnestra, Hecuba, Alcmene. And what of the huntresses, the virgins? Many modern Dianas and Daphnes are athletes virgins lesbians and we know very little about them. I think frankly the country would freak if it had a chance to see some of its superb team sportswomen display their speed and intricate skills and strategies in such sports as lacrosse and field hockey, traditionally played and developed by women in favorable school circumstances. I'd like to give a badminton demonstration myself. I was keeping an ace up my old blazer sleeve and that's badminton. People have the worst misconceptions about this light weight racket sport. They see it as some kind of feather dusting. A silly game no more demanding than jacks or croquet which are fairly demanding. Badminton is a sleek incredibly fast and space consuming game with a terrific range of strategic subleties. It's psychologically the most satisfying game I've ever played. Unlike tennis in which your arm and your racket are very much of a piece from preparation, swing, and follow through your arm is an extension of the racket and the elbow is a vital hinge as it bends or gives somewhat and then straightens out in the completion of the swing still the arm and racket are one large simple unit and your footwork and stance and profile positioning to the net are very important in permitting arm and racket their full play on the ball whereas in badminton the arm is comparatively free of the racket in the sense that the racket becomes the tail end of a whiplash in which the arm behaves very much the way it does in throwing a ball pulling the shoulder way back and the bent elbow behind the shoulder and a cocked wrist above the elbow is the same preparation for a forehand badminton swing and the swing itself is quite the same as a throw with the difference that the follow through entails a heavier spapping wrist action as you let the racket which unlike a ball of course stays in your hand terminate the whip of the arm you get a beautiful swish of the racket through the air and a popping squsshy smash on impact with the birdie whose projectile is perhaps the key element as it is in any sport to the speed and strategic range of the game. The birdie is

an amazing object. The cork of its slightly weighted bottom that
connects with your racket strings sends the thing like a cannon
shot (excluding of course net play in which arm and racket action is reduced to ping pong level) for perhaps two thirds of its
journey until the feathers slow it down and it soars or drops just
like a bird for which it's named. Naturally the higher you send it
the greater the float at the other end thus affording your opponent
all the better opportunity to position herself for the return, but
you don't send it up like that unless you're driving your opponent
into the back of the court where hopefully her return will be weak
enough to permit you a smash or a drop shot or a cross court flat
hit close to the net and like that it's an infinitely variable game of
sudden turns and changes or great unpredictability and challenge
to your control over an eccentric swing in which arm and racket
behave like the segments of a crooked snake as they whip around
a twisting body. I must sound as though I did nothing but com-
pete ferociously at this swift delicate drastic game but really in
the six years I played it most consistently I had the best fun just
volleying with a friend while rapping endlessly over a net about
our schoolgirlish affairs back and forth swish tap smash and rap
all alone on a court that was also for stunts and basketball I could
I spose play badminton sleep walking several lives from now at
an advanced age pick up a racket and startle the inhabitants of
Venus for whatever fun it might be that would still be what it
was all about. Fun and heroism aside, you might remember what
Oscar Wilde said of football and I change the football to badminton, it is all very well as a game for rough girls but it is hardly
suitable for delicate boys.

August 19, vermont, Richard says judy thinks he's already fucked
up, so she pays care to winnie. also he sd, not telling winnie i'm
a lesbian is like my mother not telling me about my father. I'm
thinking occasionally about telling richard about the richard in
st. louis. The mystery of the mystery is why these matters have

remained a mystery. Richard says his father is afraid of him being seen with me and identified as his son. Winnie says she wants
to put her poems and stories together into a book and go to rad-
cliffe and have two children and marry a doctor so she can have
a horse.

August 22, feeling zapped over photo in newsweek. I cooperated
on their "homosexual" article thinking it was just good to get the
information into the motel lobbies across amerika; in Europe they
located me for an interview in London. (I remember telling them
in answer to their question regarding my attitude toward men
that I had an excellent attitude toward men, emerging as I did
from my female oriented society, and that was that we were all
equal.) In New York their own photographer had taken dozens
of pictures of me one day outside Casey's and they didn't use a
one, they went out of their way apparently to find something that
made me look like a bleary dopey lush, in other words somebody
whose words could be discounted.

August 24, tell Brenda I couldn't call her last night cuz I was
necking at the cloisters.

August 25, Brenda says she's interested in a gay-straight consciousness raising group and Gloria had said to count her in.

August 29, dream: two girls lying suspended up high on maybe
scaffolding embracing, etc., and playing with I dunno a huge bill-
board of poster of mother and baby and the baby's tongue hanging out (bottom right) and then a MOBILE hand playing with
the tongue—police approach—maybe in dream I changed girls
playing with poster—possible the mother's nipples to an isolated
hand (mobile hand) playing with tongue because of approach
of police.

August 30, Martha Shelley: The projection of Gloria by the media (ie, newsweek cover) is a way of putting other women down. Yoko called me a paranoid bitch.

September 4: Dinner Gregory's. Brenda plus Mark. And Susan Braudy, writing piece about me for Esquire. Susan sd after Brenda had done reading in my record book she got quiet and began twirling her hair. I told my de Menil London story umpteenth time. Susan wants to interview my mother, I sd she could talk to my son.

September 20: I gave Rosemary Polly's cherry pink happy underwear latex bra, and Susan W. Helen's green pullover sweater. R. akst me if I was going to put Susan B. in my column and I sd not now and Susan B. sd she had a fantasy of revenge against her ex old man that she'd appear in my column as a homosexual lover.

September 26: News from Aphra ("world's first feminist magazine")—Aphra "presents the mothers and the daughters, telling in their own words how it was, is and can be—laying the basis for a new and scandalous alliance that all their brothers and their uncles and their sons said could never happen . . . We're all lesbians, we all loved our mothers first."

Eliz. Cady Stanton, 1852: I am at length the happy mother of a daughter. Rejoice with me all womanhood, for lo! a champion of the cause is born.

September 27, Reading Craveri's Life of Jesus and Regine Pernoud's life of Joan.

September 29, talk to Kate on phone. She says the Pres. of NOW (who's been described as a "real dyke") says officially now it's okay to be a lesbian. Following the former purge of queers.

Letter from Leticia (Kent): I hear that you're starting a salon, that Sontag, Steinem and Millett have been asked to join. Shades of de Stael, of Stein & of Steinem. Kate said it sounds like a summit meeting.

October 1, Vermont
Nature dying in its color festival.
It's the best riot going.

October 2, NYC Went to Gianni's to meet Kate after her CR group elevenish and she was late so I went off with a 17 year old Karen who had been interrogating me inside the door as to whether I was me or not and buying me gingerales.
Kate's for breakfast.

October 3, DOB dance. Jane. Kathy. Lois. Etc.

October 4 Yesterday sunday breakfast chez Brenda. —curlers, dryer, etc. depressed over money disaster. couldn't decide whether to go back to country/Dick hanging up on me pretending Richard wasn't there. Debate going to Gloria's to say g'bye to Jane Lewis going to Africa. Go. Pink and white champagne. Go to Soul East and I continued on martinis. Pushed Gloria on lesbian bit, she got very uptight, said she'd *never* been attracted to a woman. (B. says today I should work on the future, she doesn't like to be called a liar about herself.) G. gave us black and red SOLD stickers and I put one on my crotch.

My encounter with the uptown feminists was on its last lap. I couldn't sustain their straightnesses and they couldn't tolerate my challenges. Three so-called consciousness raising meetings

about finished me off. This piece published October 14 is my
postmortem epilogue to the affair woven into the tale of my last
Yoko and John episode, in Syracuse.

ANYBODY DYING OF LOVE

It was the foolhardiness of the adventure that made it so appeal-
ing. Nothing is quite true and this isn't quite true either. I woke
up six days ago 3 a. m. and decided to cancel the summit meeting in the woods. I was about to do something moderately terrible again and not hire anybody to protect people from myself.
God forces me to think abominations that I might experience Her
grace. We don't even have those magnificent attitudes of not
giving a damn anymore. Except when I'm going someplace with
Gregory. I have a feeling a lot of people love me and nobody
loves me but I think Gregory loves me so when we're driving
crosstown in his mg saying preposterous things on our way to
LaGuardia for an outlandish event in Syracuse I experience
that fatuous luxury of not giving a damn. Even when we see
overhead a flock of thick black felt birds flying with capes of
solid chrome. Contra quam est nota natura. We've come to an
impasse. We can't disagree on anything. I took a lesbian nation
friend to dinner who said she only likes lesbians. I said well
Gregory is a lesbian. She said she could tell when she saw the
moustache and also that she'd be very embarrassed to appear in
my column which made Gregory say it's good for you and she
said thanks I hope your penis falls off in the kitchen. She kept
commenting on her remarks and then commenting on the comments to her remarks. A straight one who does this said also my
column is definitely a problem. It certainly is. The only time I
need to use quotation marks are when the words I write are mine.
You have to have a grand strategy to cope with all the hostilities

and your own excesspools and spillikins. Already four hours of sleep aren't enough for a gemini chemistry to maintain herself through the first one woman exhibition in America in a museum by the wife of a Beatle and another night of only four again and up before dawn for a flight from Syracuse to Albany where she decides to hitchhike south because her van is being driven from the city to the woods by a friend and stands at the NY thruway entrance an hour in a cold windy drizzle before a somewhat scary slob picks her up and deposits her too far from another friend who eventually comes anyway to make sure she gets to her own Woodloo of Woman who are she is convinced determined to understand their own lesbianism by talking about it nothing more. My popular position now is Martha Shelley's that I won't be straight until all of you are gay. Susan B. says she feels apologetic whenever she leaves me and I forget to say how abjectly apologetic I felt for so many centuries over being gay and not even being able to apologize for it in case they should find out you had something to be apologetic for. In Syracuse Rosalyn Drexler said Jill how did you get to be so free. Huh. The husbands and brothers of the women of historical days could not, we are told, have allowed their women to rave upon the mountains. No and that's why the women went off by themselves to rave and they did. Rosalyn also said all my old happenings seemed to be flying apart. I didn't know I was Dionysus then. Dionysus is unique in the frequency with which he is defeated bound imprisoned routed and even destroyed, and in the number of times he must be rescued. Rosalyn held my hand going up in the press plane at LaGuardia and I complained when we landed she didn't hold my hand on the way down so she said it was because she felt absolutely safe and didn't want to call my attention to the landing. We were supposed to number 69 on the Mohawk charter but I could've brought my son for the last minute empties like Charlotte Moorman didn't make it and appeared later at the museum having paid her own way including a full fare for her cello and I had suggested to Brian Hirst that Richard could write up the event for his school paper but I should've just said I was bringing an assistant like Gregory did. I had to sit very close against Gregory's assistant in the mg. I met him the night before at a Guggenheim opening where I stood both of them up when a beautiful young woman stepped rightout of a Renoir and into my arms once again an angel appeared to resolve the problem of being in a threatening area at one level paranoia is the only intelligent response to the world. I fell in love for the whole night. Anybody dying of love these days should go down in history. I think I was in love with Gloria for a week in August when I even composed a letter I didn't send asking at the end if she'd like to have lunch or lust after having said a lot of incredible calculated garbage concerning what any of us were supposed to do now that everybody had been informed by Newsweek that she was the one sought by us all. I didn't have to do anything much. Brenda won't claim the credit for it but it was she who suggested a gay-straight consciousness raising affair and notified me that Gloria had said to count her in. And I said let's wait till Susan S. returns from Europe and I thought if we could get Jane Fonda and maybe Jackie Kennedy and a royalty or two and of course Kate would come, and Anselma, and Phyllis, and we could bring everybody up to my forest and provide a lot of rope and a case of rum that I'd have the makings of my most exquisite disaster to date and we did. The passivity of Dionysus may in part be associated with the fact that so many myths take place in childhood, but he is at all ages unable to cope with Hera and reacts to any threatening gesture she makes with panic or paralysis or both. There's a masochistic sensuality about these tales—a voluptuous savoring of degradation and disintegration. In Syracuse I saved myself up for the summit the next day so all I could manage was a dashing flying exit down the ramp at the airport for the camera men who were also making a movie of us on the plane (David shielded his face the way criminals do) and innumerable suggestions to Rosalyn and a May Ann alternately that we spend the night together in our hotel and repeated attempts to ascertain the cost of the whole venture to the Lennons and refusing to run with the pack when John & Yoko made a lightning brief appearance scuttling like rabbit between rooms it was a hard day's night clip all after One Beatle and asking the director at the press conference if they planned to have another exhibition by a woman (he said art was art whether by man or woman) and asking Yoko & John if they planned more cocktails and hors d'oeuvres and dinner for us and Yoko if she'd grant me a personal audience and Yoko & John if they'd please send me all their records as promised to play on my new machine I need some records and changing into a seethru black shirt in some bookstacks during the luncheon. At the conference Gregory said I'm going back to the hotel before I get on the plane and Rosalyn said yes you *should* use your room. Yoko made a speech thanking us for coming and saying many people question why we do an art show in a museum when people are starving and the world is in such crisis. She told us the world is now divided into two classes: those who can communicate and those who can't. John said his statement was that he agreed and they kissed. The museum is lots of Yoko's work and I think it's quite a nice show. As late as the 17th century monarchs owned so little furniture that they had to travel from palace to palace with wagonloads of plates and bedspreads, of carpets and tapestries. The telescope piece was my favorite. Looking thru a telescope positioned on a balcony you can see the words evidently printed about 25 yards across the gallery on a wall "Please look at me. I am so small." Above the words is an oval mirror. Rosalyn said it was such a sad piece so I cried a little. Rosalyn is very perceptive. I don't know if I really wanted to go to bed with her or not. She's larger than anybody I've been to bed with and that might be interesting. Anyway I reminded her she used to make passes at me regularly, including putting her hands on my bare breasts once in a

doorway on East Broadway. Certainly I like older people. My
first lover was 52 and my second was 65. Why is everybody so
young now. I have a feeling a lot of people love me and nobody
loves me but on the plane Rosalyn said she and Sheindi love me
so when it's all over maybe there'll be a few old friends and
we'll sit in rocking chairs the most impressively numinous temples
are caverns of twilight reminiscing of the tattoos we had with
our names on them that fell off. It's pride and presumption that
precede a fall. Kate said the weekend was such a catastrophe,
that what was supposed to happen could never happen, that they
just belong to a different sorority, that's all. I should've brought
Yoko from Syracuse to complete the problem. She might've enjoyed hitchhiking with me in the rain outside Albany too. This
a.m. I woke before the lesbian contingent that stayed and awakened Kate to whisper like boarding school over the difficulty of
names. She doesn't know what to do about names either. Nobody has a clear view, we can console ourselves. Gregory's the
only person who doesn't give a damn. We're into the silliest human affairs. It's so ridiculous. And we think it's so important.
That's what Kate thought too this morning after I said hey look at
the rain and the leaves driven down to the Bach but last night
she was storming at me how I had a nerve getting only three
hours sleep and crying in the sink and challenging people so
heavyhanded getting them all uptight and scaring them when
there was such important work to do and all these people had
come and the opportunity was gone forever and like that until I
smashed a bottle of pickles to stop the assault and said later in
the aftermath at least a couple of old friends know how mushy
and feminine and ridiculous I am and how necessary it is in order
to attract attention, to dazzle at all costs, to be disapproved of
by serious people and quoted by the foolish. Anyway I was convinced it was all my fault & I had done everything wrong but
Jane said you have to be perfect to do everything wrong. Glorious a perfectly proper person. I never met such a nice perfectly

proper person. She's a very nice properly person. Dionysus represents not so much irrationality as the liberation of natural emotions from the tyrannies of ideology and culture. At Syracuse
John in the press conference said he's always been a radical because he was always in trouble. Fate offers us misfortunes worthy
of our characters. The world is hemophiliac. David wasn't ec-
static to see that his ice tray contribution to Yoko's Water Piece
wasn't labeled or even filled with water. He thought if John Cage
had sent it in they would've filled it with water. John Cage probably sent nothing or wasn't asked since he didn't accept the gift
Yoko offered him a Box of Smile a few months ago although I
accepted the same gift and I wasn't asked either. I was included
however in the newspaper press release collection brochure
passed out by the hostess on the plane with a controversial couple of paragraphs I wrote about Yoko in 1961. Charlotte showed
me an original of this clipping out of a manila folder she was
carrying. Charlotte was Yoko's roommate at that time and she
managed that concert which was Yoko's uptown debut. Charlotte
said in that piece of Yoko's she sat on a toilet making weird
sounds with the cello. I'm glad Yoko found a use for this old review I wrote because she remains determined to be hurt that I
shouldn't have included it in my book while it happened that a
piece I wrote from London in 1968 including some mention of a
performance by John did get into the book. We fought over this
& other worldshaking matters for an hour on the phone long before Syracuse so I didn't understand why she said she and John
loved me too. In Syracuse David remarked you're on such a
down trip Jill, just because you don't like Yoko there's no need
to extend it to the food and everything. I said I like Yoko but she
isn't very nice to people. David said she can afford not to be. I
said that makes me like her even better. And I didn't have a very
strong sense of sisterhood that day. She's getting off the best way
she knows. From washington Snowshoe wrote her theory on
karma is that whatever you get thru in this life you don't have to

repeat and anything you settled in previous lives you don't have to worry about this time regardless of how many others are hung up on it. She thinks we all knew each other before in greece the return of the amazons & children of the dawn and everything we were but last time we made it starting from the top the aristocracy and this time we have to make it from down below, add that & understanding of how does it feel to be on your own and level out elitism even though we're obviously still beloved of the goddesses and gods whom many lack. Nobody's credentials as a radical are impeccable. For the woman woods party I really wanted Garbo Harlow Hepburn Dietrich Smith Sayre Plath Monroe Joplin etc.—Garbo is okay cause she's alive and well and she won't sue. We know Janis was gay, and some lesbian sisters are certain they could've saved her. Maricla said the meeting sounds very elitist Jill and I said absolutely. Further transformations also run true to the hero myth. Oedipus could think of nothing worse than a base origin. Dionysus represents an essentially masochistic solution. The Angry Mother is the Straight Mother. The challenge from her son creates her counterattack and revenge. Now a Gay Woman who is still Straight in her head is also an Angry Mother. The selfdestruct of Dionysus the DaughterSon is a way of dissolving the boundaries in distress. Kate says I don't know my own influence and a soft pitch here and there would have a proper effect. Kate's pretty heavy herself. She's almost as demanding as I am. She just asked me how to spell cunnilingus. The party was a huge success because we became friends and Jane came and so did Susan S. who is eloquent even if conservative and '50s an original hero of mine I wanted very much to introduce to Gloria Kate Anselma Brenda etc., and I danced with Phyllis who's warm and squeezy and has the best rap going about the old and new amazons, and Anselma cried a little, and Susan B. was exhausted, and Brenda I hope left the meeting to go directly to the White House with Gloria. Now's the time since her old man is in Paris on business. Seeing a kindred shape we swoon away. As for Dionysus in the end it is almost as if the defeats and persecutions were the important part of the story—they are often dwelled upon more fully than his triumphs. And even if a lot of people love him and nobody loves him there's always in one lifetime or another a Geoff Hendricks in a long beard and old denims in a Syracuse dining room writing a dedication in your new record book beginning this is a kind of love letter for I love you in a deep kind of way although we have never talked with each other until recently there has been some very basic kind of vibration communication. . . . and Dionysus felt that way too and loves him back and that's the way the world will end even with a whimper and even if our greatest talent as with the greeks remains our facility for mutual destruction. . . . And the rest of this is the story by Kate.

❈   ❈   ❈

MOVEMENT SCHMOOVEMENT

Snowshoe: what with everything that's going on a letter probably is in order since my new woman of the week is from seattle and I'd rather splat out a letter than compose a piece if you still don't mind or believe in living free as you said might include here a small adjustment to another type of intrusion into your wilderness as well as an exercise in suspending belief when you're reading along and think hey she wouldn't write that in a letter it's true I'm still not free enough here to splat out a piece the way I liberally compose a letter what with everything going on I wonder if my new woman of the week from seattle is like your new genderless folk out there and if so we're coming soon. I never made it north of Mendocino. The last time I was seriously impressed by a woman was in fact in a tiny ghosttown Caspar five miles up from Mendocino spent about 10 days with a head

amazon over six feet high and she was great too and now this
Denby aged 19 also stands over six feet but as a de facto meso-
morph meaning she hasn't stopped growing yet so you might say
she's trying to become an ectomorph which was the incredibly
gangling gawky majestic & flying hair broomsticky look of my
friend back in Caspar. Denby wouldn't ever look that way tho
even if she did grow skinnier into her 190 pounds. She's a round
one really. A smiling pumpkin head. Ruddy all american out-
doors perfect teeth pale blue smart eyes sandy short straight hair
wholesome is the word people use she told me. The other day on
a talking gig in new jersey the women afterward brought in the
problem subject of elitism in the movement and someone said
well we do proceed by models from model to model as it works
and I described my new model is a triumph of size and cool. She
makes some sort of immediate sense & according to Jane who sent
her on to me to help reclaim my camper broke apart last week
on a northern turnpike enroute another talk gig she doesn't have
a paranoid sense of privacy so I'm safe for a day and I was writing all this while she cut up some cabbage and celery for salad
speaking of what you said ah but there's other places & times &
distances & fugitive presents and you and another survivor snowshoe walking the creek throwing a big branch in watching it on
its majestic way downstream with an escort of sunken leaves
going down too swirling on the bottom . . . it was for me also
that way walking along an eastern stream here one early afternoon with Denby bubbling under her beaver black top hat and
huge inside her gray vest and carrying her napsack and a heavy
tin box of tools we were hitchhiking out of a remote little acre
thru the dead and dying rusty brown orange hills I felt very
happy like we were sisterberry finns & whitewashed fences forever on the road to noplace particular . . . immediate sense
. . . and throwing our gear into the back of a light blue truck for
a short windy hop to a lonesome corner . . . and stopping at the
wire to a cow enclosure where Denby approached with a declara-

tion of sweetheart and tramping on told me how the cows don't like the machines and miss the human hand and how back home she sometimes took a drink directly off the teat if she was playing hard near a pasture and got thirsty and also how she and her pals had a few milk fights . . . and parking our gear for an on-coming car trying to decide who should be in front and if one should sit down and who looked more like a girl and what to re-move each time she took off the top hat and me my shades and once my jacket and joked about the rest I know it must sound like city innocence in rural paradise to you all this but I have to explain in order to purge myself of the polluted politics that recently con-gested my head and lungs. Your letters predict my immediate fu-ture it seems. The college gigs are okay cause I make a formal ex-hibition and sound as authoritative as the situation demands and even bask a little in the illusion of my own heroism created by a modest amount of adulation and then it's time to split and that's easy politics. For the rest, the heavy numbers in the city, of which Ti-Grace Atkinson if you know who she is was a charter casualty, I might invoke a nice oldfashioned Huxley line "in some cases man's dreadful inhumanity to man has been inspired by the love of cru-elty for its own horrible and fascinating sake" to describe my final impression of movement politics. Movement Schmoovement. There were only a few encounters and this last one I knew it was all over when I threw a handful of crackers at the leader and like every reprimanded child went to bigger and better worse things. Z-gad, as Denby would say, I'm being swallowed by a boa-constrictor. Anyway for sure if you're having fun you're not having a move-ment and I like to have fun so I've decided to refuse myself the dubious political pleasure of causing someone and then myself to hurt by walking into a living space of another person and act-ing as if they're in another century, or have a culture that we don't have. The first phase ended in reform and was succeeded by reaction. I said to Phyllis the culture is behind me and she said it's against you, not behind you. Mixing oil and water. Three

straights who talk and act straight. One gay who talks somewhat
straight and acts all gay. One gay who talks all gay and acts gay
and a little straight. One straight who talks all gay and acts
mostly straight. Two gays what talk and act all gay. The new
term I heard in jersey is fuzzies for those straights thinking about
having a "Lesbian Experience." Did you ever hear the Yeats line
about how things are torn down and built again and those that
build again are gay? Anyway I guess Jane was my true ally and
we probably felt like doomed conspirators at the end of some
futile crusade. Higher consciousness may be moving to the country and not talking to anybody or it could be moving to chinatown and trashing everybody. Or at least assuming an air of
helplessness involving fraudulent appeals for direction thru a
show of ignorance. I'm sure someone can invent appropriate
other possibilities as well. Anyhow I let them off the hook by
exhibiting my distress. A good model doesn't throw crackers or
try to blow their nose in aluminum tinfoil. So like what you wrote
for me too that politics we cannot handle on any level at the moment and agree for the most part that the only true social inter-
action will come when we bring it from the inside out and that
it won't work from all these platforms erected outside, and I'd
add that as women we're not going to discover what our differences are until we become human since as one of these leaders
has noted women have internalized the disesteem in which they
are held, despising both themselves & each other so I refuse
now to go anyplace where my name might be added to the casualty list they call a movement. Wherever Ti-Grace is I'm with
her and I reaffirm that I constitute a movement totally myself
complete period. If we're going to be casualties I prefer the type
Denby sustained a couple of years ago a car rammed her mo-
torcycle. She's philosophical about it and takes good care of herself and still rides bikes. I think the accident broke her leg in
nine places so she limps slightly but improves all the time. I
wondered and didn't ask if there was any connection between

the accident and her height. She laments her present six foot one total and the stop her parents put to her growth when she was 13 and they convinced her that the six foot ten the doctors predicted as her outcome was not suitable for getting along in life. The top hat is perfect. When I first saw her I was really happy. She's huge and huggy and funny and together and dependable and considers herself quite lucky since she wasn't raised to buy her clothes at J. Jacobs but to coach a football team and build a house and stuff like that. She was her father's number one son she says. Though recently returning home to visit she was put out a lot when he introduced her to a friend as my son Lindsay and she had to explain that she didn't like that a bit since she's gotten her head together as a woman now she knows a woman can be a woman and build houses and coach football teams too. We talked about heroes awhile. Her big one was Vince Lombardi. I told her I collected photos of Gary Cooper a long time back. You had to pick a star then and put them in a scrapbook and Shirley Temple was unthinkable. I asked her about reading too. She loved Lord of the Rings and regardless of the chauvinism in it no matter what anybody says she's not willing to stop loving the things she loves just because she's developed a higher consciousness. My son Richard loves the Lord of the Rings too. Once last year we went on a difficult hunt around where he lives for Bored of the Rings. I've made the inevitable switch so you must be thinking uh she wouldn't write this or this way in a letter it's true but maybe someday I'll pretend I'm writing a real letter and then send it as a piece or vice reversa. I'm putting you the cider your letter Denby and Jane together and pitching it all against the dire blackness and ill humor of the politics of women at war with themselves. The immensity of Denby was a moment of truth. The combined images turned my head. Sitting on my speaker in the white work suit and black clodboots laced to the knees explaining my broken motor and how she didn't have the proper tools to fix it. Deep in a sling chair laughing over how it's good to play that game "use the alphabet & tell me everything I am." Arriving late in a foggy moonless night towing the camper and steaming the tires of Phyllis's buick stuck on the wet leaves in the last stretch of driveway. Playing the Chambers brothers full up to blasting any barn away. Noticing a remarkable pale green bug in the rocks below the door sill. The entire expedition I rambled on about the sisterberry mutt & mutt or jeff & jeff team going hopefully noplace and not waiting for any godope either but being gorgeous outsized girl marvel bums on the bounty. If this was a letter I might add that I think the clincher that made me realize I've been unseasonably heavy was when standing on my head Denby came over and drew a funny face in purple ink on my stomach it's time again to be irresponsible and irrelevant and irreverent and fuck civilization and movements . . . from wherever I am in the dead leafy season. . . .

 L., Jill.

AN AMAZON IN THE WHITE HOUSE

There is got to be a disparity between what we are talking about and your momentum. I been staring at that line and not making any meaning out of it. Now I see it & now it's gone. Now it's okay and reverse it that the disparity is between our momentum and what you are talking about and both ways of putting it add up to a confrontation which must be why I liked it before it made sense although it doesn't have to, make sense. Anyway I had a confrontation. I'm sure it was another line that provoked it. She's so impressionable. Living out her lines. In the beginning, there was woman, etc. Chasing after the sun and installing herself in the center of it, etc. Things used to be so simple when you just named them to make them exist and now you line them as well and that way eliminate a lot of experience but also make things

more complex and demanding. Now I can ignore an object or a
collection of objects unless they come alive in a line. And I can
be sure that I won't experience anything before I've enjoyed a
line that described its possibility. Not the other way around as I
thought before, although just as a circle defines it own end I
could never be sure. Especially since I know now I might suddenly be doing something I'm surprised about doing or having
just done and later find out there's every probability I happened
to be doing it because of a provocative line. This could cause a
profusion of identity. This is what we want. But why am I wearing a marine jacket? It seemed so essential to obtain a marine
jacket. And there she sat looking quite unhistorical. And then
she waved goodbye and told Jane to tell Phyllis to invent a salute.
So that war it. Warn't that some line P. had going there about a
woman's army. Hook line and sinkher. And Phyllis got it from
Helen Diner. And Diner got it from Bachofen Ephorus Phere-
cydes Isocrates Hellanicus Cleidemus Eusebius Dionysus Scytho-
brachion Herodotus Diodorus Plutarch Pliny Strabo Pompeius
Trogus and many others she said. Yeah. This book quote unquote
tells the exciting story of female dominated societies that existed
in earlier civilizations. This book avowedly endeavors to remain
as onesided as possible. This book according to its author is the
first feminine history of culture and it has an introduction by Joseph Campbell who concedes politely and cautiously and even a
little courageously that Diner speaks with a knowledge and wisdom antecedent to the world and footnotes of her son and spouse,
the male—who has just pushed things too far in his own favor
and you can order the book at your local 8th st. bookstore by the
way it's called Mothers and Amazons and all we know so far
about Helen Diner is that she was a Viennese society woman
who wrote several books between the two world wars under the
pseudonym Sir Galahad. I've heard Mothers and Amazons is
coming out in paperback in a few months. So you can wait for
your marine jacket. Just don't talk to Phyllis in the meantime.

Long distance is the best place to be. It's almost better not to know. But it's true, nonetheless. The myths are true. The myths are truer even than I thought in their clear function as the psychology of history. They're true because the lines and their actualizations work both ways. The fairy tales are merely an entertaining surrealistic crumble-jumble of actual events. Which emerged out of the psychic organ of their conception and explanation. Both ways. And this poem will be a new country pasted over some old one. It's like comparing one map with another map without reference to the territory. Very often the line is a kind of a descendant of an immigrant who can't remember her country of origin. Like when you travel astrally and you can't send a letter home exactly since the places have no names. Then they say oh you're making that up and if you're a good story teller they'll hire you to entertain the guests or to write it up as a bulfinch, otherwise they'll say you're psychotic or something and put you out of sight. Plato is still in trouble a little over his description of Atlantis. Why is it so important about the name? I mean we know now that not far from where Plato lived a volcanic disaster buried a land mass which was a whole city or community or small civilization but even its archaeological discovery doesn't confirm its existence as the place named by Plato although a number of people now feel reasonably certain that what Plato described in the Timaeus as the island of Atlantis that disappeared in the depths of the sea from violent earthquakes and floods in a single day and night all your warlike men in a body sank into the earth for which reason the sea in those parts is impassable he said and others feel certain that that was the catastrophe of a Minoan counterpart of Pompeii occurring around 1400 b. c. but many will continue because of the difficulty over corpse identification to think as did Edith Hamilton and Huntington Cairns not long ago in their Bollingen edition of the dialogues that Plato was making up a fairy tale, the most wonderful island that could be imagined. The island interests me, but not as much as Clito, who is the namesake of the female organ, and who according to Plato was safeguarded on this very island in the center of a fence of alternate rings of sea and land by her lord and master Poseidon. And where did I see the reference to Amazons and Atlantians? Anyway I conducted an archaeological investigation into the Robert Graves volumes for Clito and Clito is missing in Graves. Poseidon it seems going by Graves had every woman in the world but Clito. He married Amphitrite. He had a nymph called Thoosa. He had Libya and Tyro and Andromeda and another nymph Caenis and probably Aphrodite, everybody had Aphrodite, and Pasiphae and even Medusa who by the way became the monster we know because of this very act, by conversion of Athene, who was enraged that they had bedded down in one of her own temples. Anyhow no Clito. Jane doesn't think she's in the Oxford Classical Dictionary either. But Hippo and Lampado and Marpesia were Amazon queens. And I've got Eleanor of Aquitaine and Marie de Champagne and Blanche of Castille on my list too. Three archdykes of modern poetry. We want an Amazon in the white house, not an Aphrodite. Nor an Athene. The militant virgins who crown the kings will continue to burn. There is got to be a disparity between our momentum and what you are talking about. The house of one generation was the tomb of the next. The tombs are attractive modern antiseptic buildings for say about 1100 youth aged five to 14 or so. She traveled northward in her marine gear and didn't know she had read recently that modern protest movements depend heavily on a willingness to make a scene and not to be intimidated by a social milieu not that she didn't know this but you realize many of her confrontations take place in the center of a fortified island fighting paper dragons. Now she's prepared to learn karate and various samurai techniques and horsewomanship and archery and boatcraft and ski soldiering and all manner of arts of becoming invisible. But not in the service of the battles between the boys and the men. We're through with the sons and fathers. They've messed it all up, blown their chance. I told

Richard this. He has to do it himself next time. Like there I was
some kind of Joan or Athene charging up to the gates to unhand
the enemy of the boy and not only do I disapprove of my involvement but I've forgotten my skills as well. We've been
trained to be dancers. Every last woman. I may be very stylish
in my advances but I'm still the sort of parent who gave their
kid the power to confront what they are unable to resist themselves. At least in the form of an assistant principal who's a thug
or a bouncer. The suitable size and mentality. Already the prison
found me endearing by my visitation as a spy hobo combat marine in red hunter's gloves and warrior jewelry. Already I was
prepared to dynamite the place for implying that I should disapprove of my son the way they did. That's the way they get you.
How can you expect to emulate our miserable lives if you don't
accept oppression? Participating so eagerly in the frustration
they endure. God knows if Richard had had his arm around a
boy instead of a girl. It seemed to be all about sex and bad language. "He can't use four-letter words around here, this is a conservative community, and I don't want any boy grabbing my
daughter." —Grabbing! I said I suppose that's translated to mean
you don't approve of sex for young people. No he didn't. And
Richard was also reprimanded for acting happy. Parents under
the old method felt they had done their job well if the child was
obedient even if he turned out dull unimaginative surly sadistic
& sexually incapacitated. We needed the cross, the standard. The
cross is necessary to ward off the elders. The elders are younger
than me and very often five or 10 or 20 years old. Two incom-
patible processes are taking place at once: The elders are expressing anger, while pretending to themselves that the causes
of that anger do not exist. The assistant principal's neck was
twitching. He said no boy can swear in front of ladies. So
promptly I swore a bloody fucking filthy stream of piss shit crap
and corruption and jumped up onto my snorting firebreathing
charger & wielded my jewel studded sword and clanked all my

armor and yelled a secret war whoop and caused the whole building to fall down. Tell Phyllis we need a salute. And an oath. When Zeus Poseidon and Hades took over they shook lots in a helmet for lordship of the sky sea & murky underworld. That's not an oath I guess. But Kleonike asked Lysistrata what sort of an oath they were supposed to swear and L. said The Standard—the one where you slaughter a sheep and swear on a shield, but Kleonike sd you don't swear an Oath for Peace on a shield, so they decided on an enormous black cup, hollow up, and next to the cup to slaughter a jar of Thasian wine and to swear a mighty Oath not to dilute the water. Whatever that means. I don't like Lysistrata any better than Athene or Aphrodite. No oath, no salute, no skills, nothing. Only a marine jacket. And some fabulous lines. The Romans always found many female corpses in German battlefields and the archaeologists have unearthed many skeletons of Germanic women with the insignia of war and in full armor. I was terrified and satisfied. After the confrontation in the office in front of as many young elders and old youngers as possible and telling them all I wouldn't consider letting my son attend their prison for another minute and I was waiting for Richard in the corridor and being playful with a couple of girls and Richard arrived to kiss a girlfriend goodbye we were bodily dismissed and I thought for a second it was Chicago. Leaping into the branches of a nearby tree she looked down from a safe height on the foe she had escaped. I think his neck was still twitching. No one likes to admit they've been spending their lives in a foolish evil or crazy manner.

Her Command of Impermanence

Now that we've found ourselves here. Everybody says I'm an intellectual but actually I'm some kind of sandhog. Or snow plow.

Natural disasters such as floods hurricanes blizzards & so on gen-
erate a cheerfulness which would seem inappropriate if we didn't
all share it. It's as if some natural balance between woman and nature had been restored and with it our true function. Making a
woman in white in snow and giving her a mythological background to invest her with authority and numinosity. So what else
is old? The moon is fully total and L. is bleeding and B. seemed
in love and J. came by trailways and R. is a pyrophile and S. fell
down while standing still and D. thought I should be able to
make love in the same room with her and F. but I was too giggly
and young and innocent and I refuse to rise above that. She don't
mind stumbling over the consequences of her past inhibitions.
Her orgasm is still more important than the challenging prospect
of defeating her desire with the exhilaration of embarrassment.
Besides she has to rise above exurbia in the a. m. and confront
each mechanical invention furnished to create new difficulties out
of the problems they were devised to correct. Weather this is
true or knot the flak is that betweed you and the grape good life
stands your landlord and your landau winch is oaf again hacking
seized up according to john or mike and lennie or steve and kur-
tinly one last bastid naked tom or cat who keepsaking over and
ornery aboot the motor it was just fight, just fight, and it wasn't.
D'you think up in heaven we'll all have a rolls that works all the
time? That's what happens in this country—everything that was a
symbol becomes a fashion. It was nice just to have a single headless snowwoman fading away daily. She has a sense of sequence
that isn't ours. She's all we occasionally expire to be. But we realize that for centuries classicists have been trying to reerect the
fallen statue of grief antiquity, but unsuccessfully, for it is a
colossus around watch modern wo(men) crawl like pygmies.
The will to form remains the same throughout the entire development, only it passes thru all the stages from utmost culture to
utmost primitiveness. She said she didn't think of herself as a
Renoir and thought if anything she was a Rubens but she'd much

prefer to be called a de Kooning. But I wouldn't go to bed with a de Kooning. For herself she said she was going to bed with a celebrity. That was long before the snow set in. Which should excite anyone who detests easy seductions. The heat stops. The electric stops. The phone stops. The pipes freeze. The cars die. The world is beautiful and inconvenient. The machines arrive to frustrate their own purposes. The men arrive traditionally handling the problem by being given completely free rein to novel technological fantasies to make us breathlessly wonder what new disruptions are in store for us. In this case each new invention is not even a refuge from the misery it creates. Since none of it works Marsha said after numberless hours reading the instructions for the snowplow and understanding its mechanism that she could start it with a car, I guess the way you pull the thing out in a motorboat, but none of the cars worked. And everybody kept falling down. But the disaster was turning into a disgusting triumph. Denby and Francine arrived to play in it. Sandy was practicing her horn. Jane brought the messiah. Phyllis brought a whiskey egg nog. Mickey found a sled. Budda and Linda took Richard shopping. And Martha demonstrated her command of impermanence by exposing herself to gradual erosion outside the frame the sliding window door one could observe the record the phenomenon. Modes of destruction and positive statement. Each hero brings her decor with her. She was a seated Lachaise. Her right arm is a Giacometti now. Her right scapula a de Kooning. A dirty gash. Nov. 28: One of her nipples melted. The nipples actually were not intentio auctoris. The ass was plentiful and the breasts plump and pendulous but she had no nipples and noticing this omission returning from a walk Jane and/or Jill insolently stuck them on. Thus every manifestation of style has its climax. These feelings are intensified when we consider sensitive parts as members in a structural orgasinim. With Cleopatra, the nose is enough, we know that the rest is not far behind. We had her stand up and put her clothes back on. Chaque matin quand je me leve/Une femme se dresse devant moi/Elle resemble a tout ce qu'hier/J'ai vu de l'univers. The practical aim of greek construction was merely to provide the statue of the divinity with an enclosed space, safe from all the inclemencies of the weather. In the room the women come and go, speaking of Marthaangelo. The hunters in their bright reds walking by on the road. The constable in his camper truck. The postman in his chevie. The electric company in their cherry picker. The garbage people in their garbage machine. The snowplow in their blades and shovels. The levelers and uprooters and tunnelers and builders up and tearers down and fillers in and blowers up. Each new enlightenment being the forerunner of new obscurities. While a doe ventured hesitantly down the snow blue hill after the moon went down on the other side of our lady to see what it wasn't all about. Protect us from the people who can put things into action because they have no vision. What of the inventor who is said to make a discovery by continually thinking about it. The great shifting of emphasis in investigation from the objects of perception to perception itself. It needed but a little change to transform her slight limbs into chill waters, after that her shoulders, her back, her sides, her breasts disappeared, fading away into insubstantial streams, till at last, instead of living blood, water flowed thru her softened veins, and nothing remained for anyone to grasp. Does it excite you or does it make you calm. She said when it was close to my having an orgasm it was like pink petals and it had some orange in it. The slenderest parts of her body dissolved first of all. It was broad nightlight out. I have a history of making love to statues. Submit sloping prone in a hangdog crouch. You're aware that according to aristootle it isn't a tragic death to be slain by a statue. A classicist enjoys an immense advantage in that much of the preliminary work in her discipline has been done. Just hanging around looking meaningful. Just refusing to become a fashion by remaining a symbol. Just having a sense of sequence that isn't ours. And being all we occasionally expire to be. She's leaning forward now, and the Giacometti arm is a tendon of pale white swiss cheese. Her ass is still prominent but spongy in perforations. Her left hip and thigh is a shoddy Rodin, her bones growing fluxible. Ravished by sun and rain and a german shepherd came along to pee on her lap. The headless queen, the greatest in the world of shadows. Sanguine and phlegmatic. She only said she couldn't be counted on for tragedies. Like this one remaining vehicle here from detroit has everything wrong with it but it won't blow up or stop going because it's idiot proof. Anyway most people would rather die quietly than "make a scene." Jane said she saw an outstanding Fragonard with billowing breasts waiting on line for the ladys room appearing to be in motion while standing still. And she had a head and hair too? She got dewy tresses? Ummmmmm, hair, it's so nice, it hangs down, gets in yr mouth, gets in yr way. So what else is old.

♀ AMAZONS AND ARCHEDYKES

In the beginning, there was woman.

A misrepresentation of the world image through paternalistic prejudices can be freely compensated in the consciousness of mankind if its soul experiences the renewed image of sufficiently pure female-oriented societies, with their matriarchal precepts. It is intended that the woman shall thus receive a tradition, so that she should not seem without tradition in her own eyes in relation to those things that she can do. (Helen Diner, xii)

A similarity between her virility and freedom from the fetters of being an object of the male makes the homosexual woman resemble the image of woman in matriarchal times. This similarity applies particularly to the more masculine type of lesbian. The wide range of activities, the undoubted capacity to manage her life without dependence on men, is the ideal of the homosexual woman. Female homosexuality is inseparable from the very qualities which were the prerogative of women in early history. It is of no consequence to these conclusions whether the matriarchate existed as a definite period of history, which I believe it did, or in mythology only. Mythology *is* history, transcending concrete data and revealing their true meaning.

(Charlotte Wolff, m.d., *Love Between Women*, p. 82)

So long has the myth of feminine inferiority prevailed that women themselves find it hard to believe that their own sex was once and for a very long time the superior and dominant sex. In order to restore women to their ancient dignity and pride, they must be taught their own history, as the American blacks are being taught theirs.

Recorded history starts with a patriarchal revolution. Let it continue with the matriarchal counterrevolution that is the only hope for the survival of the human race.

. . . it is man's fear and dread of the hated sex that has made woman's lot such a cruel one in the brave new masculine world. In the frenzied insecurity of his fear of women, man has remade society after his own pattern of confusion and strife and has created a world in which woman is the outsider. He has rewritten history with the conscious purpose of ignoring, belittling, and ridiculing the great women of the past, just as modern historians and journalists seek to ignore, belittle, and ridicule the achievement of modern women. We must repudiate two thousand years of propaganda concerning the inferiority of woman. (Elizabeth Gould Davis, *The First Sex*)

A small but significant number of angry and historically minded women comprehend the women's revolution in the visionary sense of an end to the catastrophic brotherhood and a return to the former glory and wise equanimity of the matriarchies. We don't know how this will take place exactly, nor the nature of the resultant new social forms, we know that it *will* take place, and in fact that the process of its development is now irreversibly underway. Of supreme importance in this process is the recovery by modern woman of her mythology as models for theory, consciousness, and action. We know that male history has rigorously suppressed and distorted the great female models, just as the american white male has severed the blacks from their origins and distorted their image to suit the white male version of american history. For women, who had perhaps reached the nadir of their degradation and destitution by the Victorian age, it was the research of a few male scholars and anthropologists toward the end of that age which initiated the moment of reversal in all these dark ages of patriarchal history. The Swiss patrician Jacob Bachofen was one of the first to discover "the female era at the lower seam of history, with its sacerdotal, political, and economic female dominion." (Diner, 27) The fruits of this research were until recently unavailable except to a few initiates and they now form a cornerstone of the second wave in the feminist revolution. We now know that matriarchy prevailed in the most advanced and the most ancient city cultures. We know that all forms of matriarchy at one time were overthrown by the patriarchy and that almost all of recorded history is the story of the patriarchies. Woman's preeminence in history was systematically deleted in the records as it was destroyed in reality. Woman's preeminence wherever it emerged within patriarchal systems was likewise deleted if not demeaned and distorted. Women have come down to themselves virtually as a people without history except in the secondary capacity of servant or helpmate to the man. Women are now flabbergasted by their ancestral oblivion. History in the dawning Aquarian Age is a new book and it will be written by women as we reclaim ourselves from the tombs and dustbins of male matricide. We are living in the ginnunga gab. The prophecy of the future was Joyce's Finnegans Wake which he ripped off from his crazy daughter. The ginnunga gab is the time of transition. The civilization of the patriarchies is over. The legal sanction of the act of Orestes is coming to an end. Legalized matricide. The furies have returned to avenge the murders of our mothers. The feminists are the contemporary furies. The furies in the time of Orestes were living already in a patriarchal world and their defeat was an expression of this, as their indictment and pursuit was an expression of the vestiges of a matriarchy of which they were its last furious representatives. In their anthropological investigations of the 19th century the male uncovered the source of his own undoing. Besides Bachofen there was Marx's great collaborator Engels, who picked up Bachofen's theory of mother-right from the American Lewis Morgan's Ancient Society published 1877. In 1972 the most illuminating aspect of the Communist Manifesto is the first footnote by Engels explaining that the theory of class struggle delineated in the Manifesto was written *before* the discovery of the primitive communal societies and the true nature of the *gens* and its relation to the *tribe*. "With the dissolution of these primeval communities society begins to be differentiated into separate and finally antagonistic classes." The cyclical overthrow of class systems observed and predicted by Marx and the earlier Engels could later be seen as a struggle between oppressor and oppressed that followed in the wake of the oppression of women as the first subjugated class. The first sentence of the Manifesto reads: "The history of all hitherto existing society is the history of class struggles." And Engels' footnote "that is, all *written* history. In 1847 the pre-history of society, the social organization existing previous to recorded history, was all but unknown. Since then, Haxthausen discovered common ownership of land in Russia, Maurer proved it to be the social foundation from which all Teutonic races started in history, and by and by village communities were found to be, or to have been the primitive form of society everywhere from India to Ireland." It was Bachofen (1815-1887) who was the first to point out that the patriarchal social orders of both classical and biblical antiquity had been preceded in time—and are even now exceeded in space—by a more ancient, indeed primeval, social order of "mother-right" in which the claims of motherhood alone, not fatherhood, are accorded social and religious recognition. (J. Campbell, Introd. to Diner's *Mothers and Amazons*) Such an order would naturally correspond to the biological situation of woman as parent prime. The catastrophic brotherhood would appear to be a perversion of this natural order. Marx's program for social revolution in the form of communally owned property and the abolishment of private ownership was, unbeknownst to him, a form that once existed as it was defined matrilineally. What else would the ownership of the means of production mean? —woman being the original producer. Marx too, however, was a prophet of the end of the patriarchies. "The real point aimed at is to do away with the status of women as mere instruments of production." —"Bourgeois marriage is in reality a system of wives in common . . ." —"On what foundation is the present family, the bourgeois family, based? On capital, on private gain." The original communism was the community of women. When the boy became a husband and father the autonomy of women was undermined. The story of Greek myth is the gradual reduction of women from sacred beings to chattel. The story of civilized societies all over the world is the loss of female autonomy in some fierce struggle waged by the man to capture the primacy of parenthood through the secondary means of culture—the ownership of the instruments of (re)production in his own name and through the legal apparatus for inheritance. Yet fatherhood remains the fiction that it ever was when it is presumed that "in bygone days, before the facts of parentage were known, the earth was thought of as mother and husbandless, sufficient herself for all her childbearing, or vaguely fertilized by the dead spirits of men buried in her bosom." (Slater, *Glory of Hera*, 423) Such primitive races as the Australian aborigines believe that women may be impregnated by almost any means other than men. Fathers at the beginning of consciousness were only brothers. Just as they still are until the child reaches an age of acculturation and is "taught" who her "real father" is. In reality there is no "real father." There is only a real mother. The fiction of fatherhood is a giant religion called christianity. The invisible almighty father. In France they call their great cathedral Notre Dame, knowing in some region of consciousness the true ·source of this religion. "Human destiny always has been decided anew from its magical wells by the aboriginal phenomenon of female primacy, while the male principle, separated from the female, appears later and matures later into independence and creativity." (Diner, 4) The story of the evolution of culture is the eclipse of the Mother by the Son. The Son ascends to the Father and the Father denies the Mother. In Greek mythology all the phases of the drama are represented. Two tales that best represent the male claim are the birth of Athene from the head of Zeus (like Eve out of the ribs of Adam) and the birth of Dionysus as a splinter out of the thigh of the same versatile Zeus. Born without female intervention. The Greek authors competed like their heroes in the determination of parental primacy. In Homer Hephaestus seems to be the son of both Zeus and Hera while in Hesiod he is Hera's son alone giving birth without prior male assistance, like Leto who brought forth Apollo, who, however, was so prodigious, attaining to manhood in three or four days, that for all intents and purposes he was not of woman born and was immediately so loyal to the father that he imagined heredity to be transmitted only through the male. At a later date a true believer like Aeschylus (in the Eumenides) could support the claims of the great hero, attempting to minimize the woman's role in procreation in all its breathtaking unreasonableness: "Not the true parent is the woman's womb/That bears the child; she doth but nurse the seed/New-sown: the male is parent; she for him/As stranger for a stranger, hoards the gem/Of life, unless the god its promise blight." —One of the mysteries of Dionysus was that he was his own father, self created and reborn. These myths being early accounts or explanations manifested in the initiation rites of young boys into the surrogate motherhood of the male fraternity.

Dionysus of course was a woman because he remained the son. The Mother and the Son still being the One. The Dionysian solution was narcissistic homosexual indulgence and the insanity of mergence with the mother rather than the Apollonian distance of mastery and control. Sex antagonism is obliterated in the madness of (re)incorporation. Dionysus is a figure at the crossroads. Behind her lay the great matriarchies, before her the embattled patriarchy. The gods Herakles and Apollo and Perseus and Pentheus and Theseus etc., and the mythological figures of Orestes, Oedipus, etc., represent the various singular and compounded solutions to the fear, awe, and contempt of women that preceded and/or accompanied the patriarchal revolution. The solutions we well know were rape, abduction, murder, incest, enslavement, prostitution and marriage. The nuclear family. The female goddesses and figures of mythology represent the types of resistance and cooperation in the downfall of women. The Great Mothers, like Hera, held their own, but their daughters, like Hebe, were under siege. The sacrifice of Iphigenia by her father Agamemnon was the cause of Clytemnestra's wrath. The cooperation of Electra in her brother's murder of their mother was a man's story. The culminating mother-daughter myth in the Greek gamut was Demeter-Kore, or Persephone, which may be seen as the great compromise before the fall. The rape of Persephone and her abduction to the underworld by Pluto, or Hades, is analagous to the murder of Iphigenia by Agamemnon. The barrenness over the land caused by the mother Demeter in response to the abduction of her daughter represents the real power that the woman once held exclusively in the world of mother-right or matriarchy. The abduction graphically illustrates the new patriarchal regime. The compromise whereby Persephone was permitted to return to her mother some part of the year represents the intermediary state between mother-right and father-right. Demeter was the goddess who governs the fruits of the earth. In this myth she retains the power to yield or to withhold her fruits by traditional privilege of women still in control of the disposition of her own body. The reunion of Demeter and her daughter is the occasion of the earth emerging in its annual spring bloom. A rite of death and resurrection. A variation of the Dionysian and Christian celebrations of sacrifice and new life. Jesus ascends to the Father. Persephone to her Mother. An understanding of the Demeter-Persephone myth for modern western women seems extremely important to the recovery of the feminine principle. The heroic warrior-maidens are the most obvious models of inspiration and there are lessons in all their stories: the collaborator Athene, the competitor Atalanta, the independent but pursued Diana & Daphne figures, the man hating Deianeira, the successful Agave and Artemis. All aspects of one figure. The besieged female. The female at that stroboscopic arrest in history struggling to resist the moment of her coercion. Especially the militant virgins who refused to cooperate with the gods and championed their sisters. These are the metatypes of the extinct Amazon tribes, who constitute the only historical models of a pure feminist society that we know of. The psychological archetype of feminine reintegration appears in the Demeter-Persephone myth. The loss of the daughter to the father is the lamented transition from matriarchy to patriarchy in which the mother-daughter became estranged from herself in service to her captor and legislator. Doesn't every mother cry at her daughter's wedding? Isn't every mother-in-law a nuisance to her daughter's husband? The reunion of the mother and daughter constitutes the essence of the Eleusinian Mysteries of classical Greece. Persephone is the primordial virgin. Her return to her mother is the return to the mother of her primordial maidenhood, her intactness, her inviolate integrity as woman or total being. The anima of a woman is her own special ancestral soul identity. The maintenance or the recovery of that state is what Jung meant by "individuation" as distinct from the woman in relation to man—the *femme a homme*—the woman whose identity is defined by the man—the generalized state of woman all over the world in this her final state of dependence and degradation. Although Joan of Arc was a kind of Athene in her mission to assist the man, I believe she was more basically a young woman in flight from the man. For a medieval girl she was very bold in flatly refusing to marry the boy or man who claimed she was promised to him. One can read her exploits at the substratum of archetypal psychology as a militant defense of her own virginity. Her credibility at the outset depended on her purity, and all along the way she maintained this inviolability by her attitude, her armor, her appeals to the sanctity of her mission through God & Church, her contempt for the women who followed the soldiers, her physical repulsion of the English when they attempted to molest her in gaol and so forth. Joan was a militant virgin par excellence. I don't think she saw the Dauphin as a man in any ordinary sense. Rather he was a Divine King, the representative of God on earth. Possibly the psychology of her mission would include the objective of His continued protection of her purity once she had established full credibility as his Savior. An impossible mission for a girl. If the French didn't get her, the English would. There must have been so many like Joan, unknown and uncelebrated. Church and State double binded every young girl. Demanding both virginity and motherhood. Joan's "vision" can be interpreted as her fight from two contradictory commands. A not uncommon solution today as yesterday. These commands are profoundly internalized and reach far back into the primeval history of the species. The split occurs somewhere in the past where motherhood means any loss of autonomy for the woman. I presume that before this split, before the man became invader and captor and legitimized this position through the patriarchy, that virginity and motherhood were not contradictory states. The original birth, in other words, was virgin. Or parthenogenetic. Joan, through her vision or insanity, correctly understood her original self perpetuating unity. Her militant posture was a defense against the civilized male who would usurp her identity. By 1430 apparently no woman was capable of maintaining her integrity without the most absurd heroic individualism concluded by sacrifice and martyrdom. "You can take me but only dead." A one woman revolution. We are living now in a time of the "reconstructed virgins." Originally, the great life mothers were all moon women. "All of them remained virgins, which was to say *unmarried, not chaste.*" (Diner, 16) Before the patriarchal revolution the dependence of the female on the male for impregnation to reproduce herself, if such was actually the case, never seriously impaired her rights to her own destiny. The characteristics of the matriarchies were the inheritance of name and property through the female and the relative non-status of the father as an outsider and a preference for female children to continue the line and the woman's completely free disposition over her own body. The early civilizations of the matriarchies surely emerged out of a once purer state in which the human species was unisexual—male and female combined in one self-perpetuating female body. "Geneticists and physiologists say that the Y chromosome that produces males is a deformed and broken X chromosome —the female chromosome. All women have two X chromosomes, while the male has one X derived from his mother and one Y from his father." Davis postulates that "this small and twisted Y chromosome is a genetic error—an accident of nature, and that originally there was only one sex—the female." The clue to woman as prime creature is in the fact that all men start off as females. (Davis, 34) If indeed the man is a late mutation from an original female creature, the ancient social development from matriarchy to patriarchy that is now becoming clear to us should make the present feminist revolution a comprehensible instinctive reaction formation in the evolutionary design for (re)integration. Man and his destructive culture in the name of progress has reached its outer limit of potential genocide. The man remains incapable of tolerating his position as a biological "outsider." His subjugation of the Great Mother and his persistent fratricide and patricide are all manifestations of an apparently intolerable insecurity and instability apart from the source of his origin and continuation. A man apart from women is not altogether a man, and must continually "prove" his identity negatively—by stressing what he is not. "The woman holds her soul within herself (she can see the child emerge from her own body). Who impregnates her is of little importance, she need not guess whether something of herself continues on in a new organism . . . the soul of the man resides *outside* himself—as men have been lamenting for centuries, his immortality is out of his own control. Not only must a woman bear his child, but he cannot know for certain whether the child she bears is his own." (Slater, 234) The present urgent project of women is to reestablish harmony in the world by reclaiming the social prerogative which is in agreement with her natural biological position as parent prime. The male has discovered the technological means of his extinction. The female must seize the initiative for the completion of her natural evolution back towards her self perpetuating unity before she is swept along with the male in his (unconscious) efforts to abort the project. Every woman can and does enact with her own body the double role of the child and the mother. The male element is essentially mortal, the female essentially indestructible. The massive phallic structure of Culture is man's frantic effort to perpetuate himself in stone, in memorials and monuments testifying to his Deeds. A deed is a contract for real estate. A deed is a performance and a contract with the same objective: immortality through conquest in default of the basic equipment for just *being* immortal. The man does, the woman is. The man, however, does in the faustian sense of restless incompletion. The woman does in the profound sense of *being* already what she does. To say now merely that the woman *is* is to call up the unfortunate cultural image of the passive inert woman to whom something is done. The pedestal woman. The woman in reality is the ultimate actor. The virgin birth is still a natural occurrence.

"Virgin conception reaches far into our animal ancestry as parthenogenesis, through epochs incomparably longer than those that have passed since its termination and more: The original female in the animal species not only reproduces herself but also is the sole creatress of the male; the male never is anything without the female . . . Asexual reproduction by females, parthenogenesis, is not only possible but it still occurs here and there in the modern world, perhaps as an atavistic survival of the once *only* means of reproduction in an all female world. Since the discovery of the proof of parthenogenesis by Jacques Loeb in 1911, 'it has been known that the male is not necessary for reproduction, and that a simple physicochemical agent in the female is enough to bring it about.' " (Diner, 4, 34-35) The order of the day for all women immediately is *psychic* parthenogenesis. Women are experiencing their own rebirth through their fugitive collective enterprises of consciousness raising groups, writings and research into our history, role model identification, anarchic political structurings, mirror imaging primarily through the supreme experience of lesbian unification. The inspiration of historical models provides authenticity to the contemporary struggle. Although myth and legend are the true stuff of history, there is a way in which materials as historical evidence are discredited through the implicit condemnation of them as *merely* legendary or *merely* mythical. Certainly it was by this implication, myth as harmless fabrication, that I never thought Amazons really existed. In any case the word was always a pejorative. To be called an Amazon was to be impugned as a "real woman." Nobody ever called you an Amazon. An Amazon is big and tough and not nice. No tactful person would say you were an Amazon. Now I look around me and pick out the women of the revolution—the Amazons. The Amazons were real. Amazons live! Lesbian nation is amazon culture. The extremist intermediary state in the transition back to the matriarchies. There were a number of Amazon tribal cultures at a critical juncture in history. "The tradition of the Amazons is established before Homer, for whom they inhabit the Sangarios area (Iliad, iii, 184) and Lycia (Iliad, vi, 181), but already there is a trace of the Amazon foundation legends of Aeolis in the mention of the tomb of Myrine in the Troad (Iliad, ii, 811). These warrior women, in my opinion, belong to the stories of the strange folk who dwell at the edge of the known world, and though perhaps misunderstandings of native customs may have shaped parts of the story, no attempt to identify them with any particular people, Cimmerians, hairless Mongols, seems to me to have succeeded. . . . The original habitat of the Amazons was pushed further east with the advance of Greek geographical knowledge. It became established doctrine that their home was at Themiskyra on the Thermodon. Then the eastern end of Pontus became familiar ground to the Greeks, and it became necessary to explain why Amazons were no longer to be found there. This gave rise to the second great Amazon cycle, the Amazon expedition of Herakles. . . . Before Alexander there are three great cycles of Amazon legends: 1) Post-Homeric epic, particularly Arctinus, developed the Homeric mention of Amazons into the story of the participation of Penthesilea and her Amazons as allies of Priam in the Trojan War. With this were usually associated the Amazon foundation legends of Aeolis and Ionia. Myrine, Kyme, Gryneia, Pitane, Mytilene, Smyrna, Anaia, Pygela, Latoreia, and in one version Ephesus, were all Amazon foundations. 2) The Amazon expedition of Herakles, somewhere about the time of the colonization of the Black Sea coast. 3) The story of Theseus and the Amazons." (W. R. Halliday, *Plutarch's Greek Questions*) The story of Theseus and the Amazons may be the best known tale concerning these independent women. Plutarch commented on Theseus: ". . . he seemed to resemble Romulus in many particulars. Both of them born out of wedlock and of uncertain parentage, had the repute of being sprung from the gods. Both of them united with strength of body an equal vigor of mind; and of the

two most famous cities in the world, the one built Rome, the
other made Athens be inhabited. *Both stand charged with the
rape of women"* (my italics). In Plutarch's account of the tale
. . . "Theseus made the voyage . . . with a navy under his command, and took the Amazon (Antiope) prisoner . . . to take
her, he had to use deceit and fly away; for the Amazons . . .
were so far from avoiding Theseus when he touched upon their
coasts, that they sent him presents to his ship; but he, having
invited Antiope, who brought them, to come aboard, immediately
set sail and carried her away. This was the cause and origin of
the Amazonian invasion of Attica which would seem to have
been no slight womanish enterprise. For it is impossible that they
should have placed their camp in the very city, and joined battle
close by the Pnyx and the hill called Museum, unless, having
first conquered the country around about, they had thus with
impunity advanced to the city. That they made so long a journey
by land, and passed the Cimmerian Bosphorous, then frozen,
as Hellanicus writes, is difficult to be believed. That they en-
camped all but in the city is certain, and may be sufficiently confirmed by the names that the places here about yet retain, and
the graves and monuments of those that fell in the battle. Both
armies being in sight, there was a long pause and doubt on each
side which should give the first onset; at last Theseus, in obedi-
ence to the command of an oracle he had received, gave them
battle . . . the Athenians were routed, and gave way before the
women, but fresh supplies coming in from the paladium, Ardet-
tus, and the Lyceum, they charged their right wing, and beat
them back into their tents, in which action a great number of the
Amazons were slain. At length, after four months, a peace was
concluded between them by the mediation of Hippolyta . . ."—It
has come down to us that the Amazons were warrior tribes akin to
head hunting cannibals. Undoubtedly they were well trained in the
arts of defense and attack. It is unlikely, however, that they were
aggressive just for the hell of it. There are no such stories in any

case. Greek male legends of Amazons invariably involve rape and the women's retaliation. They resisted invasion and took revenge against crimes of abduction. No doubt they were constantly on the defensive and were superbly trained as a result. According to one Emanuel Kanter, in *Amazons, a Marxian Study* (1926), "it is from the disruptions of primitive communist tribes which are on the point of becoming patriarchal in character, either through internal or external economic and military pressure, that they arise. So that women warriors must appear under special conditions for them to be considered Amazons." Amazons were fugitive matriarchies. Clearly the matriarchies were under siege and large numbers of women removed themselves from the immediate sites of their dissolution under pressure from the males to usurp their matriarchal prerogatives and formed independent exclusive communities. Certain so-called Amazon tribes fighting in men's wars are tales co-opted by male history. If women's tribes really did fight alongside men they were not true Amazons but more likely anachronistic matriarchal cells. (Contemporary Irish women fighters an example.) There is the well known story of the triumphant conquest of the East by Dionysus, who in one version of the story was assisted in his conquest by a tribe of Amazons "on the analogy of the women votaries who successfully resisted attempts at state repression by Pentheus and his congeners when Dionysus first invaded Greece." (W. R. Halliday, *Plutarch's Greek Questions*) The Amazon solution was an extreme reaction to the violent physical coercion of women that was apparently the prime mode of change in the patriarchal revolution. It is still in fact the means by which males control women, even in its so-called civilized forms of courtship and romance. We can surmise that the Amazons thrived quite happily apart from the male oppressor. Lesbianism among Amazons was entirely suppressed in male history of pre-historical phenomena. *Time* recently reported findings of Amazon tribes in South America, mentioning that certain symbols "positioned side by side" suggested lesbianism. Male history aside, as Plutarch noted long ago, it is not to be wondered at that in events of such antiquity, history should be in disorder. Nonetheless, we know our history in our cell memories. Any proud contemporary lesbian would scoff at the idea that these independent tribes of women did not enjoy each other apart from their well known annual custom of descending on a male tribe for purposes of reproductive copulation. These were women identified women who slaughtered their male children or sent them back to the men, and kept their females to bring them up in their own image. More than likely they enjoyed the full benefits of their autonomy including the supreme satisfactions of lesbian sexuality. In the Amazon society there is no struggle to maintain mother-right, except to resist invasion from the foreigner. The society *is* by its nature a mother-right society. It turns around on itself in its own image. A society without fathers brothers or sons. The intruder has been totally removed. All beings without fathers are sacred. Having no beginnings, no origins. All male saviors, heroes, founders of cities and religions, have claimed to be without father born. "There is a general and primordial belief in parthenogenesis and in the excellence of such an origin. It is greatly valued by all those who would excel: saviors, heroes, gods, demigods, ancestors, kings, and magi. Buddha and Quetzalcoatl, Huizipochli and Plato, Montezuma and Genghis Khan claimed to have been born of virgins. The ainus of Japan, the tribes of central Asia, Chinese philosophers, Siamese demigods, Indian (American) heroes, and Tibetan prophets—they all want to be considered the products solely of their mothers and disclaim any bodily fathers." (Diner, 6) The anomalous explanations of birth concocted in the stories of Eve and Athene were desperate theological expedients to rid women of their matriarchal condition and demote them from their ancient position as chiefs of the immortals and creators of the races of Greeks and Semites. Athene was the patron deity of Athens. After the invention of the tale of her birth from the head of Zeus she was converted into a "man's woman"—a traitor to her sex. Athene cast her vote for Orestes. The present feminist revolution is a battle not only to wrest control from the men but to confront the women ourselves with the spectacle of our collaboration with the men in maintaining our helpless position. The tool of revolution is consciousness. In the course of time we all became Athenes and Joans. When we do our historical research we first realize that the myths were male creations expressing the psychology of the male who perpetrated his needs through his stories in influencing the transition to the patriarchies. If Athene betrayed us in the Eumenides, she was made to do so by the man. A few decades ago Otto Rank wrote a very impressive essay "The Myth of the Birth of the Hero." Central to all the stories of these heroes was the virgin birth. Rank collected the common characteristics of the tales and then made a Freudian analysis relating the myths to the fantasies of children. He concluded that both phenomena represented the growing dissatisfaction and disillusionment of the child with his real parents out of which a neurotic fantasy of a second set of parents is created. The royal couple and the peasant couple. The subjects of so many fairy tales. The child imagines that his "real parents" are not really his parents and that he was royally born and he develops the heroic project of returning to his real or royal parents, who correspond to the omnipotent and perfect parents of the infantile conception, before disillusionment (or parental restraint). That's a simple breakdown of Rank's conclusion. Apparently Rank was not in a position to comprehend his own significant data from the vantage point of the battle for parental primacy. His child is a boy. The boy grows up to be all those wandering knights in search of the grail and the dragon and the princess. The boy also grows up to be all those mad Kings who lock up their daughters from the attentions of those wandering suitors. What are these boys after? What is the significance of the virgin birth? The denial of the real parents. The exalting of the fantasy parents. The primary

questions: Who is my real father, and Who is my real mother—
these are the ultimate political questions. Mother-right and
father-right. Why did those Kings lock up their daughters in response to all those oracles proclaiming the return of a son or a
grandson who would depose him? Why a son or a grandson? I
didn't know myself when I read the important Rank essay. But
again it seems many of these tales represented the transitional
state from matriarchy to patriarchy. Here is Rank: "He (the
father) locks her up in some inaccessible spot, so as to safeguard
her virginity (Perseus, Gilgamesh, Telephus, Romulus), and
when his command is disobeyed he pursues the daughter and
her offspring with insatiable hatred. However, the unconscious
sexual motives of his hostile attitude, which is later on avenged
by his grandson, render it evident that again the hero kills in him
simply the man who is trying to rob him of the love of his
mother; namely, the father." (p. 84) Here is Elizabeth Gould
Davis: "King Acrisius of Argos . . . to prevent his daughter
Danae from marrying and depriving him of the throne he had
acquired through marriage to the queen, had Danae incarcerated
in a bronze tower." The real significance of the tale is "the absolute right of the daughter to inherit the throne and the machina-
tions perpetrated by her male relatives to deprive her of this
right." (p. 185) The return of the boy to claim the rights to the
mother, the daughter. Love and Sex and Position, or Property,
seem to mean the same thing. The virgin birth is a repudiation of
the father as well as a device or a wish for perpetuating the
guardianship of the older male. In the earlier virgin birth the
woman is the active principle. In the later, or immaculate conception, she is the passive receptacle for the god. A way of re-
pudiating the mother. To claim his rights the male must kill off
himself, the father, and he must also murder the mother, i.e.,
Orestes. That's a picture of the world as it is. Imminent genocide.
The daughters of the 20th century are reasserting their rights to
themselves. The daughters are the self perpetuating unities.

Their claims to the thrones are the claims to their own self reproducing bodies. The thrones are those seats of the king's estate or dignity. The woman's accession to the throne will mean the Rulership of her own estate and dignity or body. The restoration of the holy temple of her body. The daughters were the original saviors or children born without fathers. My mother was a Vestal, my father I knew not. By the matriarchate I mean in all cases a form of woman power, historically and futuristically, not necessarily akin at all the patriarchy in its domination of one sex by another; I do mean that form of society in which women have complete control over their own bodies, destinies and produce. That, I believe, was a society consisting primarily of mothers, daughters and sons, a society in which the adult male was not admitted under conditions of power accruing to males in the sense of dominating the policies and decisions in the political life of the community.

> Throughout the ancient world the ram became the symbol of patriarchy, just as the bull was that of matriarchy. It is a curious fact that according to astrology the age of the bull, the Taurian Age, coincided historically with the last two thousand years of the gynarchates—4000 to 2000 B.C., while the Arian Age, the age of Aries the ram, coincided with the age that immediately preceded the Christian era, the time of the patriarchal revolution. The Piscean Age, the age of the fish, embraced the Christian era, the two-thousand-year period from which we are just now emerging, and it is therefore appropriate that the fish became the symbol of Christianity.
>
> The Aquarian Age, upon whose threshold we now stand, will be "inimical to man," as Macrobius prophesied in the early days of the Piscean Age. The "new morality" of the Aquarian youth of our day perhaps bespeaks a return to matriarchal mores too long suppressed by the materialistic patriarchal values that

have prevailed for the past two thousand years in the Occidental world. The Aquarian Age of the next two thousand years will see an end to patriarchal Christianity and a return to goddess worship and to the peaceful social progress that distinguished the Taurian Age of four millennia ago. (Elizabeth Gould Davis, 134, 353)

On a Clear Day You Can See Your Mother

Some old lines and some new ones thrown on to each other for the Town Hall affair

The title of this episode is new approach: All women are lesbians except those who don't know it naturally they are but don't know it yet I am a woman who is a lesbian because I am a woman and a woman who loves herself naturally who is other women is a lesbian a woman who loves women loves herself naturally this is the case that a woman is herself is all woman is a natural born lesbian so we don't mind using the name like any name it is quite meaningless it means naturely I am a woman and whatever I am we are we affirm being what we are the way of course all men are homosexuals being having a more sense of their homo their homo-ness their ecce homo-ness their ecce prince & lord & masterness the 350 years of Abraham intersample Abraham lived for 350 years because the bible ages are only a succession of sons and fathers and grandfathers intensely identifying with their ancestors their son so identified naturely with the father that he believed he was the father and of course he was as was Abraham and Isaac and Jacob and Esau and Reuben and Simeon and Levi and Judah and Joseph each one lived for 350 years, but who are the daughters of Rachel and Ruth and Sarah and Rebekah the rest we do not know the daughters never had any daughters they had only sons who begat more sons and sons so we have very little sense, from that particular book, of the lineage and ligaments and legacies and identities of mothers and daughters and their daughters and their mothers and mothers and daughters and sisters who were naturally not lesbians if they had nothing of each other save sons so now we must say Verily Verily, I say unto thee, except a woman be born again she cannot see the Kingdom of Goddess a woman must be born again to be herself her own eminence and grace the queen queen-self whose mother has pressed upon her mouth innumerable passionate kisses so sigh us . . . . There is in every perfect love/A law to be accomplished too: that the lover should resemble/The belov'd: And be the same. And the greater is the likeness/Brighter will the rapture flame—even as John there St. John of the Cross raptured on his pal Jesus whose son he was his father his son as when Jesus in another time said to his lovers and haven't you heard it a deluge of times And he saith unto them, Follow me, and I will make you fishers of men. And straightway they left their nets, and followed him. Ah lover and perfect equal! I meant that you should discover me so, by my faint indirection; And I, when I meet you, mean to discover you by the like in you . . . I want she who is the tomboy in me . . . I want she who is very female in me . . . I want she who is British about me . . . I want she who is ugly American about me . . . I want she who is mayonnaise about me . . . I want she who is the cunt and the balls and the breasts of me and the long straight browny hair and the gangly boarding school adolescent in a navy blue blazer and gold buttons of me . . . narcissme, qui consiste a se choisir soi-meme comme objet erotique . . . and I want the men to carry my boxes of books for me and carry me upsy daily pigback and pay for me everywhere and adore me as a lesberated woman . . . Over the inevitable we shall not grieve . . . This is the body that Jill built . . . Ecce Leda the Lesbian . . . Ecce Greta the Gay the gay Gertrude the gay gay gayness of being gay, of being, to be equal

we have to become who we really are and women we will never
be equal women until we love one another women and say Woe,
and behold, a voice from Hera saying This is my beloved daughter in whom I am well pleased O Women of America the World
you are your own best friend, your own closest friend, you are
the best company for yourself . . . you should go through and
study even right back to your childhood, and of course if you
have the great ability to go back to your previous lives you
should do so Women of America the World you are your own
best friend . . . These are the series of sayings we are saving
the world with: the lamentations of Mary and Marilyn Monroe.
Lord help you, Maria, full of grease, the load is with me! Her
smile is between her legs and her moustache is in her armpit and
she ordered that history should begin with her with her this is a
muster of elephental cuntsequence the lost and foundamental
situation of the feminine is the primordial relation of identity between mother and daughter the mysteries of Eleusis of the reunion of Demeter and her daughter Persephone to be born again
and again and Arethusa and Artemis and Hebe and Hera and
Diana and Daphne and Doris and Dora and Dolly and the Da-
naides all but one murdered their husbands on their wedding
nights our case revives their stories for more than a hundred years
I wander about in it without coming to the end of her body the
most we can do is to dream the myth onwards, and rewrite the
stories we will reunite Electra and her mother Clytemnestra and
Jocasta will be well pleased in her daughter Antigone who will be
more involved in her mothers and her daughters than in the
proper burial for her brother and we will remember the histories
of say how Eleanor of Aquitaine made a crusade to the holy land
and dressed all her ladies in waiting as Amazons in leopard skins
and dressed herself as Pan Athenea and that's how they rode
through Greece for the queendom of heaven *is* as a woman travelling into a far country who called her own servants and delivered unto them *her* goods for Whole the World to see a woman

finds pleasure in caressing a body whose secrets she knows, her own body giving her the clue to its preferences giving each the other their sense of self tracing the body of the woman whose fingers in turn trace her body that the miracle of the mirror be accomplished between women love is contemplative caresses are intended less to gain possession of the other than gradually to recreate the self thru her own self among the women and the women the multitude on the way to the way the world was before it began it is now the world is heading definitely toward a matriarchy more often to return to the source of things we must travel in the opposite direction, Wring out the clothes! Wring in the dew! Before all the King's Hoarsers with all the Queens Mum Her birth is uncontrollable and her organ is working perfectly and there's a part that's not screwed on and her education is now for by and about women and presided over by woman All women are lesbians except those who don't know it of course since whereas both sexes (even as Sigmund sd) are originally more attached to the mother and it is the *task* of the girl to transfer this attachment to the father naturally they we are but don't know it yet that woman is now approaching her ancient destiny as woman I am and therefore lesbian which means nothing we could say it over and over again over lesbianlesbianlesbianles-bianlesbianlesbianlesbianlesbian—Special from the White House, the President of the United States announced last night the appointment of a lesbian to his cabinet . . . it's nice if you can invite them in, they usually come in without knocking . . . Womens lib and let lib new official position on lesbians: Hey ladies it's okay, like Red China is there so we might as well recognize it . . . yupyop . . . Liberal Schmiberal . . . Maybe . . . uh . . . we should invite . . . uh . . . her . . . uh . . . one of them to dinner . . . One of what, dear? Uh, well, uh, she is a bit odd isn't she? I mean, you know how we'd feel if a black man was interested in our daughter—Aaaaaaaaaaaaa. . . . Oh god, and she might make a pass at my wife . . . Agh . . . But if she just

doesn't *talk* about what she is . . . We could pretend . . .
Whaddyou say to the naked lady please please sorry thank you
we are getting to the bottom of women's lib we are going down
on women's lib I am beside myself with love for you when you
are beside me my love the beginning of the unifirst is rite now if
all tinks are at this momentum being cremated and the end of the
unihearse is right now for all thinks are at this momentus passing away we went to see the Dairy of a Skinzopretty girl O why
dint her mother straighten out her teeth when she was young O
she is envolved in many strange and wondrous adventures O in
short she had come into that abnormal condition known as elation O she did not yet love and she loved to love; she sought
what she might love, in love with loving . . . O what can she
say now that is not the story of so many others O do not fail me
she says you are my last chance, indeed our last chance, to save
the West . . . and who vants the Moon ven ve can land on
Venus . . . and O how would you like to be the heroine of yr
own life story (she's looking forward to it extremely) and O don't
be nervous be mermaid be she whom I love who travels with
me and sits along while holding me by the hand she ahold of my
hand has completely satisfied me o natural woman woman vimmin virmin woreman woeman of America the World until until
women all the women see in each other the possibility of a primal commitment which includes sexual love they will be denying
themselves the love and value they have readily accorded to men,
thus affirming their second class status for within the heterosexual
institution no woman can be the equal it is a contrafiction in
terms the heterosexual institution is a male institution a homo ecce
homo institution and you can't ever change the absoluteness the
institution is political is built out of the institutionalized slavery of
women so it *is* a contradiction in terms—such an institution must
only collapse of its own accord from within the heterosexual institution is over spiritually over and the new thing now that is happening is the withdrawal of women to give each other their own

sense of self a new sense of self until women see in each other the possibility of a primal commitment which includes sexual love they will be denying themselves the love and value they readily accord to men thus affirming their second class status. *Until all women are lesbians there will be no true political revolution* until in other same words we are woman I am a woman who loves herself naturally who is other women is a lesbian a woman who loves women loves herself naturally this is the case that a woman is herself is all woman is a natural born lesbian so we don't mind using the name it means naturely I am a woman and whatever I am we are we affirm being what we are saying therefore *Until all women are lesbians there will be no true political revolution* meaning the terminus of the heterosexual institution through the recollection by woman of her womanhood her own grace and eminence by the intense identities of our ancestors our descendants of the mothers and the daughters and the grandmothers we become who we are which is to say we become our own identities and autonomies even as now we are so but except those who don't know it yet will be quite upset about it for some time to come as I would more properly be as majorities would have it leaning on my sword describing my defeat some women want to have their cock and eat it too and lesbian is a label invented by anybody to throw at any woman who dares to be a man's equal and lesbian is a good name it means nothig of course or everythig so we don't mind using the name in face we like it for we can be proud to claim allusion to the island made famous by Sappho the birds are talking to us in Greek again and continue on making a big thing out of it over all these centuries time we can do that we don't mind it's nice in fact for we all all of us women are lesbians why not and isn't it wonderful what a lot of devotion there is to us lying around the universe especially to those all envolved in some penis they're wrapping their cunts around. . . . Oh well . . . Lillian over and out . . . he sd I want your body and she sd you can have it when I'm through with it . . . Keep yer hands off me you worldwide weirdo, I just want to be noticed, not attacked—we had a big argonaut about it . . . The age of shrivelry is abonus again . . . A Lord was not considered defeated in a local war until his flag had fallen from the main tower of his castle . . . svastickles falling outen da sky . . . the current dispute would be settled if the central figure was no longer present (*at this moment our leader Norman Mailer akst me to read my last line and I said I'd like to forego the question and my friends appeared on stage and I made love before notables and my circuitry got overloaded and the men in the audience voted they dint want to hear me no more and I don't remember too much except leaving and wishing later I'd kissed Germaine before we walked off*) . . . Flash from the White House: last night the President of the United States, clad only in a scanty tribal costume, announced the resignation of the American Government . . . His life was an empty record of gambling cockfighting titting balls and masques vimmin and vine clothes . . . Better latent than never . . . aliquem alium interum . . . there's no such thing as sexual differentiation in the spiritual nature of wo(man) . . . This is the problem passion play of the millentury . . . O this Restoration Comedy—it's going to be a beautiful reunion . . . plunderpussy and all spoiled goods going into her nabsack and some heroine women in wings of Samothrace . . . Is it to drown her passengers that you have bored a hole in her? Rubbish, what bunkum these people talk . . . Events are preshipitaking themselves in the harpiest confusion . . . cunnilinguist . . . Listen. If you recognized an aspect of yourself that you love in these ancient new womens heads I too have recognized an admirable aspect of myself in your willingness to be as beautiful as you are who you are My mother was a vestal, my father I knew not no prince nor lord nor master-ness but the nipples and navels of the whirld a wonderwoman the mothers and the daughters and the great grandmothers and daughters of Rachel and Ruth and Sarah and Rebekah the rest we will know now the daughter the mothers and sisters will have daughters who beget daughters so we will more sense, from this time, of the lineage and ligaments and legacies and identities of our mothers and daughters and their mothers and mothers and daughters and sisters who are naturally of course lesbians if they have of each other and saying Verily Verily except a woman must be born again she cannot see the Queendom of Goddess a woman must be born again to be herself her own eminence and grace the queen queenself whose mother has pressed upon her mouth innumerable passionate kisses . . . Sail away where the wind blows sweet . . . and take a sister by her hand . . . Lead her far from this barren land . . . ON A CLEAR DAY YOU CAN SEE YOUR MOTHER.

CONCLUSION

Within just two years the meaning of the word lesbian has changed from private subversive activity to political revolutionary identity. Although sexual relations between people remain a private affair for the most part in the actual doing of it it is now recognized that your choice of mate or mates is a political choice. It just isn't possible any more to overlook the feminist analysis of the heterosexist institution by which women are oppressed. The new definition of the lesbian emerges from this analysis. The choice of mate can no longer be regarded as a purely personal one. Until now all women and men have been coerced by social conditioning of the established heterosexual institution to choose each other. Choice has been further limited by class and race. What choice there is left over for, say, a particular woman, is for a particular man within her class and race, and of course the man traditionally is less limited in his choice through his social prerogative as the aggressor. Although within this system exceptional women may receive special treatment from exceptional men, we know now that women, defined as a class, suffer from their secondary status under the laws and customs and psychology of this institution. This choice then benefits the man and not the woman. The purpose of feminist analysis is to provide women with an awareness of their servitude *as a class* so that they can unite and rise up against it. The problem now for strictly heterosexually conditioned women is how to obtain the sexual gratification they think they need from the sex who remains their *institutional* oppressor. Many feminists are now stranded between their personal needs and their political persuasions. The lesbian is the woman obviously who unites the personal and the political in the struggle to free ourselves from the oppressive institution. I think it is generally acknowledged that the conditioning is so deep that there is practically no man in any case who transcends the supremacist psychology of his class. The lesbian argument is first and foremost withdrawal at every level from the man to develop woman supremacy, which does not necessarily mean the diminution of the man the way male supremacy has meant the diminution of women as though one can't be up without the other being down, but it does mean the (re)-development of the moral physical spiritual intellectual strengths of women whatever the social consequences of that may be.

Proceeding from the premise that women are oppressed by the heterosexual institution, that women are an oppressed class, that from this point of view the man has become (if he was not always) the natural enemy of women, it follows that the continued collusion of any woman with any man is an event that retards the progress of woman supremacy. The continued economic dependence of women upon men, both individually and through the social institutions, is perhaps the central concrete factor holding back the liberation of women, the psychic aspects of liberation being held in check by the power of men to threaten survival. The self sufficiency of women in the end will have to mean much more than any apparent individual solution to the problem. We remain fugitives.

It is the banding together of fugitives which constitutes the phenomenon of revolutionary opposition. Ti-Grace Atkinson has said "It is the association by choice of individual members of any Oppressed group, the massing of power, which is essential to resistance. It is the commitment of individuals to common goals, and to death if necessary, that determines the strength of an army. In war, even political warfare, there is no distinction between the political and the personal. (Can you imagine a Frenchman serving in the French army from 9 to 5, then trotting 'home' to Germany for supper and overnight? That's called game-playing, or collaboration, not political commitment.) It is this commitment, by choice, full-time, of one woman to others of her class that is called lesbianism. It is this full commitment, against any and all personal considerations if necessary, that constitutes the political significance of lesbianism." Atkinson correctly placed the lesbian as that tiny minority within the Oppressed who refused to play out its proper political function in society. As such the lesbian or "this minority is labeled by those in power, the Oppressor, as the 'criminal' element." When the criminal element is politicized it becomes a revolutionary force. Black men in jail have defined themselves as political prisoners. Lesbians are defining themselves as political outcasts and as such constitute a political group legitimate by its own creation and challenging by its very existence if not by any overt action the exclusive political dominion of the heterosexual institution by which women are maintained as the subservient caste. By this definition lesbians are in the vanguard of the resistance. If driven back from a position as a group with political consciousness the lesbian would become again a private suffering fugitive, or criminal, or sick person by the psychiatric terminology, and permitted to exist only under the old conspiracy of silence.

Historically the lesbian had two choices: being criminal or going straight. The present revolutionary project is the creation of a legitimate state defined by women. Only women can do this. Going straight is legitimizing your oppression. As was being criminal. A male society will not permit any other choice for a woman. The women therefore can't expect anything from the

men except token concessions and class privilege. The totally
woman committed woman, or lesbian, who shares this consciousness with other women, is the political nucleus of a woman's or
lesbian state—a state that women cannot achieve by demand
from the male bastion but only from within from exclusive
woman strength building its own institutions of self support and
identity.

The word lesbian has expanded so much through political definition that it should no longer refer exclusively to a woman
simply in sexual relation to another woman. The word has in fact
had pornographic implications, as though a lesbian was a woman
who did nothing but enjoy sex, an implication employed as a tool
of discrimination. The word is now a generic term signifying ac-
tivism and resistance and the envisioned goal of a woman committed state. And in such a state a woman or lesbian will also be
free to reproduce herself as she pleases, that is on her own terms
in a woman supportive environment in which the child has a
legal identity derived from its mother, still the only clear parent.
The essence of the new political definition is peer grouping.
Women and men are not peers and many people seriously doubt
whether we ever were or if we ever could be. The male remains
the biological aggressor and as such especially predisposed to take
cultural-political advantage of the woman. It is against this advantage that feminism deploys itself. The psychology of male
supremacy emerged of course from the cultural institutions of
oppression by which women more and more internalized the political reality of their status to believe in their own innate inferiority. It is extremely difficult for women to think back or ahead
to a condition that pre- or postdates the artificial realities of social constructs. One thing we can be certain of however and that
is that women en masse are peers and as such equals. Lesbians
know this better than any other women. We also know how to
achieve a certain illusory equality with the man by playing his

game and being taken in as a special or token woman who performs various functions for the man, like assuaging his guilt, or making woman as a class think that if one woman can do it all women can and thus reinforcing both the woman's sense of inferiority, insomuch as only a few make it through, and her notion of herself as a *person*, not politically classified. It is perhaps our mistrust of the man as the biological aggressor which keeps bringing us back to the political necessity of power by peer grouping. Although we are still virtually powerless it is only by constantly adhering to this difficult principle of the power inherent in natural peers (men after all have demonstrated the success of this principle very well) that women will eventually achieve an autonomous existence.

BIBLIOGRAPHY

Aldington, Richard, ed., *Oscar Wilde*. New York, Viking, 1946.

Altman, Dennis, *Homosexual Oppression and Liberation*. New York, Outerbridge & Dienstfrey, 1971.

Bachofen, J. J., *Myth, Religion and Mother Right*. Princeton, N.J., Princeton University Press, 1967.

Becker, Raymond, *The Other Face of Love*, translated by M. Crosland and A. Daventry. London, Sphere Books, 1969.

Briffault, Robert, *The Mothers*. New York, Grosset & Dunlap, 1963.

Brown, Norman O., *Life Against Death*. Middletown, Conn., Wesleyan University Press, 1959.

————, *Love's Body*. New York, Random House, 1966.

Campbell, Joseph, ed., *Myths, Dreams and Religion*. New York, Dutton, 1970.

Colette, *The Pure and the Impure*. New York, Farrar, Straus & Giroux, 1967.

Craveri, Marcello, *The Life of Jesus*. New York, Grove Press, 1967.

Dalton, David, *Janis*. New York, Simon and Schuster, 1971.

Davis, Elizabeth Gould, *The First Sex*. New York, G. P. Putnam's Sons, 1971.

De Beauvoir, Simone, *The Second Sex*. New York, Knopf, 1953.

De Mott, Benjamin, *Supergrow*. New York, Dutton, 1969.

Diner, Helen, *Mothers and Amazons*. New York, Julian Press, 1965.

Engels, Friedrich, *The Origin of the Family, Private Property, and the State*. New York, International Publishers, 1942.

Euripides, *Three Tragedies*, edited by D. Grene and R. Lattimore. Chicago, University of Chicago Press, 1959.

Ferenczi, Sandor, *Thalassa*. New York, W. W. Norton, 1968.

Figes, Eva, *Patriarchal Attitudes*. New York, Fawcett, 1971.

Freud, Sigmund, *Dora: An Analysis of a Case of Hysteria*. New York, Avon, 1962.

———, *Three Essays on the Theory of Sexuality*. New York, Collier Books, 1963.

Gay Revolution Party, "Realesbians, Politicalesbians and the Women's Liberation Movement," *Ecstasy*, New York, 1971.

Ginsberg, Allen, *Howl and Other Poems*. San Francisco, City Lights, 1956.

Graves, Robert, *The Greek Myths*. Baltimore, Penguin, 1955.

Hall, Radclyffe, *The Well of Loneliness*. New York, Covici-Friede, 1929.

Halliday, W. R., *Plutarch's Greek Questions*. Oxford University Press, 1928.

Harrison, Jane, *Ancient Art and Ritual*. Oxford University Press, 1951.

———, *Prolegomena to the Study of Greek Religion*. Cleveland, Meridian, 1959.

———, *Themis*. Cleveland, Meridian, 1962.

I Ching, translated by Cary Baynes. Princeton, N.J., Princeton University Press, 1961.

James, Alice, *Diary*, edited by Leon Edel. New York, Dodd, Mead, 1964.

Johnson, Virginia, and Masters, William H., *Human Sexual Response*. Boston, Little, Brown, 1966.

Jones, Ernest, *Hamlet and Oedipus*. New York, Doubleday, 1954.

Joyce, James, *Finnegans Wake*. New York, Viking, 1959.

Jung, C. G., and Kerenyi, C., *Essays on the Science of Mythology*. Princeton, N.J., Princeton University Press, 1969.

Kanter, Emanuel, *The Amazons, a Marxian Study*. Chicago, Chas. H. Kerr & Co., 1926.

Laing, R. D., *The Politics of Experience*. New York, Ballantine, 1968.

Mailer, Norman, *Advertisements for Myself*. New York, G. P. Putnam's Sons, 1959.

———, *Prisoner of Sex*. Boston, Little, Brown and Co., 1971.

Milford, Nancy, *Zelda*. New York, Avon, 1971.

Mill, Harriet Taylor, and Mill, John Stuart, *Essays on Sex Equality*. Chicago, University of Chicago Press, 1970.

Millett, Kate, *Sexual Politics*. New York, Avon, 1971.

Mitchell, Juliet, *Woman's Estate*. New York, Pantheon, 1971.

Morgan, Robin, ed., *Sisterhood Is Powerful.* New York, Random House, 1970.

Neale, J. E., *Queen Elizabeth I.* Garden City, N.Y., Doubleday Anchor, 1959.

Neumann, Erich, *Amor and Psyche.* New York, Pantheon, 1956.

———, *The Great Mother.* Princeton, N.J., Princeton University Press, 1963.

Pernoud, Régine, *Joan of Arc.* New York, Stein & Day, 1969.

Plath, Sylvia, *The Bell Jar.* London, Faber & Faber, 1966.

Plutarch, *Lives,* translated by T. North. Cambridge, Mass., Harvard University Press, 1926.

Radicalesbians, "Woman Identified Woman," *Notes from the Fourth Year.* New York, 1971.

Rank, Otto, *The Myth of the Birth of the Hero.* New York, Vintage, 1964.

Rubin, Jerry, *Do It.* New York, Ballantine, 1970.

———, *We Are Everywhere.* New York, Harper & Row, 1971.

Seale, Bobby, *Seize the Time.* New York, Random House, 1970.

Shattuck, Roger, *The Banquet Years.* New York, Vintage, 1968.

Slater, Philip, *The Glory of Hera.* Boston, Beacon Press, 1968.

———, *The Pursuit of Loneliness.* Boston, Beacon Press, 1971.

Solanis, Valerie, *The SCUM Manifesto.* New York, Olympia Press, 1968.

Sontag, Susan, *Styles of Radical Will.* New York, Delta, 1970.

Teal, Donn, *The Gay Militants.* New York, Stein & Day, 1971.

Tibetan Book of the Dead, edited by W. Y. Evans-Wentz. Oxford University Press, 1960.

Velikovsky, I., *Oedipus and Akhnaton: Myth and History.* New York, Doubleday, 1960.

Weinberg, George, *Society and the Healthy Homosexual.* New York, St. Martin's, 1972.

Wittman, Carl, "The Gay Manifesto," *Liberation,* February, 1970.

Wolff, Charlotte, *Love Between Women. New York,* St. Martin's, 1971.

Woolf, Virginia, *A Room of One's Own.* New York, Harcourt, Brace & World, 1957.

———, *Three Guineas.* New York, Harcourt, Brace & World, 1963.